Deconstructing history

Postmodernism has changed how we study the past. In *Deconstructing History*, Alun Munslow examines history in the postmodern age. He provides an introduction to the debates and issues of postmodernist history. He also surveys the latest research into the relationship between the past and contests that, not only is history defined as the textual product of historians, but that narrative may provide the textual model for the past itself.

The author details both empiricist and deconstructionist issues and considers the arguments of major proponents of both schools. He includes an examination of the character of historical evidence and an exploration of the role of historians as well as a discussion of the failure of traditional historical methods.

Deconstructing History maps the philosophical field, outlines the controversies involved and assesses the merits of the deconstructionist position. Alun Munslow debates the importance of history as the textual product of historians. He argues that instead of beginning with the past, history begins with representations of the past.

Alun Munslow is Principal Lecturer in History, Staffordshire University.

Deconstructing history

Alun Munslow

London and New York

First published 1997
by Routledge
11 New Fetter Lane, London EC4P 4EE

Simultaneously published in the USA and Canada
by Routledge
29 West 35th Street, New York, NY 10001

Reprinted 1998, 2001

Routledge is an imprint of the Taylor & Francis Group

Typeset in Times by
M Rules

Printed and bound in Great Britain by T.J. International Ltd,
Padstow, Cornwall

British Library Cataloguing in Publication Data
A catalogue record for this book is available from the British Library

Library of Congress Cataloguing in Publication Data
Munslow, Alun, 1947–
    Deconstructing history/by Alun Munslow
    p. cm.
    Includes bibliographical references and index
    1. History–Methodology. 2. Historiography. History–
Philosophy. 4. Narration (Rhetoric). 5. Literature and history.
    I. Title.
    D16.M963 1997
    907'.2–dc21 97-2974 CIP

ISBN 0-415-13192-8
    0-415-13193-6 (pbk)

Contents

	Acknowledgements	vi
1	**Introduction**	1
2	**The past in a changing present**	17
3	**History as reconstruction/construction**	36
4	**History as deconstruction**	57
5	**What is wrong with deconstructionist history?**	76
6	**What is wrong with reconstructionist/constructionist history?**	99
7	**Michel Foucault and history**	120
8	**Hayden White and deconstructionist history**	140
9	**Conclusion**	163
	Glossary	179
	Guide to further reading	191
	Notes	197
	Index	218

Acknowledgements

This book is the result of a prolonged period of teaching and thinking about the ways in which it is possible to write the past. As a consequence there are many colleagues who, often unwittingly perhaps, have made me reassess my thinking as a historian. I am grateful to them all. As ever, my final thanks are to Jane, who has always known that history is a story.

1 Introduction

APPROACHING HISTORY

It is my intention to navigate through the central debate to be found in history today, viz. the extent to which history, as a discipline, can accurately recover and represent the content of the past, through the form of the narrative. Put plainly, to what extent is the narrative or literary structure of the history text an adequate vehicle for historical explanation, and what implications can we draw from our answer? It is now commonplace for historians, philosophers of history and others interested in narrative to claim we live in a postmodern age wherein the old modernist certainties of historical truth and methodological objectivity, as applied by disinterested historians, are challenged principles. Few historians today would argue that we write *the* truth about the past. It is generally recognised that written history is contemporary or present orientated to the extent that we historians not only occupy a platform in the here-and-now, but also hold positions on how we see the relationship between the past and its traces, and the manner in which we extract meaning from them. This book is called *Deconstructing History* because at its core is my belief that history must be reassessed at its most basic level. It is not enough merely to criticise historical method, but rather to ask can professional historians be relied upon to reconstruct and explain the past objectively by inferring the 'facts' from the evidence, and who, after all the hard work of research, will then write up their conclusions unproblematically for everyone to read?

Even if, as many might argue, history has never been nor is now precisely as positivist a research process, or as unreflective a literary undertaking as that description suggests, the crude empiricist or reconstructionist emphasis on the historian as the impartial observer who conveys the 'facts' is a paradigm (defined as a set of beliefs about how to gain knowledge) that obscures history's real character as a literary undertaking. I will argue that the genuine nature of history can be understood only when it is viewed not solely and simply as an objectivised empiricist enterprise, but as the creation and eventual imposition by historians of a particular narrative form on the past: a process that directly affects the whole project, not merely the writing up stage. This understanding, for convenience, I shall call the deconstructive consciousness. This use of the term is not to be confused with its original use by French cultural theorist Jacques Derrida, who employed the term more narrowly to mean the process whereby we grasp the meaning of texts without reference to some originating external reality. The deconstructive consciousness not only defines history as what it palpably is, a written narrative (the textual product of historians), but additionally, and more radically, suggests that narrative as the form of story-telling may also provide the textual model for the past itself. Recognising the literary dimension to history as a discipline does not mean that we cannot ask ourselves is it only our lived experience that is retold by historians as a narrative, or as historical agents do we experience narratives – as people in the past? In other words, does the evidence reveal past lives to be story-shaped, and can we historians retell the narrative as it actually happened, or do we always impose our own stories on the evidence of the past?

Whatever we decide, it follows that history cannot exist for the reader until the historian writes it in its obligatory form: narrative. What do I mean by narrative? When we explain in history we place its contents as events in a sequential order, a process usually described as the telling of a story. No matter how extensive are the analytical apparatuses borrowed from the social sciences and brought to bear on the past, history's power to explain resides in its fundamental narrative form. As the pro-narrative philosopher of history Louis Mink said in the early 1960s: 'Where scientists . . . note each other's results, historians . . . read each other's books.'[1] So far as this book is concerned, the *reality* of the past is the written report, rather than the past *as it actually was*. I will argue that history is the study not of change over time *per se*, but the study of the information produced by historians as they go about this task. In *Deconstructing History* I am attempting to highlight the essentially literary nature of historical knowledge and the significance of its narrative form in the constitution of such knowledge. In our contemporary or postmodern world, history conceived of as an empirical research method based upon the belief in some reasonably accurate correspondence between the past, its interpretation and its narrative representation is no longer a tenable conception of the task of the historian. Instead of beginning with the past we should start with its representation, because it is only by doing this that we challenge the belief that there is a discoverable and accurately representable truthfulness in the reality of the past.

SOME BASIC QUESTIONS ABOUT THE NATURE OF HISTORY

Four specific questions about the nature of history flow from the belief that history as it is lived and written is structured as much by its form as by its content. Although we can distinguish these questions for the purpose of listing, in practice it is very difficult to keep them separate.

- Can empiricism legitimately constitute history as a separate epistemology?
- What is the character of historical evidence and what function does it perform?
- What is the role of the historian, his/her use of social theory, and the construction of explanatory frameworks in historical understanding?
- How significant to historical explanation is its narrative form?

These questions prompted the writing of this book and lie at the heart of the status crisis besetting history today.

Epistemology

The first question confronts the basic issue about history as a form of knowledge: is there something special in the methods deployed by historians to study the past that produces a reliable and objective knowledge peculiar to itself, and which makes it possible to argue that there is such a thing as a discipline of history at all? Historical knowledge, as it is usually described, is derived through a method – called a practice by those who believe in the possibility of an accurate understanding of the past – that flows from its techniques in dealing with the traces of the past. The most basic function of the historian is to understand, and explain in a written form, the connections between events and human intention or agency in the past. Put another way, the historian has to work out some kind of method or means whereby he/she can grasp the relationship between knowledge and explanation in order to find the foundation of truth, if one exists.

One method would be to imitate the natural sciences, and although there has always been a large minority following among historians (especially among those with a positivist or social science training) for this flattery, it has never achieved a dominant methodological status. History cannot claim to be straightforwardly scientific in the sense that we understand the physical sciences to be because it does not share the protocol of hypothesis-testing, does not employ deductive reasoning, and neither is it an experimental and objective process producing incontrovertible facts. Moreover, the better we do it does not guarantee we will get closer to the truth. Scientific method works on the assumption that data are connected by a universal explanation, and consequently the scientist selects his/her data according to this belief. The historian, however, selects his/her data because of his/her interest in a unique event or individual acting intentionally in response to circumstances. Evidence is chosen for what it can tell us about that unique event or individual, rather than any and every event within a general category being explained.

What particular consequences flow from this for history as an epistemology, or special form of knowledge?[2] Can we gain genuine and 'truthful' historical descriptions by simply following the historian's literary narrative – her or his story? This is certainly the opinion of several commentators. The British theorist of history M.C. Lemon considers that the 'very logic' of history as a discipline revolves 'around the rationale of the narrative structure'.[3] In respect of what peculiarly constitutes historical explanation, Lemon argues that its essence lies in the manner in which historians account 'for occurrences in terms of the reasons individuals have for their conduct'. In other words, history can be legitimately defined as the narrative interpretation and explanation of human agency and intention.[4] The special character of narrative that makes it so useful to historians is, as Lemon points out, its 'this happened, *then* that' structure which also, of course, is the essence of historical change. It is a process that saturates our lived experience. In other words, the past existed and will exist as knowledge transmitted to us according to the basic principles of narrative form.

What, then, is the relationship of history to its closest neighbour, literature? The bottom line seems to be one of referentiality. I take this to mean the accuracy and veracity with which the narrative relates what actually happened in the past. As Lemon argues, while literature is not wholly 'devoid of referentiality', it is 'not referential in the same manner' as the historical text.[5] It follows that, like literature, *the past* and *written history* are not the same thing.[6] Not recognising this permits us to forget the difficulties involved in recreating the past – something that does not exist apart from a few traces and the historians' narrative. Because we cannot directly encounter the past, whether as a political movement, economic process or an event, we employ a narrative fulfilling a two-fold function, as both a surrogate for the past and as a medium of exchange in our active engagement with it. History is thus a class of literature.

The most basic assumption that informs my book is that the past is negotiated only when historians represent it in its narrative form and that historical interpretation should not close down the meanings of the past to pursue what at best must remain an ersatz 'truth'. Indeed, we ought to be more open to the possible meaninglessness or sublime character of the past. Although mainstream empiricists may dispute it, I shall argue that there cannot be any unmediated correspondence between language and the world as a discoverable reality. Of course, even if this is the case, it does not stop us from asking, although we cannot provide a definitive answer, is it possible that the past unfolded as a particular kind of narrative the first time around and can we recover it more or less intact, or are we only selecting and imposing an emplotment or story line on it derived from our own present? Are stories lived in the past or just told in the present? Do we explain our lives at the time like the unfolding of a story? The most important question, then, is not the dog-eared modernist one of whether history is an accurate science, but the postmodernist one of how and why when we write about the past, we cast it in a particular narrative form. Further, how adequate is the cognitive power of narrative? What is its capacity to explain the past plausibly?

Just as it is impossible to have a narrative without a narrator, we cannot have a history without a historian. What is the role of the historian in recreating the past? Every history contains ideas or theories about the nature of change and continuity as held by historians – some are overt, others deeply buried, and some just poorly formulated. The theories of history mustered by historians both *affect* and *effect* our understanding about the past, whether they are explicit or not. To the extent that history is a narrative interpretation built in part out of the social theories or ideological positions that historians invent to explain the past, history may be defined essentially as a language-based manufacturing process in which the written historical interpretation is assembled or produced by historians. As the pro-narrative philosopher of history Arthur Danto put it, 'to tell what happened . . . and to explain why . . . is to do one and the same thing',[7] or in the words of Lemon, the historian regularly encounters questions of 'selection, relevance, significance and objectivity' in his/her description of events.[8] I will suggest, therefore, that history is best viewed epistemologically as a form of literature producing knowledge as much by its aesthetic or narrative structure as by any other criteria. In addition, as we acknowledge history's literary and fabricated character, I shall also address the past as *a* narrative, as well as describe it *in* narrative.

Evidence

The second question concerns the raw materials in the history industry's manufacturing process – the traces or evidence of the past. We should be beginning by now to see that because of the central role of language in the constitution of knowledge, our historical understanding is as much the product of *how* we write as well as *what* we write, so that history's so-called raw 'facts' are likewise presented either wholly or in large part to us in a written or literary form. Even raw statistics have to be interpreted in narrative. If you, as a student of history, were asked to give an example of a historical 'fact', the normal response is to quote an incontrovertible event or description that everyone agrees upon. That slavery was the ultimate cause of the American Civil War is clearly not such a 'fact'. It is a complex interpretation based on the relating of disparate occurrences, statistical data, events and human intentions translated as actions involving outcomes. But if we say in cold factual terms that the American President James Madison was 'small of stature (5 feet, 4 inches; 1.62 metres), light of weight (about 100 pounds; 45 kilograms), bald of head, and weak of voice' this seems unproblematic – Madison was or wasn't this tall, was or wasn't slight, was or wasn't bald, was or wasn't weak voiced. The important point, however, is the meaning that these 'facts' about Madison produce in the mind of the reader, rather than the inherent veracity of the 'facts' themselves.

Because he was short, slight, bald and had a squeaky voice, does this incline us towards an interpretation that he was weak, could not therefore hold his cabinet together, and eventually became a dupe of Napoleon?[9] History is about the process of translating evidence into facts. You and I as historians do this. Even when straight from the dusty archive, the evidence always pre-exists within narrative structures and is freighted with cultural meanings – who put the archive together, why, and what did they include or exclude? 'Facts' are literally meaningless in their unprocessed state of simple evidential statement. The evidence is turned into 'facts' through the narrative interpretations of historians; but facts usually already possess their own narrators, and then they gain further meaning when they are organised by the historian as strands in a story producing a particular, appealing, followable, but above all a convincing relationship. Historical interpretation is the written explanation of that perceived relationship.

As we can see, 'facts' are never innocent because only when used by the historian is factual evidence invested with meaning as it is correlated and placed within a context, sometimes called the process of colligation, collation, configuration or emplotment, which then leads the historian to generate the 'facts'.[10] Traditionally, this process of contextualisation is undertaken by the historian as part of the process of interpretation as he/she relates masses of apparently unconnected data with an eye to producing a meaning. The evidence of the past is processed through inference, with the historian construing a meaning by employing categories of analysis supposedly determined by the nature of the evidence. The traces of the past are thus traditionally viewed as empirical objects from which to mine *the* meaning, or as sources out of which social theories of explanation can be constructed.

However, this positioning or organising of the evidence in relation to other examples – what I choose to call the process of emplotment – is where the historian's own views and cultural situation usually emerge. In writing history it is impossible to divorce the historian from the constitution of meaning through the creation of a context, even though this is seemingly and innocently derived from the facts. It is at this point that the historian unavoidably imposes him/herself on the past, whether it be through the apparently wholesome practice of mining the evidence for its true meaning, or more obviously through the creation and use of social theories, but most importantly, I would suggest, because of the emplotment or story-line (narrative structure) deployed to facilitate explanation and historical interpretation. I will examine the implications of the role played in writing history by the evidence and our representation of it. Evidence is there for us to infer meaning from and thus create historical knowledge. However, the inference of meaning emerges as we organise, configure and emplot the data. It does not, I would argue, just turn up or suggest itself as the only or most likely conclusion to draw.

Theories of history: constructing the past

The third question in this debate comes out of the belief, held by hardcore empiricists, that history is a practice founded on the objective reconstruction of the facts, through which we get close to what actually happened in the past. This is what the English philosopher of history R.G. Collingwood called 'naïve realism', and it is based on the idea that experience can be the object of historical knowledge.[11] In order to sustain this position, such empiricists deny that historians should intervene or impose on the past by suggesting that they must be not only impartial and objective in their treatment of the evidence, but also that they should reject social theory models in interpreting the past. This latter process is viewed by them as a crude construction or invention of the past.

However, since the 1920s, social and cultural history has been popular because it demands the construction of explanations of how post-industrial society has been able/unable to cope with the massive social changes that have occurred in the train of capitalist industrialisation. This modernisation process could not be explained without recourse to a new and utilitarian kind of history in which historians played an active role in its construction. They play this role either by empathically rethinking the thoughts of people in the past to ascertain their intentions, or by constructing social theory explanations rather than just waiting for them to suggest themselves. Hard-core empiricists (Collingwood's naïve realists) today embrace the idea that historians must not yield to this twin siren call to justify historical interpretations by imagining or empathising with past historical actors, nor less construct universal explanatory theories (usually described today as meta-narratives) that can explain the past. Such empiricists refuse to accept the changing character of contemporary thought, not least what has now become a commonplace argument among the majority of historians, that historical knowledge is not objective but has upon it the fingerprints of its interpreters.

As twentieth-century Western society has experienced total war, social, political and ecological revolutions, and new technology, the growing need has been to make the past intelligible to the present, and that means historians speculating on the causes of change, the nature of continuity, and the endless possibilities in the past. Such speculations cannot simply rely upon empathy or its corollary historicism – seeing the past in its own context or terms. Although the most obvious example of twentieth-century constructionism is the Marxist school of history that stresses the social theory of class exploitation as *the* model of historical change, the advent in France in the 1920s of the *Annales* school of historiography also produced a parallel constructionist-social science-inspired history that proposed alternative behavioural and demographic theories. From the 1970s an anthropologically indebted social history has also emerged that challenges class as the major construct in historical explanation in favour of taking single events and decoding them for their wider cultural significance. In addition, the modernisation school has stressed the benefits of model-making to comparative history. The New Economic History of the 1960s and 1970s emphasised quantification. Constructionism has thus been subject to fashions or trends.

Sociological and anthropological constructionism is one of the key sources of what has become known as the New Cultural History and what I shall designate as deconstructionist history. As a variant of constructionism, the New Cultural History works on principles derived not only from anthropology but also from the broader intellectual movement of post-structuralism which itself emerged from literary critical theory in the 1970s. Deconstructionist history regards the past as a complex narrative discourse, but one, as the French cultural critic and historian Michel Foucault has pointed out, that accepts that representation is not a transparent mode of communication that can adequately carry understanding or generate truthful meaning. Deconstructionist history is a part of the larger challenge to the modernist empiricist notion that understanding emanates from the independent knowledge-centred individual subject designated variously as Man, humanity, the author or the evidence. Modernist empiricism is in crisis because of the objection that meaning is generated by socially encoded and constructed discursive practices that mediate reality so much so that they effectively close off direct access to it. This situation is compounded when language is considered not to be a pure medium of representation. Is it any longer possible to write history when not only are we looking at it through our constructed categories of analysis – race, class, gender – but the narrative medium of exchange itself confounds the realist and empiricist dependence upon what one commentator has called an 'adequate level of correspondence between representations of the past and the past itself' as it once actually existed?[12]

The leading practitioner of the narrative or rhetorical version of constructionism is the American philosopher of history Hayden White. White insists that history fails if its intention is the modernist one of the objective reconstruction of the past simply according to the evidence. It fails because the process involved is the literary one of interpretative narrative, rather than objective empiricism and/or social theorising. This means that writing history requires the emplotment of the past not just as a way of organising the evidence, but also taking into account the rhetorical, metaphorical and ideological strategies of explanation employed by historians. The study of rhetoric as the mode of historical explanation is summarised in the claim that history is literary artifact, as White says, as much invented as found.[13]

History as narrative

Because history is written by historians, it is best understood as a cultural product existing *within* society, and as a part of the historical process, rather than an objective methodology and commentary *outside* of society. This brings us to the fourth key question – posed by White along with Collingwood, and more recently by Louis Mink and Arthur Danto – what is the significance of narrative in generating historical knowledge, and what is its relationship to the previous three questions? But, first of all, what do we mean when we talk of historical narrative? The modernist empiricist historical method handed down from the nineteenth century requires and assumes historical explanation will emerge in a naturalistic fashion from the archival raw data, its meaning offered as interpretation in the form of a story related explicitly, impersonally, transparently, and without resort to any of the devices used by writers of literary narratives, viz., imagery or figurative language. Style is deliberately expunged as an issue, or relegated to a minor problem of presentation. This vision of the history as a practice fails to acknowledge the difficulties in reading the pre-existing narrative constituted as evidence, or the problems of writing up the past.

We historians employ narrative as the vehicle for our reports but usually neglect to study it as an important part of what we do. For most analytical philosophers of history the essence of historical understanding is the ability to recognise, construct and follow a narrative, that is *a* story based upon the available evidence. A historical narrative is a discourse that places disparate events in an understandable order: as Lemon says, 'this happened *then* that'. Such a narrative is an intelligible sequence of individual statements about past events and/or the experiences of people or their actions, capable of being followed by a reader while he/she is pulled through time by the author towards the conclusion. All such narratives make over events and explain why they happened, but are overlaid by the assumptions held by the historian about the forces influencing the nature of causality. These might well include individual or combined elements like race, gender, class, culture, weather, coincidence, geography, region, blundering politicians, and so on and so forth. So, while individual statements may be true/false, narrative as a collection of them is more than their sum. The narrative becomes a complex interpretative exercise that is neither conclusively true nor false.

The commonsense version of the general empiricist and reconstructionist position on the essential role of narrative is well described by the philosopher W.B. Gallie:

> Historical understanding is the exercise of the capacity to follow a story, where the story is known to be based on evidence and is put forward as a sincere effort to get at *the* story. . . .[14]

Gallie is suggesting that the actual events as they really occurred in *the* story of the past have a striking resemblance to the shape of *the* narrative eventually produced by the historian – the narrative is found (discovered?) by the historian in the events themselves and then reproduced. The narrative here has referentiality. While philosophers of history like Keith Jenkins, Louis Mink and Hayden White believe that we do not live stories but only recount our lived experience in the story form, the American philosopher of history David Carr supports Gallie and French philosopher of history Paul Ricoeur in holding that there is a basic continuity or correspondence between history as it is lived (the past) and history as it is written (narrated).[15] Are we justified in claiming that because our lives are narrativised and written history is a text, then surely the past itself conforms to the structure of narrative? White reverses the argument – *the* narrative does not pre-exist but *a* narrative is invented and provided by the historian. Consequently, there are many different stories to be told about the same events, the same past. While still constrained by what actually happened (historians do not invent events, people or processes), as the French historian Paul Veyne suggests, the meaning of history as a story comes from *a* plot, which is imposed, or, as Hayden White insists, invented as much as found by the historian.[16]

The argument runs that just as there are no grounds for believing that an empiricist methodology can guarantee an understanding of the past as it actually was, neither is there a discoverable *original* emplotment. However, the self-reflexive and self-conscious historian may argue that it is possible to offer an interpretation that, although not claiming to be *the* true narrative, is nevertheless a plausible and therefore quite acceptable rendering of it. The range of emplotments upon which people in the past, and the historian, draw, though wide because of the combinations possible, is formally limited to the four main kinds – romance, tragedy, satire and comedy. This is no different to other narrators who operate in the realm of fiction. Of equal significance to the narrative emplotment, however, is the dimension of figurative description or style.

Historical story-telling, like all other kinds, employs the four primary figurative devices known as tropes. These are more commonly known as the four primary figures of speech: metaphor, metonymy, synecdoche and irony, and their use constitutes what is called the troping process. Troping means turning or steering the description of an object, event or person away from one meaning, so as to wring out further different, and possibly even multiple, meanings. When we use these four master tropes we describe objects, events, persons or intentions, in terms of other objects, events, persons or intentions, according to their similarities or differences, or characterise them by substituting their component parts for the whole – like hands representing workers, the one element or aspect representing the essence of the other (as a synecdoche), or sails for ships, the one aspect again representing the other, but now in a part–whole relationship (to be read as a metonymy). Metaphor is, however, the most basic kind of trope, with metonymy, synecdoche and irony as secondary kinds. Metaphor refers to one thing by denoting another so as to suggest that they share a common feature. To deny literal meaning is to use irony. Troping is as crucial to the writing of history as it is to other forms of literature because it permits us to create meanings that differ from those of colleagues and to disrupt the expectations of readers different to those anticipated.

Later I shall examine emplotment and troping in White's formal model and his argument that there is no continuity between lived experience and its narrative representation, that narrative as a form of historical explanation is ultimately inadequate, and that writing history is also an unavoidably ideological act. Narrative is normally deployed, therefore, not to defend the correspondence theory of empiricism so much as to act as its vehicle – getting at *the* story – but always at the expense of the historical sublime. By this, White means the celebration of the undiscoverable, possibly meaningless, and open-ended nature of the past. Such a meaninglessness is the only invitation that potentially oppositional and dissenting groups of historians may get to challenge certaintist (e.g. fascist) history. They, and we, empower ourselves when we can find no objective certainty in the past – in the sense of a factual correspondence of evidence with Truth – that can be used to validate the authority of those in power over us.[17] From a strictly philosophical point of view, the existence of a past reality does not in itself verify the correspondence theory, since it does not mean *the* truth of past events can be found in any correspondence between the word and the world as statements of past reality. Paradoxically, most historians, even leftist dissenting ones, prefer to believe it does.

Michel Foucault challenges this by arguing that the idea of Man (Man = historian for our purposes) is not able to stand outside society and history and thus generate objective and truthful knowledge. He concludes (as does White) that language is an ideologically contaminated medium, and what it can and cannot do is dependent upon the use to which it is put, and for what social and political purposes – usually to maintain or challenge systems of authority and views of what is right or wrong, allowed or banned. As he says, '"Truth" is to be understood as a system of ordered procedures for the production, regulation, distribution, circulation, and operation of statements. "Truth" is linked [to the] . . . statements of power, which produce and sustain it.'[18] Foucault is pointing out here how historical agents – you and me – become confederates in our own subjectivity rather than just victims. Through the functioning of language we cannot avoid being placed in subject positions where the repression of the word fixes us all – like moths pinned to a collector's board. In this sense, the organised study of the past (history as a discipline which includes both its meanings: as a profession, and as a collection of methodological practices) as an organised narrative is itself founded on the dispensation of authority/power in contemporary society. How we write history is as open to the uses and misuses of power as any other narrative.

Written history is always more than merely innocent story-telling, precisely because it is the primary vehicle for the distribution and use of power. The very act of organising historical data into a narrative not only constitutes an illusion of 'truthful' reality, but in lending a spurious tidiness to the past can ultimately serve as a mechanism for the exercise of power in contemporary society. As White suggests, even when we acknowledge and describe the messiness of the past, the very act of narration imposes an unavoidable 'continuity, wholeness, closure and individuality that every "civilised" society wishes to see itself as incarnating'.[19] All historical narrative is thus subject to the complex and subtle demands of ideology, and in its turn gives effect to it.

Viewing history as a literary artifact recognises the importance of narrative explanation in our lives as well as in the study of the past, and it ought to liberate historians as we try to narrate the disruptive discontinuity and chaos of the past for and in the present. This desire is, in itself, a product of our own age's preoccupation with understanding the nature of our seemingly chaotic lives. Chaos Theory, for example, a 1990s methodological innovation, is a new aid to our historical understanding. Interestingly, one of the leading exponents of Chaos Theory maintains that its use still requires a narrative to explain the past.[20] This illustrates how history itself is historical, that is, its methods and concepts as well as the debates about its nature are the products of historical time periods. In the 1890s American history turned towards explaining the peculiarly American origins of the nation's history, and in the 1950s the strains of the US–Russian Cold War produced a consensus among historians on the ideological coherence in American history in the face of an implacable and potentially divisive enemy. The millennial rediscovery of the importance of narrative as an access to the sublime and possible worlds of the past is very much the product of today and, like all historical understandings, will presumably pass away with time. This book and the issues I raise in it are, indeed, very much products of our time.

POSTMODERN NARRATIVES AND HISTORY

The deconstructionist view of history – as a constituted narrative rather than the report of an objective empiricist undertaking – results from the wider end-of-century postmodern intellectual context.[21] It is a context that the French cultural critic Jean-François Lyotard, in his highly influential 1984 book *The Postmodern Condition*, described as centring on the vexed relationship between the acquisition of what he called scientific knowledge and the functioning of narrative. In defining narrative, Lyotard suggested that it is the characteristic and essential feature of cultural formation and transmission.[22] Lyotard agrees with Foucault that narrative is about the exercise of power. For Lyotard it is a kind of self-legitimation whereby constructing it according to a certain set of socially accepted rules and practices establishes the speaker's or writer's authority within their society, and acts as a mutual reinforcement of that society's self-identity.[23] As a western cultural practice, history has been challenged by the loss of our self-identity. Meanwhile, historians who stick to their realist belief in commonsense, science-inspired, objective empiricist paradigm remain inured to what they see as mere 'distractions' in the pursuit of truthful historical knowledge (even though they realise that technical problems with the evidence, social theorising, or simple bias may prevent its attainment).

Science, from the eighteenth up to the early twentieth century, has depended upon powerful, socially constructed, political and philosophical 'master' narratives to support, protect and legitimise it – what Lyotard calls meta-narratives. In the epistemological hierarchy the key master or meta-narratives were the eighteenth-century Enlightenment (as focused in the upheaval of the French Revolution), promising as it did human freedom through emancipation from monarchical despotism and feudalism, to be followed by the nineteenth-century narrative of human consciousness leading towards some perfectible future (as elaborated in the philosophy of Hegel). Consequently, Lyotard claims that scientific knowledge cannot describe its truth without resort to these other two meta-narratives of emancipation and self-consciousness. Science denies narrative as a form of legitimate cognition (that is, it is not scientific) while depending on it for its own social acceptance and intellectual and cultural legitimation.

If by implication, history, like science, is now under challenge today, it

is presumed to be partly because of the traumatic events of the twentieth century which have meant a loss of confidence in our ability to relate
the past or, as Keith Jenkins describes it, 'the general failure . . . of that
experiment in social living which we call modernity'.[24] The meta-narrative of scientific objectivity and the unfolding of progress through our
grasp of the past is now under challenge. The rise of fascism, two world
wars, de-colonisation, seismic technological change, environmental and
ecological disaster, the information explosion, the growth of exploitative
and non-accountable global capitalism, with its commodification of
labour in the 'developed' West and the worsening dispossession of the
toiling masses across the undeveloped globe, have all but destroyed the
meta-narratives that legitimised both science and history as foundations
of what has been regarded as an inexorable trend towards individual
freedom and the self-conscious improvement of the human condition.

As a consequence of all this, at the close of the twentieth century,
narratives both grand and petty, beliefs, attitudes, values, disciplines,
societies, and meaning itself, appear to be fractured or fracturing. The
future is one of gloomy uncertainty. It now seems quite incredible that
anyone could have ever believed in the hierarchy of master narratives
like liberalism, science, Marxism, socialism, or a view of history that
emphasised either the discovery of the past as it actually was, or even
the inevitability of progress. So it is that Lyotard describes the postmodern condition as an incredulity towards meta-narratives. We have
now lost the old, modernist sense of history as the fount of wisdom or
teacher of moral or intellectual certainty. What this means is that any
study of what history is cannot be other than located within its social
and cultural context. History, as a form of literature, is like music,
drama and poetry, a cultural practice. As a text or series of texts (evidence and interpretations), history can be understood only when it is
situated, as the philosopher of postmodern history F.R. Ankersmit said
in the late 1980s, 'within present day civilisation as a whole'.[25] For our
purposes this means studying both the content of the past and its interpretation in its narrative form. As a self-reflexive historian, I define
written history as a socially constituted narrative representation that
recognises the ultimate failure of that narrative form to represent either
accurately or objectively. We can study the past only by first probing the
nature of history as a discipline.

CONCLUSION

This definition of history, as a literary, cultural practice, places it within
its present postmodern context. From this perspective, the explosion of

written history, as well as in its many other forms, will continue to fill the space provided for it. Historiography well illustrates this eruption in our knowledge of the past, as well as our irruption into it. Not only is there more history but historians agree on it less.[26] That the past is never fixed is the message of the deconstructive consciousness, whether in terms of its epistemology, treatment of evidence, the construction of explanations, or the precise nature of our explanatory narrative form. This postmodern or deconstructive history challenges the traditional paradigm at every turn – hence its description variously as the deconstructionist, deconstructive or linguistic turn. Deconstructionist history treats the past as a text to be examined for its possibilities of meaning, and above all exposes the spurious methodological aims and assumptions of modernist historians which incline them towards the ultimate viability of correspondence between evidence and interpretation, resulting in enough transparency in representation so as to make possible their aims of moral detachment, disinterestedness, objectivity, authenticity (if not absolute truthfulness) and the objective constitution of historical facts – allowing the sources to speak for themselves. Because today we doubt these empiricist notions of certainty, veracity and a socially and morally independent standpoint, there is no more history in the traditional realist sense, there are only possible narrative representations in, and of, the past, and none can claim to know the past as it actually was. It is to this claim that I now turn by addressing the four key questions in more detail.

2 The past in a changing present

INTRODUCTION

Never before has there been such a vast array of methods available with which to study the past, such a range of subject-matter and variety of audiences, and all to be understood within the broad sense of irony that seemingly encompasses Western culture today.[1] Never before have so many historians also accepted that written history deploys a system of language that is a part of the reality being described – a representation that is itself a complex cultural as well as a linguistic product. Living as we do in an age conceived and understood predominantly in terms of an ironic consciousness, and heavily influenced by the profusion and confusion of structuralist, post-structuralist, symbolic and anthropological models of the relationship between explanation and theory, even the strongest supporters of the traditional empiricist paradigm occasionally ask how can the reality of the past be known to us – or more precisely, how accurate can be its representation as a narrative? The debate on the relationship between postmodernity and history centres on the connection between the empirical and other methods of understanding as used by historians.[2]

Specifically, the impact of postmodernism on the study of history is seen in the new emphasis placed on its literary or aesthetic aspect, but not as before only as stylistic presentation, but now as a mode of explanation not primarily dependent upon the established empiricist paradigm. Even the staunchest defender of empiricism, Peter Gay, has noted that 'style . . . is worn into the texture of . . . history. Apart from a few mechanical tricks of rhetoric, manner is indissolubly linked to matter; style shapes, and in turn is shaped by, substance.'[3] This should be seen not as subversive but as liberating for the writing of the past. The collapse of the old universal standards upon which modernity as a phase of history was primarily founded – science, liberalism and

Marxism – has meant that history, while it can no more depend on undisputed notions of truth, objectivity and factualism, can speak to new and even more challenging questions about how we gain knowledge about the past.

THREE APPROACHES TO HISTORICAL KNOWLEDGE

In the introduction, I argued that historians are today addressing four basic questions about the method or form of history as well as its subject-matter or content. The first of those distinct, but inter-related, questions is the big one of whether or not history is an epistemology with its own rules for gaining and using knowledge. Does history exist as a separate empiricist discipline, or is it at best only a branch of the constructionist social sciences, or possibly a form of literature; or is it so vague an intellectual undertaking that it can be either or both, depending upon the choices made by the individual historian? The answers to the other three questions, on the treatment of historical evidence, the role of social theory, and narrative as the form of historical explanation, animate our answer to this, the big question. In the welter of history today I have already briefly noted three major approaches which I have characterised as reconstructionism, constructionism and deconstructionism. The reconstructionist, or as it is sometimes called the contextualist, approach refers to the established consensus or 'commonsense' empiricist tradition handed down from the nineteenth century. That it actually covers a variety of empiricisms is demonstrated in the work of hardened reconstructionists such as G.R. Elton, Gordon S. Wood, H. Trevor-Roper, Lawrence Stone, John Tosh, Gertrude Himmelfarb, Arthur Marwick, J.H. Hexter and Oscar Handlin, and in the work of those we might call the practical realists such as Peter Novick, Joyce Appleby, Lynn Hunt, Margaret Jacob and David M. Roberts. Both groups construct historical explanations around the evidence while maintaining a foundational belief in empiricism and historical meanings ultimately deriving from sense experience as mediated by their constructed narratives.[4] Elton and Marwick are among the most outspoken advocates of the modernist 'craftsman' approach to historical study, maintaining that history is still about objective and forensic research into the sources, the reconstructing of the past as it actually happened, and the freedom of the whole process from ideological contamination and/or the linguistic *a priorism* of emplotment and troping.

Constructionism refers to the 'social theory' schools that appeal to general laws in historical explanation, as exemplified, for example, in the French *Annalistes,* attempt at all-encompassing total explanations, and other sociologically inspired case-study and biographical work of historians like Norbert Elias, Robert Darnton, Marshal Sahlins and Anthony Giddens.[5] Modernisation theory is yet another variety of constructionism which found favour, especially in the USA, in the early 1960s. This theory looks to the past for models that might be applied today as a means of studying the present development of the Third World. The most famous of all constructionist approaches, of course, is the Marxist/neo-Marxist school as exemplified in the work of Eugene Genovese, George Rudé, Perry Anderson and E.P. Thompson and political scientists who have strayed into history such as Alex Callinicos.[6] The question usually asked of all varieties of constructionism is how can such history approximate what actually happened in the past when, in effect, all it does is generate explanations grounded in contemporary cultural practices, and hence is ideologically tainted? This question will remain open for the moment, but I shall return to it because it is an open issue that deconstructionist historians must also face.

The final group of approaches, loosely defined as deconstructionist, derive their focus from the postmodern historical understanding found in the work of a growing number of historians and philosophers of history like Hayden White, Dominick LaCapra, David Harlan, Allan Megill, Keith Jenkins, F.R. Ankersmit, Philippe Carrard, Joan W. Scott, Patrick Joyce, Roger Chartier and many other 'new wave' intellectual and cultural historians, where the emphasis is placed less on traditional empiricism or explicit social scientific theorising, than on the relationship of form and content (sources and interpretations) and the unavoidable relativism of historical understanding.[7] The deconstructionist consciousness accepts that the content of history, like that of literature, is defined as much by the nature of the language used to describe and interpret that content as it is by research into the documentary sources. Deconstructionist historians tend to view history and the past as a complex series of literary products that derive their chains of meaning(s) or significations from the nature of narrative structure (or forms of representation) as much as from other culturally provided ideological factors. Because we historians choose our words with great care, it seems wrong to ignore them as a significant part of our attempt to explain the past. I will now outline all three approaches in more detail before assessing their significance to the writing of history.

Reconstructionism

The Western tradition of history-writing is built on the correspondence theory of empiricism firmly rooted in the belief that truthful meaning can be directly inferred from the primary sources. It is further held that this is enough to constitute history as a separate and independent epistemology.[8] Reconstructionism thereby rests on the assumption that the more carefully we do it, like experienced craftsmen and women, the more accurate we can become, and the closer we get to fulfilling Leopold von Ranke's nineteenth-century dictum *wie es eigentlich gewesen*, or knowing history as it actually happened. The central tenet of this variety of hardened empiricism in historical study is an antipathy to the testing of preconceived theories of explanation. Such empiricists verify their knowledge of the past by insisting that their experience of the real world must be as unaffected by their perception of it as possible – they remain objective in other words. We can gain a useful insight into the conservative heart of empiricism by reading G.R. Elton's aptly entitled 1991 book *Return to Essentials*. Elton insists that the most valuable aspect of the historian's work is the 'rational, independent and impartial investigation' of the documents of the past.[9] Arguing that this reliance on commonsense empiricism does not constitute a theory of knowledge but is history as it should be properly understood, he goes on to dismiss relativism in history – other theories of knowledge – as 'Ideological theories . . . imposed upon the reconstruction of the past rather than derived from it.' For Elton, ideology is the arch-enemy of empiricism.

In a further rejection of the taint of ideology, bias and the interventionism of the historian, Elton also forcefully rejects the notion that writing history may involve a 're-enactment in the historian's mind'. In disparaging the two most well-known relativist historians, Benedetto Croce and R.G. Collingwood, who in the first half of the twentieth century suggested that historians play an active role in constructing history by rethinking the past, Elton's claim that the 'history of ideas' has now been 'suddenly promoted from the scullery to the drawing-room' is not far from the mark.[10] Most historians today feel that they cannot 'do' history without actively thinking about their role in the process of deriving historical knowledge – they do not share Elton's faith in empiricism. Indeed, there is a continuing debate (sometimes called the *Historikerstreit*, or conflict of the historians) between postmodernist and modernist historians over whether we can ever have a genuine knowledge of the real past, given the opacity and instability of language in its constructed narrative form as well as history's ideological dimension.[11]

From the Eltonian reconstructionist position, the infection of ideology produces the greatest of all ills in the fall from the grace of objectivity witnessed in the imposition of the intrusive authorial voice of the historian. This can lead only into perspective – a degraded history written from a particular point of view. The voice of the historian should never drown out the voice of history. For Elton, the impositionalism either of social theory or ideology is 'one of the most pernicious commonplaces of the contemporary analysis',[12] and each generation must avoid writing history in its own image. With 'strident' feminist historians in mind, Elton describes this 'corruption' as often the result of 'bigoted idleness'.[13] In spite of his bellicosity, Elton raises an important point about whether historians should measure the past according to present standards of method and/or morality. This is clearly a real problem if history is assumed to be the objective pursuit of truth. His answer is firmly that it is and that we do history for history's sake and not to comment on life today.

Conservative reconstructionist historians are ill at ease with importing the discipline of philosophy (usually described as the history of ideas) into their practice. Some (like Elton) are simply anti-theory in any shape, whilst most just oppose the theory or categories of analysis of which they do not personally approve. Elton, for example, rejects not only the 'ideological theory' of Croce and Collingwood, and more recently the methods advocated by the influential British historian E.H. Carr, but also a range of other theories derived from the social sciences which, he claims, tend 'to arrive at their results by setting up a theoretical model which they then profess to validate or disprove by an "experimental" application of factual detail'.[14] Elton finds Marxism to be especially pernicious, and gets substantial support from another hard-line reconstructionist, Arthur Marwick. In Marwick's late modernist view, history is not a social science and is, therefore, a non-theoretical exercise. In spite of their shared suspicion of philosophy, their views are supported by a number of philosopher-historians like Chris Lorenz, James Kloppenberg, J.H. Hexter, C. Behan McCullagh and Michael Stanford.

Marwick and Elton argue that history and the social sciences are distinct because the raw material of history, in the form of unique or singular documents and relics of the past, precludes the formulation of 'theoretical constructs', and if the attempt is made, 'these constructs are nearly always of a more abstract character than the historian would be prepared to accept'.[15] In the early 1990s another sober reconstructionist, Lawrence Stone, took up a hard-line position when he publicly denounced 'attacks from extreme relativists from Hayden White to

Derrida' on the 'hard won professional expertise in the study of evidence that was worked out in the late nineteenth century'.[16] History, according to Stone, Elton and Marwick, deals with the historical concrete, not the speculative constructions of social scientists and even less those of deconstructionist philosophers of history and language. Imposing paradigms or models of explanation on the evidence means that the past cannot be thought, in practical effect, to have existed independently of the historian who works to understand it. Using theory means that we, as historians, impose models of explanation on the evidence of the past which are derived from social sciences, or increasingly from other modes of organisation knowledge like structuralism, post-structuralism, anthropology and literary theory. In this sense deconstructionism, for empiricists, is just one more kind of constructionist-type imposition on the past. Hard-core reconstructionist history is history proper, and proper history has no social theory or philosophical axes to grind.

Constructionism

Constructionism is essentially a sub-species of reconstructionism. It grew in the course of the twentieth century out of the weaknesses of the traditional reconstructionist paradigm.[17] The great complexity and variety of constructionism today results from the fact that most historians range themselves around the methodological point at which constructionism branches from reconstructionism. Historians today are probably more open to new ways of doing history than ever before. This branching begins with the recognition of the frailty of empiricism. The first practitioners of constructionist history in the nineteenth century – Karl Marx, Auguste Comte and Herbert Spencer – were dissatisfied with reconstructionism's simple descriptive narrative of discrete and singular events. For these nineteenth-century precursors of social theory, and subsequently for many others in the twentieth century, history can explain the past only when the evidence is placed within a pre-existing explanatory framework that allows for the calculation of general rules of human action. These general rules are revealed as patterns of behaviour, and singular events are seen as part of a discernible pattern. In the twentieth century the starting-point of this constructionist history was the New History movement of the 1920s, associated with the French school of historians who gathered around the journal *Annales*, and the American New Historians Frederick Jackson Turner, Charles Beard, James Harvey Robinson and Vernon L. Parrington. As the result of the branching process, the close of the twentieth century has seen an ever-greater variety of ways in which reconstructionism (narrative single event history) and social theory constructionism can be combined. The richness of constructionist history is witnessed in its development in the French *Annales* school from the work of Marc Bloch through to Fernand Braudel, to Emmanuel Le Roy Ladurie and Robert Darnton today, and in the work of anthropologically inspired historians like Natalie Zemon Davis. What is sometimes called cultural Marxism is another example of the development of narrative empiricism into a form of constructionism and is well represented in the work of self-styled empiricist Marxist historian E.P. Thompson. For such practitioners, constructionist model-making is not taken necessarily to involve fitting events into a preconceived pattern. For all these historians, as with those of the Modernisation School, the imposing of an explanatory framework does not diminish human agency, intentionality, or choice in the past, but rather enriches our understanding of it.

As modernist visions of history, reconstructionism and its constructionist cousin branched not over what is their shared belief in the separate existence of factual knowledge derived from observable evidence, but upon the empiricist claim that it is possible to build high order and well-justified interpretations upon observable and singular evidence alone. What is challenged by sophisticated constructionism is the implicit reconstructionist belief that historical investigation can resolve historical issues by evaluating unique events as the peculiarly historical litmus test of knowledge.[18] Very few reasonable reconstructionist or constructionist historians today endorse the rigidly conservative Elton–Marwick view of history as a purely evidence-based undertaking that is a non-philosophical and non-theoretical practice. History cannot be written as if it were in some way entirely removed from the experience of the present, of our everyday life or the dominant ideas within the broader intellectual community. Nor less is it able to avoid explanatory frameworks that must be to some greater or lesser extent culturally provided.

Many historians clustering around the point at which reconstructionism branches from constructionism accept that they mediate past reality through a complex mixture of professional if not social convention, and shared categories of analysis and conceptualisation if not actual ideological positioning. The more ideologically self-conscious social and cultural historians since the 1950s and 1960s have, however, written history as an interventionist exercise of dissent and opposition. This is particularly evident in the interpretations by leftist historian-activists like E.P. Thompson, Philip Foner, Christopher Hill, John

Saville, Mike Davis, George Rudé, David Roediger, Victor Kiernan, Herbert Gutman and Raphael Samuel – just a few among many. Although Elton severely disapproves, the present varieties of social history are evidence that history is more and more constructed and written as a form of political commitment to marginalised groups – racial and ethnocultural, gendered, class, colonial, sexual and regional. Much social and cultural history now being written assumes that the historian's personal beliefs and commitments cannot be suspended, but that this does not diminish the value of our historical understanding. It is also more and more widely recognised that there is, in addition, another important dimension to the writing of history – the form it takes. Notwithstanding claims by some in the *Annales* camp to the contrary, even the most positivist of constructionist history has to be written as a narrative. The main point of deconstructionist history is this recognition, that the primary function of historians, whether they are ostensibly reconstructionist or constructionist, is to narrate a story based upon their understanding of other narratives and their pre-existing interpretations.

This recognition was signalled by a concerned Lawrence Stone first in 1979, and again in 1991/92. In his 1979 article 'The Revival of Narrative', Stone claimed to detect the end of social theory (constructionist) history and, as the article title suggests, the return to an earlier kind of narrative-based history (reconstructionism).[19] Developments in the next decade or so prompted a second foray of 1991/92 in which he characterised the relationship between 'History and Post-Modernism' (the title of the article) as producing three new threats to history – from linguistics, anthropology and the new historicism.[20] Despite responses defending the new historicist turn in social and cultural history which noted that for all practical purposes the events and processes of the past are indistinguishable from the forms of their documentary representation and the historical discourses that constructed them, Stone remained convinced that history was in danger of losing sight of the essential character of its elemental empiricist and contextualist foundation, as he said, because of 'the extreme position that there is no reality outside language'.[21]

One of Stone's antagonists, the British social historian Patrick Joyce, claimed that there was a crisis in the history profession and that it centred on a three-fold consideration: first, that language constitutes meaning in the social world; second, the historical object of study is always created by the historian; and last, our access to the past is only ever through a text – the text as the historian's written interpretation, or as documentary evidence: diaries, statutes, graveyard memorials, wills, films, or whatever. As a result, history is also about the relationship between such texts and our past and present social life as mediated through language-use. Since the late 1970s, literary theory has established its influence over historians as it has over many other people working in the humanities and social sciences. We historians are increasingly aware, for example, of the literary rules that govern the production of our texts and the nature of historical narrative representation. Leading French historian Roger Chartier concludes that all texts (whether literary or historical, evidence or interpretation) are best viewed as the result of a constructed production and reading by the historian. They are *a* representation of the past rather than the objective access to *the* reality of the past.[22] As the historian consumes the evidence of the past, he/she also produces a meaning. How we organise/emplot the evidence creates the past for us and our readers. This understanding is at the heart of deconstructionist history.

Deconstructionism: narrative and history

Historians of the deconstructionist or linguistic turn, like others aware of the indeterminate character of postmodern society and the self-referential nature of representation, are conscious that the written historical narrative is the formal *re-presentation* of historical content.[23] This consciousness has emerged in the last quarter of the twentieth century, prompting all historians to think self-consciously about how we use language – to be particularly aware of the figurative character of our own narrative as the medium by which we relate the past and written history. This means further exploring the idea that our opaque language constitutes and represents rather than transparently corresponds to reality, that there is no ultimate knowable historical truth, that our knowledge of the past is social and perspectival, and that written history exists within culturally determined power structures. As Chartier has argued, no text, even 'the most apparently documentary, even the most "objective", can ever 'maintain a transparent relationship with the reality that it apprehends'.[24]

The French post-structuralist philosopher and cultural critic Jacques Derrida coined the term deconstruction to challenge the fundamental tenet of Anglo-American and European philosophy and reconstructionist history: that there is a stable/knowable reality 'out there' that we can access accurately. It is upon such a belief that the basic polarities of real–unreal, fact–fiction, truth–untruth, subject–object, and mind–knowledge were established in our culture.[25] The thrust of literary deconstruction – that there is no certainty of meaning in language-based texts because 'out there' is always encountered as a socially constructed text – has provoked outrage among empiricist philosophers and commonsense contextualist historians. The idea that we constantly intervene in the real world through language means that we cannot achieve a direct representation of reality, and the correspondence theory of knowledge collapses. While at one level it may seem obvious that our world is known to us only through language, and that language-use makes knowing possible, this is never acknowledged by inured reconstructionists as central to the writing of history, or if it is noted by a few, it is as just another constraint among many.

As soon as we acknowledge that written history is open rather than closed in meaning, as when, for example, the history of imperialism is written from a non-European perspective – not recognised as a perspective at all in the West until the second half of the twentieth century and the advent of decolonisation – then we come closer to what postmodern history means: a recognition of the relativism of meaning, determined by where one stands and the dissolution of source-derived certainty in historical representation. But most historians clustering around the reconstructionist/constructionist axis still insist on seeking out *the* past, as opposed to *a* possible history. They accept evidence as *the* essential proof that something discoverable and recoverable happened in the past, reasoning that the source, if studied appropriately – in its context and/or the application of appropriate models of explanation – will reveal the reality behind it. The deconstructionist historian, on the other hand, maintains that evidence only signposts possible realities and possible interpretations because all contexts are inevitably textualised or narrativised or texts within texts. When we historians interpret the past we write texts to marshal ideas, to sift and sort evidence, and thereby inevitably and primarily impose a narrative or textualised shape on the past. The implications of this textual impositionalism are substantial. If deconstructionist historians are correct, and history as knowledge is not discovered, but is produced in and through language – as a text – then there can be no reality shorn of presupposition, nor the interpretative shaping of historians.[26] This is not a disagreement over historical objectivity, but more one about how thought itself can apprehend the presumed 'real' or truthful world 'out there' through an acknowledgement of the 'varieties of realities', or even recognise history's ultimately meaningless, and therefore open, nature.

STRUCTURALISM

This basic challenge to empiricism, and particularly its belief in the power of language to explain through correspondence theory, had its origins at the start of the twentieth century, in the broad intellectual enterprise known as structuralism. What we might call orthodox structuralism maintains that we perceive and interpret the real world through an innate and pre-existing or *a priori* mental grid. This grid works at the deep level of human consciousness and is exhibited in the real world in many ways, as the structure of grammar, as kinship relationships, myths, even as patterns of food consumption. This means that any body of information, like historical data, can be understood only through pre-existing or generic mental structures located in the mind of the historian. Understanding does not come unsullied with the data, and the data do not possess inherent and discoverable empirical truths, or direct and unmediated correspondences with reality. The point is that structuralism emphasises the formal qualities of what is an *a priori* internal mental system of understanding, rather than the independent power of external determinants. As the British Marxist cultural critic Raymond Williams self-reflexively pointed out, although there have been many variations in the use of the term structuralism, the 'primary emphasis is on deep permanent structures of which the observed variations of languages and cultures are forms'. The inevitable result, as he noted, has been a growing 'rejection of historical (historicist) and evolutionary assumptions' about how we acquire knowledge in the humanities and social sciences.[27] It is this structuralist insight that both Foucault and White use as springboards for their analyses.

Structuralism has had a profound effect on the way in which we think about the past as history, as well as the present and, for that matter, our future. As a theory of how we acquire knowledge, structuralism quickly placed the notion of scientific objectivity under sustained pressure as the relativist basis of knowledge emerged, resulting in the more recent intellectual developments of post-structuralism and new historicism. Its ramifications now cross all fields of knowledge – the natural and life sciences, the law, anthropology, cosmology, sociology, philosophy, literature and history. As we shall see, structuralism, but particularly its successor post-structuralism, as well as their joint off-spring new historicism, have ultimately all helped to shape the deconstructionist objections to traditional history.

It was in the study of linguistics that structuralism had its beginnings. Between 1907 and 1911, a Professor of Linguistics at the University of Geneva, Ferdinand de Saussure, delivered a series of three lecture courses. Upon his relatively early death at the age of 56 in 1913, some of his friends and colleagues published a synthesis of his lectures and notes as a book, the *Course in General Linguistics*.[28] In the *Course* Saussure detailed his ideas about the relationship between words and their social meaning. In so doing he produced two arguments that have become central to linguistics and to our understanding of the role of language in the creation of all knowledge, not just historical knowledge.

The first is that language operates according to its own rules and is quite unrelated to the 'real world', past or present. Saussure explains this apparently strange idea through his formulation of the *langue* and *parole* – the former being language's structure, the latter the actual examples of the system in operation, usually an utterance or expression. Saussure does not see language as just a huge collection of pictures reflecting the reality of things – for example, that the quality or reality of being a horse naturally corresponds to the word horse. In Saussure's opinion, words do not unproblematically correspond to the things to which they refer – their referents. There is no natural relationship between the word and the world. The relationship between words and what they signify is, therefore, arbitrary. Any referentiality we assume in language is the result of it being fixed by social convention.

Saussure's second argument follows from this lack of natural correspondence of word and world. Words are only 'signs' being, in effect, defined by their difference from other words in a sentence. Signs are constructed out of two elements – the signifier (the word) and the signified (the concept that the word represents). The structuralist view of language concerns itself only with the structure of the arbitrary connections between signifiers, instead of gazing beyond the language system at the signified. The important point about the arbitrary signifier–signified relationship is that it is socially produced. Although we all tend to use words as if they were strictly referential, they are of course based on conventional social meanings or generally accepted social values. Saussure's primary insistence on the *langue* means rejecting the historical, or diachronic, dimension of language in favour of the structural, or synchronic, as he calls it.

We need to understand the implications that this has, particularly for history. Because the importance of the sign resides in this arbitrary connection between signifier and signified, it follows that language is the complex and determining expression of our experience of life and being. We live in a social world of language, and thus language is always freighted with social meaning and is, as Foucault argues, homologous to the power relationships creating the social structure. It follows that language, in describing experience, is unavoidably ideological. Ideology may be defined as a mode of thinking that is in some way or other related to the hierarchies of society and the dispensation of power within it. Consequently, language is never innocent. The definition and meaning of words/concepts are always connected to the use of power in our society. We shall return to this very important issue again when I further discuss the special contribution of Michel Foucault to the deconstructionist consciousness.

Structuralism's notion of the text as a self-sufficient sealed system means that structuralist-inspired literary critics do not comprehend their sources – fictional texts – by studying them in their context of real life. The structuralist literary critic tries to understand them by isolating text from context, attempting to work out how the text figures according to some deep grammatical or syntactic structure. This arcane form of literary criticism is unattractive for most literary critics who prefer to relate their texts to the real world to grasp their meaning. Structuralism in its pure form insists that we have to become detached from this involvement, but this is not possible for historians, dealing as we do with society. The one implication of this structuralist preoccupation with the nature of language that is of crucial importance for historians is the arbitrary nature of signs, which emphasises the problematic nature of language as an effective medium of expression and understanding. Because language is unable to make any kind of natural, original or genuine sense of the world (including structuralism!), structuralism gives way to post-structuralism. If structuralism recognises the importance of language, then post-structuralism acknowledges its limitations as a means of understanding. Accepting the elusive nature of the text as full of gaps, silences and uncertainties of meaning – unfixed and flowing signifiers – it suggests that historical interpretation of the texts, like literary criticism, must be indeterminate and that all its readings are more or less inadequate. This does not, of course, mean that any interpretation is as good as any other; it simply means that there are no definitive interpretations.[29]

POST-STRUCTURALISM

This view of language as an infinity of free-flowing signifiers that have no knowable, and therefore no concrete, point of origination, and consequently no certain end, has been the central concern of Jacques Derrida. To explore this idea of endless chains of signification, Derrida employs the structuralist concept of *différance* whereby words are defined by their difference to other words, but meaning is continuously *deferred* as every word leads to another in the system of signification.

The French critical theorist Roland Barthes took up this post-structuralist idea of endless chains of signification in the late 1960s and 1970s, arguing that in consequence knowledge must have many second-order levels of meaning and signification.[30] What we have then is a fundamental challenge to the correspondence or referential theory of meaning.

Worryingly for mainstream reconstructionist/constructionist historians, if language is uncertain, then our knowledge we gain through it must be equally indeterminate. This means that it is impossible to construct truthful narratives as historical explanations. Despite Derrida's and Barthes' post-structuralist argument that meaning is just a stream of signifiers, most historians still insist on the eccentric practice of reading texts (historical sources and narratives) to locate *the* truth. They do this because they still believe in the commonsense reconstructionist notion that there is *a* referent for each word and that consequently there is some external presence to the text as evidence *that we can be sure of.* Many historians still continue the search for *the real* historical past as it once existed and which they believe can be truthfully recovered like treasure trove hauled from the sea bed or a fire re-ignited from the ashes.

The question is what can historians do when confronted by these issues? Most simply do not think about them. Entertaining doubts about the veracity of language leads to a critical process that requires unravelling the style and figurative dimensions of texts. The vast majority of historians are just not interested in that undertaking. They argue that they do not wish to study the literary form of their own discourse – the books they write. However, this issue of relating form to content to context quickly became a part of the new historicist movement which emerged in the last twenty years of the twentieth century.[31] Not of initial concern to historians, new historicism emerged as a type of literary criticism in the United States in the early 1980s.[32] Taking its intellectual cue(s) from a variety of post-structuralist literary critics and postmodernist thinkers, new historicism challenged literature's established disciplinary boundaries while ventilating further doubts about language as a transparent medium able to generate meaning by corresponding to the social world, past and present – a debate that paralleled and fuelled doubts about the representational power of written history.

NEW HISTORICISM

By the late-1990s new historicism had moved beyond literary criticism to assume the proportions of a much wider cultural analysis. As

Hayden White has suggested, new historicism was initially little more than 'an attempt to restore a historical dimension to . . . literary studies',[33] to relocate literary works within their historical context – to understand poems, novels and plays as texts not simply in their structuralist relation to each other, but also in their associative connections with the institutions of society and the historical events that might have influenced their production: the relationship of text to context. As a cultural analysis, new historicism was yet another twist in the continuing exploration of the socially constructed relationship between the knower and the known, between evidence, proof and truth. For worried historians like Lawrence Stone, new historicism is a threat to the traditional study of the past because it deals with political and social practices as cultural scripts, or language systems or codes, with history emptied of its association with past reality.[34]

It is important for historians to understand what new historicism is saying because, like deconstructive history, it is built on assumptions that directly challenge the empiricist paradigm.[35] First, our descriptions of real historical events like fictional ones can at best only be representations, or events under description, because there is no direct way in which historians can acquire first-hand historical knowledge. Second, history as a literary form is about the unique and contingent event and the real nature of causality must consequently always remain unresolved. Third, historians ought to recognise the overlapping of historical events and their interpretation – not just that the written history of one generation becomes the primary sources of the next, but that the historical text itself exists intertextually within the broader social and political structures of any epoch. Finally, new historicist thinking suggests that our evidence and the written discourse we produce in interpreting it are time and place specific – there are no universal historical truths to be discovered or transcendental values to be elaborated. These seemingly innocuous assumptions undermine the two mainstream approaches to history because they undercut reconstructionist foundational beliefs in an accurately discernible reality 'out there', and in the fact that we can verify constructionist theories of explanation through empirical testing.

Consequently, the distinction between cultural history and other literary disciplines has disappeared under new historicist thinking about the conventions underpinning the representation of factual as well as fictional texts. This opening up of historical analysis to rhetorical interrogation is at the heart of deconstructionist history, which recognises no practical distinction between history proper and the philosophy of history where that includes analysis of the form of history's written form.

What this means is that the analysis of emplotment and style, more usually applied to fictional literature, is also basic to the understanding of all types of historical text, including sources.[36] The narrative form of explanation is now redeemed as a central feature of the historical enterprise, and the notional distinction between historical and literary language disappears.

Deconstructionist history's reading of its sources elevates their form, in the shape of their narrative structure, use of metaphor, style, emplotment, and so forth, to the same level of interpretative analytical significance as that of content. Form must be acknowledged like empirically derived content in the production and conveyance of meaning and knowledge. This does not mean that the content of the past is secondary or unimportant. What it does mean is that, as the cultural critic Raymond Williams declares, we need to examine 'the forms of content and the content of forms, as integral processes'.[37] Because deconstructionist history no longer demarcates literary texts as qualitatively or categorically different from either historical sources or interpretations, there is no need for a privileged hierarchy between the historian's critical study of the sources and a self-effacing role for language and the narrative ordering of the data. The deconstruction of history means no longer repressing the importance of *writing* history or, more radically, being willing to view the past as well as our existence in the present as texts to be read.

DECONSTRUCTIONIST HISTORY: FOUCAULT AND WHITE

For reconstructionists, their version of history centres on the nature of evidence as the key to the accurate recovery of the past. The failings of the correspondence theory of truth, the imposition of theoretical structures, the indeterminacy of language or debates over the nature of reality are not primary concerns. Two individuals who have challenged mainstreamers to address these perspectives, however, are the French intellectual historian and historian of sexuality Michel Foucault, and the American historian of the Renaissance and philosopher of history Hayden White. Both have addressed the representational function of language in the production of historical knowledge, and specifically the relationship between historical 'discourse' and past and present cultural change. For my purposes, historical discourse is defined as a shared language-use where meaning derives not directly from the intentionality of the speaker/writer as either historical actor or historian, nor solely in respect of the content of what is said or written, but from the formal structure and context in which the utterance or text is delivered or located.[38] Taking this definition with its emphasis on history's social context, both Foucault and White have stressed the capricious nature of historical discourse that results from the arbitrary signifier–signified–referent relationship, and the consequent unsettled social world of the past and the present.

Foucault especially has acknowledged the post-structuralist question-mark over narrative's failure to encompass any genuine correspondence to, or reflection of, past reality. The traditional or commonsense reconstructionist search for historical origins is not a part of his project. He is a historian who does not believe in the empiricist notion of causality. While this lack of belief in itself clearly casts him beyond the bounds of mainstream history, he further compounds his sinning by both placing the individual historian at the very centre of the process of constituting historical knowledge, while at the same time questioning the centrality of the author as the generator of meaning. His definition of historical truth depends on the agreement between historians as to what constitutes the historically real – summarised by Foucault as the will to knowledge. For Foucault, knowledge and discourse are interchangeable, and because both are grounded in the cultural practices of society, they are inextricably related to the exercise of power both intellectual and material. The central claim of conservative reconstructionists – that the history they write is the discovery of the verifiable truth of the past – Foucault rejects as naïve, or, what is worse, as the perpetuation of a monstrous myth.

In assuming that written history is essentially a form of literature, Hayden White also addresses the issue of history as an epistemology resting on the distinction already noted between *the past* and *history*. Because for White we can never know *the* story of the past as it actually was, it means that there can be no historiographically uncontaminated past – the past exists for us *only* as it is written up by historians. History does not pre-exist in any body of facts that will allow unmediated access to *the* real past. History, as opposed to the past, is a literary creation because it is always interpreted through textualised relics which themselves are only to be understood through layers of interpretation as the historian's facts. Because the facts never arrange themselves autonomously to yield meaning, White argues that it is the function of the historian to impose a meaning through the organisation of the data as a narrative. This necessitates troping and emplotments. This is the point at which many mainstream historians reject what they see as White's cutting adrift of history from its factual anchor. White, they claim, relativises the past in the light of his now famous post-structuralist-inspired, anti-representational and anti-empiricist suggestion that historical narratives . . . are verbal fictions, the contents of which are as much invented as found and the forms of which have more in common with their counterparts in literature than they have with those in the sciences.[39]

For White, the historian's interpretation means selecting from the evidence that which is significant and that which, when strung together, produces a meaningful explanation, or, as he would say, an emplotment.

The actual mechanism for relating the evidence to the context necessitates us formally employing strategies of explanation founded on the tropes (the figures of speech I have already mentioned: metaphor, metonymy, synecdoche and irony), emplotments (the four primary ones of romance, tragedy, comedy and satire), and other strategies of explanation which he calls formal arguments (formist, mechanist, organicist and contextualist), as well as explanations through the ideological commitment of the author/historian (anarchist, radical, conservative and liberal). These aspects of historical explanation will be examined in more detail when I discuss White's model of historical explanation in Chapter 8. The important point for now is that the process of historical explanation for both White and Foucault is one of literary effect, rather than literal meaning. Historical explanation ultimately relies upon the use of the tropes that we all use to express whole–part (and the reverse) relationships, and which I have already designated as the troping process. As French historian Philippe Carrard claims, historians can try to eliminate such literary devices, but writing 'without turning to tropes is not a simple task, even for scholars who . . . have been trained to do so through such demanding exercises as *dissertations historiques*'.[40] As we shall see, metaphor, the founding trope, as well as its successive refinements in the form of metonymy and synecdoche, are basic to the constitution of narrative explanations and the human process of understanding, experiencing and explaining social change. Like people in the past (and in the present and future), because we historians cannot escape figuration in narrative we should understand the nature of its representational character.

CONCLUSION

At the start of this chapter I posed the question: why is it that history keeps on changing? The deconstructionist answer ought now to be clearer. It changes for two reasons. The first is the postmodern condition in which we live and which confronts the inadequacy of the modernist empirical method; the second, flowing directly from this, is the realisation that history is a constituted narrative discourse written by the historian in the here and now. History always comes to us at many removes from the actuality it claims to represent. Every historical interpretation is just one more in a long chain of interpretations, each one usually claiming to be closer to the reality of the past, but each one merely another reinscription of the same events, with each successive description being the product of the historian's imposition at the levels of the trope, emplotment, argument and ideology. No amount of training in the forensic skills of dissecting the sources can eliminate the unavoidable process whereby the historical work is as much invented as found. History is not a separate epistemology, but as a form of explanation is a plausible literature. The fact that the historical narrative is always figurative confounds the empirical insistence on history as a realistic reconstruction or representation of what happened by correspondence to facts. While this is at the centre of deconstructionist history, it remains unacceptable not only to the conservative minority of reconstructionist historians but to all mainstreamers who refuse to slip the anchor of empiricism. It is necessary, therefore, to examine their vision of the historical enterprise before we can move to my criticism and the implications of the deconstructionive consciousness for the writing of history.

3 History as reconstruction/construction

INTRODUCTION

As I have attempted to show, although most historians found in either of the two main tendencies agree that history is presented as a written interpretative narrative, they assume that it corresponds to what actually happened because of the research carefully undertaken in the sources. They perform this research task believing in the ideal of objectivity and attempt to produce interpretations through a value-free inductive and/or deductive method, and finally reach what is for them convincing historical explanations. In sum, their interpretation possesses referentiality and corresponds to the truth. What unifies the majority of historians is this general commitment to an evidence-based methodology which, by following basic inferential 'rules of evidence', is presumed to produce specific interpretations that allow the reconstruction/construction of the past close to the truth of what it was about. I shall now review this complex approach to acquiring historical knowledge prior to examining the issues raised for deconstructionist history.

EPISTEMOLOGY

Reconstructionism and its positivist model-making derivative, constructionist history, rely ultimately on a shared belief in both the epistemological integrity of empiricism and a recoverable past reality 'out there'. One recent commentator claims that, 'in contrast to radical scepticism', as a historian he adopts 'the realist position that it is possible by means of a resort to the tried and tested "historical discourse of the proof" (both theoretical and evidential in character) truthfully to reconstruct the past'.[1] Reconstructionists, by assuming an anti-hypothetical and value-neutral empirical method (akin to a positivist or scientific methodology), believe, as that quotation evidences, that they really can explain the past with a substantial claim to accuracy and truthfulness. The mainstream reconstructionist philosopher of history C. Behan McCullagh provides an exceptionally clear argument as to the objectives of reconstructionists and maintains that most try to discover what actually happened in the past, which explains

> why they pay such attention to the accuracy of their observations of evidence and to the adequacy of their inferences from it, and why they refuse to put forward any descriptions of the past for which there is not good evidence. If the pursuit of truth were abandoned as the goal of historical inquiry, then the main reason for insisting upon present standards of historical criticism would disappear.[2]

McCullagh concludes that

> although historical descriptions cannot be proved true beyond all possibility of error, they can often be proved probably true, given empiricist assumptions. Assuming that an historian's perceptions of data are very probably accurate, that his general knowledge and other beliefs are very probably true, and that his forms of inference are generally reliable, one can rationally infer the probable truth of many historical descriptions.[3]

Without this belief in the reliability of a historical description as inferred from the available evidence, we could never claim that history exists as a distinct epistemology. To the extent that we believe in inductive inference, we believe in the truth of historical knowledge. For McCullagh, calling the interpretation of a text correct 'is to say it would be accepted as the meaning of the text by the majority of educated speakers of the language in which it is written'. These educated speakers would, of course, be aware of the 'literary and historical contexts relevant to its subject matter and the intentions of its author'.[4] As he neatly concludes, summarising the philosophical underpinning of the mainstream position, 'to pursue reliable historical descriptions is to pursue true ones'.[5] The only ground for doubting this logic is if we deny the essential nature of empiricism, or if the historian's 'forms of inference' are in some way flawed. McCullagh is convinced that the 'objective understanding of historical texts is possible', that understanding is 'rationally justifiable' and that meaning thus derived should be accepted as correct.[6]

For most of the twentieth century this way of acquiring knowledge has constituted a consensus founded on the six key principles of empiricism:

- The past (like the present) is real and 'truth' corresponds to that reality through the mechanism of referentiality and inference – the discovery of facts in the evidence.
- For reconstructionists, facts normally precede interpretation, although constructionists argue that inductive reasoning cannot operate independently of the deduction of generalised explanations.
- There is a clear division between fact and value.
- History and fiction are not the same.
- There is a division between the knower and that which is known.
- Truth is not perspectival.[7]

The essential feature of historical truth for all mainstream empiricists resides in the first principle: that a single historical description, as opposed to an interpretation based on several related descriptions, may be regarded as true so long as it corresponds to, or resembles, one or more of a set of truth conditions. This means that we can believe a historical description is true if it accords preferably to several known criteria or at worst a single criterion of correspondence or referentiality. The criteria of correspondence are usually found through comparing pieces of primary evidence or, less convincingly, the descriptions of other historians which constitute our secondary evidence. Truthful historical descriptions may be taken to depend upon one or more of three kinds of inference: first, that most favoured by reconstructionist/constructionist historians and what I will label as the hypothesis–deduction–data–induction method, or the loop of explanation and evidence; second, statistical probability; and finally, the deconstructive notion of historical justifications derived and implied by our narratives.

McCullagh's concern, namely the extent to which historians can accurately recover and represent the past, has been reformulated by the self-proclaimed practical realist historians Joyce Appleby, Lynn Hunt and Margaret Jacob in their collaborative and provocatively entitled book *Telling the Truth About History* (1994) in which they, like McCullagh, promote and defend the correspondence theory of historical explanation. In their collective view the debate on the relationship between postmodernism and history comes down to how we bridge the gap between the records of the past, and their narrative interpretation by the historian. As moderates in this debate, they willingly acknowledge as a truism that 'the past only dimly corresponds to what the historians say about it'. While they accept the basic reconstructionist tenet of the existence of a discoverable historical truth 'out there', as practical realists they happily concede 'the tentativeness and imperfections of the historians' accounts'. Naturally, their commitment to the correspondence theory requires that they insist that this does not 'cause them to give up the effort to aim for accuracy and completeness and to judge historical accounts on the basis of those criteria'. They contrast their pragmatism with that of the 'anti-realists' or 'relativists', whom they suggest believe 'any kind of correspondence is impossible' between evidence and written narrative interpretation.[8]

Because Appleby, Hunt and Jacob have become the most widely read proponents of what we might call the moderate wing of the reconstructionist position, we should take seriously their attraction to 'reconstructing what appears in the mind when it contemplates the past'. It is appropriate then that we should isolate the six key principles upon which this reconstructionist/constructionist view of history is founded – what Appleby, Hunt and Jacob describe as the translation of words 'from the documents into a story that seeks to be faithful to the past' and which constitutes 'the historians' particular struggle with truth'.[9]

This classic, six-point, historical method assumes that advances in the techniques used to study and draw inductive and deductive inferences from the evidence will generate ever more truthful historical interpretations. This assumption is summarised in Arthur Marwick's claim that 'the powerful shoulders of our illustrious predecessors [are there] for us to stand on', and as a result there is an 'absolute advance in the quality, the "truthfulness" of history'.[10] Marwick is convinced that history is primarily about 'finding things out, and solving problems, rather than about spinning narratives or telling stories'. He insists that 'History is a human activity carried out by an organised corps of fallible human beings [acting] in accordance with strict methods and principles, empowered to make choices in the language they use . . . and known as historians.'[11] Marwick, like Elton, rejects White's and Foucault's claim for the inevitable impositionalism of the historian. Although Marwick accepts the notion of history as a discipline in the sense of a profession, he will not agree that the profession is disciplined by power relations to say and do certain things. He certainly disagrees with White's view that history has been domesticated by ideologies of all kinds from the nineteenth century onwards, and that deconstruction has reinvigorated the past by acknowledging its possibilities rather than truths to be found.

Most mainstream historians start by rejecting what they characterise as a relativist view of historical knowledge. They agree that the past once existed and that the human mind is quite capable of producing statements about it that are close enough to reality for most practical purposes. Behind this practical-realist empiricist approach is the belief that *the* truth once existed and is now discoverable because the events and actions that have occurred correspond to the evidence. We can, therefore, be fully justified in making factual statements describing that correspondence, and any provisionality of historical interpretation simply means every interpretation is just one more further genuine attempt to get closer to the truth – standing on Marwick's shoulders. The bases for historical knowledge are events and actions represented as empirical facts. This view rejects the deconstructionist position that facts are narrativised texts and always, therefore, cloudy, obscure and ultimately impenetrable.

Central to empiricism is the assumption that historians, like scientists, search for *the* truth. For historians this is the assumption of referentiality rather than a truth-*effect*. The inheritance of the early seventeenth-century English historian Francis Bacon remains today in his development of the primary historical method – inductive inference. This method derives historical meaning by drawing un-biased inferences from the detailed evidence of individual examples. Baconian-inspired inductivism reached its high tide in the years from the late 1950s to the 1980s in the work of English historians like Hugh Trevor-Roper (in *Religion, the Reformation, and Social Change*, 1967) and G.R. Elton (in *England, 1200–1640*, 1969), and Americans Oscar Handlin (*Boston's Immigrants*, 1959), Gertrude Himmelfarb (*The Idea of Poverty: England in the Early Industrial Age*, 1984) and J.H. Hexter (*Reappraisals in History*, 1969), as well as philosophers of history like Quentin Skinner (*Machiavelli*, 1981). All accepted the commonsense referentiality of language and forcefully rejected the impositionalism of *a priori* conceptualisations arrived at by deductive inference.

Unlike social scientists, reconstructionist historians do not propose general theories, or operate working hypotheses that they then proceed to 'prove' by the derivation of facts through empirical research. Inductive inference requires that theories of explanation emerge from the discovery of the evidence which translates into meaningful facts after being placed in its historical context. Having said this, as Alex Callinicos points out, in historical explanation today deductively inferred theories are invariably employed, either consciously or unconsciously. It is impossible, even for the most stainless of reconstructionist historians, to approach their evidence innocent of presupposition, since prior assumptions may, wittingly or unwittingly, await confirmation or denial through research – examples of the *a priorism* so distasteful to Elton and Marwick. In practice, deduction and induction merge as the process of historical reconstruction translates slowly into construction and back again. The more epistemologically self-conscious we have become about the possibilities in the theories we employ, and the philosophy of history to which we adhere, helps explain why our constructionist history has become ever more complex in the last twenty years.

As Appleby, Hunt and Jacob have demonstrated, few historians today deploy a pure form of inductive analysis reliant solely upon a commonsense interpretation of events that assumes, almost as an afterthought, the use of a transparent and unproblematic narrative medium. Nevertheless, most reconstructionists continue to insist that they justify their inductive inferences – and therefore sustain the epistemological integrity of the discipline – through the direct observation of the evidence of the past. The data thus observed/discovered determine the inductive interpretation, regardless of whether that interpretation differs from that which may be currently dominant among their peers. Consistency, coherence and correspondence with the observable facts remain the watchwords of reconstructionist history now as they have been for the past century.

EVIDENCE

In his defence of induction as *the* historical method, Elton insists that 'history should not be regarded as merely a form of some other intellectual enterprise: it has its own operating rules, its own independent function, and its own contribution to make to the intellectual and social life of mankind'.[12] Inductivist historical knowledge, Elton maintains, derives from the authority of the available and validated sources. But as British historian John Tosh has said, interpretation of the evidence cannot *literally* generate a meaning, without 'a command of the historical context' which will reveal that to which the evidence corresponds.[13] Reconstructionist historians cannot understand the past by only consulting the textual evidence. They must place it within the broader framework of which they are aware, the context, in order to reconstruct the past as it really was. Contextualisation is not the same as configuration or emplotment, the latter two being the active product of the historian, unlike the former, which reconstructionists assume to be merely the setting of the scene, the laying out of the adjacent pieces of evidence, the other pieces in the jigsaw.

Scrupulous attention to the evidence is the bedrock of the six principles. We could do worse than consult G.R. Elton on the importance of these principles in the processing of evidence for the reconstructionist historian. As he says:

We are looking for a way to ground historical reconstruction in something that offers a measure of independent security – independent of the historian, independent of the concerns of his day, independent of the social and political conditions imposed on him. And the obvious answer to this quest, as it has always been and must continue to be, lies in the sources he has at his disposal. *Ad fontes* remains the necessary war cry. For the historian the reality – yes, the truth – of the past exists in materials of various kinds, produced by that past at the time that it occurred and left behind by its testimony. Historical evidence is not created by the historian, and little of it was deliberately created for him; it is simply that deposit of past happenings that still exist to be looked at.[14]

Elton thus summarises the traditional key assumptions upon which evidence is treated and interpreted. This can be undertaken only by the professionally trained historian, which means the independently minded and judicial historian. This training is a mixture of language skills, a broad knowledge of the context, a deep knowledge of the extant interpretations within the field, and a close understanding of the nature of the primary sources which allows comparison and verification. But Elton is at pains to point out that the understanding of the evidence is not the same as saying that it is 'processed through the historian's personal mind'. Instead historians must all ask the same questions of the evidence – who created it, for what purposes, and how did they create it? 'Which is to say [that these fundamental questions we put to the evidence are] independent of the concerns of the questioner and focused entirely on the concerns of the original creators.'[15] The point is to divorce the historian from the past – not only to get rid of hindsight, but to avoid writing history from the perspective of the present. The historian's personal preferences, whether in terms of bias of method, or ideology (or both), must be avoided.

Firm in his belief in *the* historical method of inductive inference, Elton insists that it subjects 'every paradigm on offer to a sceptical questioning in the light of discoverable detail'. Unlike, say, literature, historians do not have the same free will to put forward interpretations constrained only by our imagination. We cannot invent details just to make our story more convincing. For Elton, reconstructionist history is thus neither science nor art:

> For it cannot expect to arrive at knowledge testable by falsification (the secret of a science), nor can it manipulate its subject matter so as to produce morally or aesthetically satisfying results (the characteristic of an art). In short, history is a study different from any other and governed by rules peculiar to itself.[16]

It is the study of evidence that not only makes history epistemologically independent but, more significantly, makes it capable of reconstructing the past as it actually happened, and without any imposition from the historian.

As a result of the practice of objective inductive inference there is always daylight between fact and value in the study of the traces of the past. This means never breaching the divide between the knower and the known when asking questions of the evidence. Questions should be separated from prior knowledge so that the evidence cannot be skewed towards an answer already lurking in the recesses of the historian's brain. This fences off the deductive method for Elton. Neither begging the question nor begging the answer has a place in reconstructing the past. In a felicitous phrase Elton summarises this as meaning 'one solicits questions from the evidence [for it is] wrong to start with exact questions carrying in-built answers'.[17] For example, it would be bad practice to interpret the late nineteenth-century American economic advance across the Pacific as a salt-water economic imperialism, while at the same time asking what social class or classes benefited. This is a value-laden question that assumes the existence of classes and which, therefore, begs answers. It would be better to inquire of the evidence of economic expansion what was its particular character in comparison to other periods of economic growth, and did the process benefit a particular group, if any? Different forms of questions produce different answers.

Keeping an open mind about the past assumes that history and fiction are not the same and that truth is not perspectival. The application of the basic principles of reconstructionist historical analysis will produce conclusions about the past that, though often incomplete or tentative, will serve the social function of keeping *the* truthful social, political and economic memory. To fall below the exacting professional standards set for the reconstruction of the past is, according to Elton, to leave 'the task of telling about the past to the untrained and largely ignorant – to the writers of fiction, avowed or disguised, to the makers of films, to the journalists and speculators of the pen'.[18] The distinction between history and fiction resides in the professionalism of the historian as much as in the constraint to recount what actually happened rather than invent it. As Michael Stanford has argued, 'a historical fact accords with a judgement about the past in which historians agree'.[19] Stanford points to the difference between interpretations and facts – the former produce no consensus among historians; the latter do. Without this dependence on facticity history cannot exist.

In the last few years, however, a new moderate or practical realist consensus has dominated reconstructionist/constructionist historical scholarship. The American intellectual historian David Hollinger summarised this consensus when he argued that the historian's preconceptions are often what makes historical interpretation possible.[20] This is not to dispute the evidence, but to acknowledge the murky turning of evidence into facts (contextualisation) to produce an interpretation. When historians attempt to reconstruct the past by studying its evidence – Hollinger's process of *Quellenkritik* (the critical examination of documentary sources) – the historian cannot be as isolated from the reconstruction process as conservative empiricist reconstructionists like Elton would have us believe.

The clearest case of impositionalism is in the application of explanatory theories to the experience of the past – the deductive method as employed by constructionist historians. Deductive reasoning assumes that knowledge is derived from premises tested by observation. Contemplating this process horrifies hard-core reconstructionists like Elton. What he calls 'interpretative and ideological theory' arises from the ambition to 'destroy the reality of the past as it had previously emerged from a study of that past's relics', and he concludes that 'all do equal harm to the independent understanding of the past'.[21] We must, therefore, now examine the role of theory in writing the past.

THEORIES OF HISTORY: CONSTRUCTING THE PAST

Constructionism covers a variety of impositionalist approaches to the study of the past, but all share the reconstructionist's belief that our historical knowledge corresponds to the reality being studied. Both mainstreams doubt what they view as the proto-deconstructionist approach to history exemplified by R.G. Collingwood, but are happier to accept the position of E.H. Carr who typifies the relativist judgement which insists that they are facts because the historian has selected them for inquiry, what Carr calls historian's facts. It follows, much to the annoyance of Elton, that objectivity is now impossible to attain. Carr's view of history is that it is concerned with the relationship between the individual and the general, and, as a historian, 'you can no more separate them, or give precedence to one over the other, than you can separate fact and interpretation'.[22] For Carr, echoing Collingwood's general position:

> the facts of history never come to us 'pure' since they do not and cannot exist in a pure form: they are always refracted through the mind of the recorder. It follows that when we take up a work of history, our

first concern should not be with the facts which it contains but with the historian who wrote it.[23]

This position has a powerful appeal to constructionist historians. Callinicos, defending the constructionist historian, claims he/she goes about his/her business by inferring answers from the questions he/she puts *to* the evidence and not *from* the sources which cannot speak for themselves. Now this may sound reasonable enough, but at the end of the day Callinicos ends up in a position similar to Elton's as they both presume to solicit questions rather than answers from the evidence. Of course the difference is that Callinicos insists that facts emerge from analysis, not analysis from facts. According to Elton, Marxism, as the most well-known form of constructionism, chooses to view historical reality as being ordered by a bastard version of a so-called covering law. A covering law ascribes causation in history and it is derived from deductive inference. An explanation of an event or particular action is made (deduced) in terms of an invariable law of nature or human behaviour. Elton's rejection of covering laws follows on from his belief that historical explanation requires understanding the motivations, goals, values and information available to historical agents, all of which constitute their individual intentions and cannot be subsumed under universal explanations of behaviour. The divergent views of the ardent reconstructionist G.R. Elton, and the equally impassioned Marxist constructionist Alex Callinicos, reveal the chasm in the non-deconstructionist historical profession between the extremes of positivism and empiricism: what Peter Burke calls theorists and historians.[24]

When social theory historians write history they set about retelling and narrating the lives, intentions and events of the past with models of explanation already in their minds – gender, race, class, or whatever. Of course, they usually stress that they are not slaves to proving the accuracy of one over-arching theory of social action or philosophy of history, unless they are overtly committed to a certain perspective as an act of faith. Instead they maintain that their models are no more than 'concepts' – though often highly complex in construction – that emerge from the evidence and act as an aid to the understanding of the evidence. Most, therefore, insist that their interpretations are quite independent of any dominant self-serving theory or master narrative, a judgement that accounts for the widespread popularity among historians today of the E.H. Carr approach to history. Almost universally among practical realist historians – that majority of practising historians existing between the two extremes – it is assumed that the function of the historian is not only to establish the veracity and accuracy of the evidence, but also to bring all the known and available evidence into an interpretative fine focus by employing some organising concepts. The dissenting left, for example, use class, race and gender in a variety of ways. At the most sophisticated level gender, for illustration, is viewed as a richly complex category of analysis that is best employed when it recognises the equally important shaping power of the other categories of experience. The ultimate object for all practical realist historians, no matter how complex their methods or whether they ideologically dissent or conform, is to use evidence to demonstrate that the concepts they use are intrinsic to the evidence.

This situation effectively blurs any sharp division between reconstructionism and constructionism. It means in practice that historians do not go about their task in two separate phases of research in the sources for the facts, and then exercise interpretation using various concepts or models of explanation. Rather the historian gets going, in Carr's own words, 'on a few of what I take to be the capital sources' and then inevitably gets the itch to write, by which he means to compose an interpretation, and 'thereafter, reading and writing go on simultaneously'.[25] For Carr this means that the feared dichotomy 'of an untenable theory of history as an objective compilation of facts ... and an equally untenable theory of history as the subjective product of the mind of the historian' is far less of a problem than conservative reconstructionists – either of the left or right – might fear. For Carr this is how people operate in everyday life, a 'reflection of the nature of man' as he suggests.[26]

This merging of the mainstreams around the E.H. Carr position is found in the ideologically liberal practical realism of Appleby, Hunt and Jacob as they conclude: 'Inferential evidence of invisible structures and patterns abounds' in history writing today.[27] Not surprisingly, the Marxist Alex Callinicos agrees, believing that historical facts are arrived at 'inferentially by a process of interpreting data according to a complicated system of rules and assumptions'.[28] Where the two mainstreams branch is often only in the ideologically informed nature of the explanatory frameworks chosen to interpret the facts. When Appleby, Hunt and Jacob argue for the importance of 'structures and patterns', they are asking the perennial question: what is the nature of the relationship between free will and determinism in explaining the past? Answers to this question tend to hinge on ideological preferences. They suggest that the forces, the social structures and patterns that influence our lives are rarely palpable, and never quite as simplistic or reductive as, say, a crude Marxist class analysis suggests. As they argue,

'The falling rain is visible, but it takes meteorologists to explain the structure of climatic change.'[29] Social structures are taken to refer to consistent patterns that can be found in behaviour and beliefs and which to a greater or lesser extent determine intentional social action. Without concepts and categories like class, gender, race, nation, city, and so forth, the complexities of the past would be inexplicable, remaining at the level of lists of events and time charts.

That it is at the ideological level that members of the mainstream diverge is evidenced in Callinicos's refusal to accept the position of the American liberal-relativist and pragmatic philosopher Richard Rorty that historical meaning is at best provisional because, Rorty argues, there is no inherent truth to be discovered in the evidence. Callinicos rejects the Rortyan position that preference between explanatory theories may be purely aesthetic. In this way Callinicos rejects the pragmatic ideologically liberal reconstructionism of Appleby, Hunt and Jacob which accepts that historical interpretation may be measured not by reference to a reality found in the evidence and engineered by social theory, but according to other ideological criteria with which he does not agree. For Marxists in general the truth is indeed 'out there', and it is Marxist rather than bogus bourgeois liberal. But they would agree, as empiricists, that it is the material nature of the real world that makes the claims of historians true or false, not the nature of language or representation. Correspondence theory for mainstreamers, regardless of ideology, defines what occurs in the real world when our statements, as Callinicos says, 'capture the way the world is'.[30]

The constructionist process assumes – regardless of ideological preference – that explanatory frameworks as suggested by the evidence must be stated in propositional terms that are then open to verification through the further study of the evidence. To take the constructed social category of class by way of illustration, historical explanations using some kind of class model are legion, and historians create ever more complex theories of class explanation for their own personal use. They normally borrow existing models from colleagues (in history, economics, sociology, anthropology and cultural theory) and then look to the evidence to refine them as their preferred explanations. As noted at the start of this section, constructionism is a loose description that covers a spectrum of impositionalist approaches to the past. The precise nature of the class model employed by any single historian is, therefore, dictated by the complexity and assumed explanatory power of the social science and cultural models of class-based human behaviour that he/she has picked over. Other historians inclining towards the reconstructionist mainstream will stick to the empiricist method in which they have been schooled, leaving the propositional theoretical dimension at the mundane level of working explanations (but still ready to be modified as the evidence dictates), rather than go in for very complex social science constructionism.

The plea for complex model-making in history was made by James Harvey Robinson in his appropriately titled book *The New History* published in 1912, in which he argued for the study of a much broader social history, rejecting the then predominant distinction between history as a method concerned to explain unique events, and other disciplines that sought general explanations.[31] Robinson, however, went only so far, fearing to make history the 'prisoner' of *a priori* hypotheses that might deny the historian's objectivity.[32] For Robinson and his colleagues among the French *Annales* school, empiricism remained the foundation of the constructionist enterprise, although they acknowledged the complexities in the relationship between knower and known, explanation and event. For conservative reconstructionists, the New History marks the start of the descent into relativism. Most historians in the twentieth century have generally refused the siren voice of grand theory or deductive positivism, preferring instead to concentrate on the collection of detailed evidence upon which they could deploy the empiricist inductive method and their low-grade concepts or categories of analysis like class. However, the *Annales* school in France developed the constructionist tradition of marrying inductive inference from factual evidence with deduction (deductive inference) based upon more general prior sociological generalisations about the socio-economic and politico-cultural structures of society. For its adherents, this development added greatly to the explanatory power of history.

Although the point at which reconstructionism historically evolved into constructionism is not easy to identify, in the founding of the journal *Annales* in 1929 we have as distinct a point of mutation as any. For the first time in the twentieth century, history was written from an explicit propositional social theory position. From the early seventeenth century and the advent of the Enlightenment, when reason, experience and science became supreme, generations of European historians built the discipline upon the search for truth. Science, like nature, is neutral, rational, factual, logical, unemotional, value-free, calculable and, above all, secular – innocent of man's faith, religious dogma or corruption. Although *Annales* history was designed to be like that, early practitioners Febvre and Bloch recognised that it could never be based on first-hand experience, observation or experiment, since there was no Cartesian calculus or geometry in historical knowledge. So, while science continued to rely upon empiricism to refine its hypotheses (as it still does), history, if it widened its explanatory theories, could also now depend upon other more rigorous mathematical, experimental and observational techniques for the confirmation of deductive knowledge.

Since the founding of the school, *Annaliste* historians like Fernand Braudel, Emmanuel Le Roy Ladurie and, more recently, Roger Chartier have all employed highly sophisticated theories of varying kinds – sociological, economic, cultural, anthropological, psychological and linguistic.[33] The analysis of the 'structures' underlying the surface phenomena of history, and of the relationship between human intention, agency and action, has not, of course, been limited to the *Annales* school. It has constituted what the historiographer Christopher Lloyd has called a 'broad structurist tradition of structural history writing . . . which is far from being a school of single coherent approach'.[34] Constructionist history as a result is characterised today by its often great complexity and sophistication, but also by its clear rejection of what Philippe Carrard describes as 'event history' or interpretations that account only for dramatic single and unrepeatable events.[35]

The high tide of constructionist empiricism arrived in 1942 with Carl Hempel's positivist-inspired article on 'The Function of General Laws in History' in which he claimed that to explain any historical event the historian should subsume it under a general or covering law.[36] Covering law theory maintains that the historical event ought to be capable of prediction given the specification of certain contextual conditions. History, like science, therefore, can operate general or covering laws which work according to the deduction of the meaning of the event (the explanandum) from statements consisting of the general law and antecedent conditions (the explanans). Hempel recognised, however, that because historians do not really work in this precise manner of formulating and articulating general laws, what they do in effect is produce 'explanation sketches' that require 'filling out' or refining until the operative laws of human behaviour become distinct.[37] It is only by this strict deductive process that history can claim to reconstruct the past. Reconstructionist historians, and their philosophical supporters like McCullagh, have nevertheless consistently rejected Hempelian covering law theory, viewing it as deterministic and as an unnecessary distraction from their empirical research into the sources and the derivation of unique historical facts. General laws, if they operate at all, do so for most historians at the far less rigorous level of assumptions which may cover only one instance or unique event. Equally, it is argued that any single event is likely to be the result of many so-called laws. Most historians today would not rely, as did Frederick Jackson Turner, for example, on a single theory to explain the significance of the frontier movement in American history – in his case the existence of free land in the West. When writing history, the historian has to take into account not only the contingent but also the difficulties of accurately deciphering human intentions.

Although people do not always act rationally, the complexities of the past still continue to be studied by constructionists employing ever more elaborate models of social and cultural institutions, which try to take into account ecological changes, gender redefinitions, class relations, race, colonisation and de-colonisation, industrialism and technology. All require more tools of analysis than simple inductive inference alone provides. The list of thinkers influencing constructionist history now includes the sociologist Anthony Giddens, with his theory that the historical agent and social institutions are produced by complex hierarchies or levels of social practices; the Weberian sociologists Ernest Gellner, Charles Tilly and Clifford Geertz, who have applied the ideas of social anthropology to historical change; the ecological perspective of the historian W.G. Hoskins; the total history of the *Annalistes* Fernand Braudel, Emmanuel Le Roy Ladurie, Robert Darnton and Roger Chartier; the recognition of power structures in society by the American Marxist social historians Harry Braverman, Herbert Gutman, David Montgomery, James Weinstein and Gabriel Kolko; or the Gramsci-influenced Marxist history of Eric Hobsbawm and Eugene Genovese, as well as that of the Marxist-feminist perspectives of Sheila Rowbotham and Catherine Hall.[38] These are just a few examples of the huge range of constructionist explanations available today that seek to locate the structures influencing apparently unique events.

All these historians grouping around the reconstructionist–constructionist axis still insist on the interrogation of sources to explain how events happened as they did. Hard-core empiricist opposition to the analysis of structures over events has been successfully confronted through the insistence that history as empiricism and social theory as proposition cannot be separate in practice. Something else that links many among these historians is the fact that while they accept language to be the vehicle for the 'concepts' and/or social theories deployed, most agree that the explicit and scrupulous defining of the terms, concepts and categories regularly employed will usually overcome any lurking problem of significatory collapse, and most refuse to entertain the notion that their emplotments may have a major effect on the nature of the past they purport to discover. As Elton notes, the assumption by the 'theory-mongers' that language is a dangerous terrain full of pitfalls for the unwary is not new, and every historian worth his/her salt has known about them, and has for many years talked about them – but in a jargon-free language we can all understand! So, what is the role of narrative in mainstream history beyond it being merely the medium of report?

HISTORY AS NARRATIVE

The function of language in creating historical understanding centres on the nature and use of narrative. While most historians agree that history is in large part a literary process, they disagree over the character and implications of its literariness, but specifically over the question of whether or not its literary form creates the past as we write it. That history is the discovered truth about the past has been the main belief underpinning the general rejection, especially by conservative reconstructionists, of social theory constructionist history, but it has provided the rationale for not regarding narrative in and of itself as a form of explanation and understanding. Constructionists tend to view narrative as non-scientific and non-explanatory because of its teleological nature, that is, as an explanation orientated towards an already likely known, if not blatantly desired, end result. Constructionists also perceive narrative history as inevitably emphasising the unique event over the discovery and recognition of patterns, because of the stress on the role of individual people in the past rather than on groups' behaviour or processes.

The rediscovery of narrative has, however, been a feature of recent developments in history-writing. Consequently, some historians increasingly view narrative in historical understanding as explanatory in as much as it is mimetic. As the American historian J.H. Hexter has said, narrative displays history's 'capacity to convey knowledge of the past as it actually was'. Most importantly for constructionist historians, Hexter insists that narrative does not deny objectivity because historical investigation, when properly conducted, can produce close approximations to the truth precisely through the discovery of patterns in the events of the past. As he claims, trying also to satisfy reconstructionists, 'reconstructing connections among the records'[39] suggests that history is a narrative reconstruction of the past that can objectively reveal what actually happened. He concludes:

The function of the historian's language . . . may best be described as 'translational'; it aims to assist the reader to translate his experience from a familiar accepted context into a context strange and perhaps initially repugnant. The *direction* of the translation is as important as its effectiveness.[40]

This recognition of the way in which historians use narrative to direct or 'translate' meaning is unproblematic for Hexter because it is an integral part of the constitution of historical interpretation. This historian is the guide and narrative the terrain.

M.C. Lemon agrees that historians communicate primarily through language's written narrative form; as he says, they 'trans-form' their thoughts into language. Translating thinking into language, however, does not *prove* the correspondence theory. What it does do is reinforce and support the basic historical method of inductive inference. As Lemon says, the reader has to infer 'from what is said, the thinking it evidences. This is the function of narrative.'[41] In order to establish the thought behind the primary or secondary evidence, readers and historians must first understand the language used. This logic follows the Collingwood–Carr approach noted already. The main difficulty with it is the extent to which language is the constitutive of reality rather than its reflection. For practical realist mainstreamers this is not a major problem because they assume that narrative is not *the* primary mechanism for historical explanation – historical explanation emerges inferentially from the study of the sources and/or the use of analytical models of explanation, not from 'this happened, then that'. Although narrative conforms to this basic structure of change over time, this is not a good enough basis on which to claim that it is *the* essence of historical explanation. Narrative is taken to be the form in which historical analysis is transmitted to its readers, but the further claim is disputed. While narratives may carry or contain explanations, they are not explanations in themselves.[42]

Since the 1970s, however, the choices that historians make about their descriptions, emplotments, figurative styles, the construction of their explanatory arguments and any moral judgements with which they engage have been increasingly discussed and acknowledged as significant features of narrative explanation. The practical realist mainstream position is clearly stated by Lawrence Stone in his 1979 article. After defining narrative simply as 'the organisation of material in a chronologically sequential order and the focusing of the content into a single coherent story', he says that narrative history differs from social theory or constructionist history (what he called 'structural history') in that 'its arrangement is descriptive rather than analytical and that its central focus is on man not circumstances. It therefore deals with the particular and specific rather than the collective and statistical.' For Stone, economic determinism, structuralism, quantification and psychohistory are poor substitutes for a narrated empiricism that produced historical understanding 'based on observation, experience, judgement and intuition'.[43]

Although the object of Stone's defence of narrative was to attack 'the attempt to produce a coherent scientific explanation of change in the past',[44] as we noted in Chapter 1, in the mid-1960s William Gallie had argued for the centrality of narrative as *the* characteristic form of historical understanding, and, like Hexter, had suggested that narrative and constructionism are not incompatible. Historians understand the past as they produce a story that they and their readers can follow, based on the causally related and contextualised evidence. Gallie argued that to follow a historical narrative may regularly require the acceptance of explanations that stretch one's credulity.[45] What he is saying is that no matter how unlikely is the story of a series of events and their changing relationship over time, if it is reasonably supported by the causally connected evidence, it should be believed. M.C. Lemon, however, insists that no matter how unlikely it may appear, narrative history is not about establishing constructionist-type mechanistic causal relationships between events. Its explanatory power arises from its in-built ability or power to track, trail or follow the individual person's intentional responses to their context. The function of narrative history lies in discovering the intentionality of people in the past and duplicating it through narrative, making the story followable and comprehensible.

More recently, the French historian Philippe Carrard has commented on how the highly sophisticated New History continues to rely upon narrative as its primary vehicle for expression *and* explanation. He claims that 'New Historians . . . still depend largely on storytelling to make sense of the world . . . [and] . . . this analytical component is still framed by a plot, and this plot retains essential cognitive functions.'[46] Like William Gallie and Arthur Danto, Carrard is insisting here that even constructionist history requires emplotments that identify the intentions of the historical agent and which also constitute explanations. Writing history seems to be a highly complex amalgam of interpretation of the sources (discovering how people in the past acted with intentionality), plus overt propositional testing (using abstract social constructions like class), translated into an understandable and explanatory narrative.

Joyce Appleby, Lynn Hunt and Margaret Jacob support the mainstream consensus by arguing in favour of the necessity for historians to combine 'narrative coherence, causal analysis, and social contextualisation', creating a process that they believe is 'exemplified in our own narratives'.[47] Mindful of their empiricist credentials, they reject 'the current negative or ironic judgements about history's role' of the postmodern deconstructionists while carefully recognising the aesthetic or literary choices that historians have to make when writing history. They summarise the judgement of the mainstream on the literariness of history when they judge its literary dimension as not being history's first consideration. Their ranking of primary choices as narrative historians are 'political, social and epistemological', and reflect their beliefs about their role in the community of historians and the nature of American society. While agreeing 'that the focus on culture and language undermines this hierarchical view by showing that all social reality is culturally constructed and discursively construed in the first instance', they still maintain their belief in the practical knowability of past reality. In accepting that narrative 'is a universal mode of organising human knowledge' and that there is a gap between 'reality and its narration', narrative remains, nevertheless, 'an inappropriate vehicle for historical explanation'.[48]

Taking narrative to be a form of report rather than of knowing is a judgement reached by philosopher of history Michael Stanford. It is his view that 'history does not have to be narrative history'.[49] As he points out, the commonsense view that life happens like a story is merely a ploy of writers and nothing more. Events do not, in reality, conveniently occur in a narrative form. This is supplied by the historian later, but what is really important, he says, is to note that 'most academic works of history are not written in the narrative mode'.[50] The reason Stanford gives for this in opposition to Gallie is that the narrative form cannot cope with the complexities of causally related events. The interweaving of the political, cultural, social and economic is so complicated that description alone cannot substitute for constructionist-type conceptual analysis.

As the result of the popularity of this view, most history written today is done through a topics or problems approach rather than describing single events in a sequence that the historian assumes will, in effect, become self-explanatory.[51] In examples taken from my office shelf, Phyllis Deane, in her undergraduate British economic history primer *The First Industrial Revolution* (1965), reconstructs British industrialisation through topics such as the Demographic Revolution, the Transport Revolution, the Iron Industry, the Role of the Banks, and Standards of Living. A second example I found from European economic history is Clive Trebilcock's *The Industrialisation of the Continental Powers 1780–1914* (1981), which is constructed around models of industrialisation associated with individual European countries. Another example taken at random, but this time from recently published American history, is Vicki L. Ruiz and Ellen Carol DuBois's *Unequal Sisters* (1994), a multi-cultural reader in American women's history from the colonial slave days up to the 1990s, which is also organised around distinct topics – housework and *ante-bellum* working-class subsistence, the marriage structure of Mission-educated Chinese-American women, the cosmetics industry and the construction of gender, and Vietnamese immigrant women.[52] The sequencing of events over time is handled differently in all three of these texts – while it is there it is always of secondary importance to constructionist explanatory frameworks.

So, although its nature remains disputed, the recovery of narrative history by the mainstream is a well-established trend. Conservative reconstructionists are willing to defend narrative only as the vehicle for conclusions inferred from the sources. Practical realists, probably along with the majority of constructionists, maintain that narrative carries meaning but remains secondary to their conceptualisations and explanatory social theories. None, however, accept narrative as either a wholly unproblematic descriptive vehicle, or so fluid in meaning as to be incapable of conveying any definitive knowledge. Reconstructionists and constructionists see no good reason to believe that just because narrative is not *the* primary instrument for creating historical knowledge it is a worthless mechanism for conveying the results of historical research.

CONCLUSION

What I have argued in this chapter is that the reconstructionist/constructionist mainstream approach depends on several related principles. The first is the acceptance of an objectivist-inspired methodology, which in serving the evidence and isolating the historian allows for the accurate, independent and truthful reconstruction of the past. Second, it follows that the truth of history can be distinguished from fiction and value-judgement, with history being about discovering what has actually happened. I noted, however, the divisions within the reconstructionist/constructionist mainstream with Elton's attacks on all forms of history produced by the fashionable 'theory-mongers'.[53] I also stressed the argument of McCullagh in support of Elton, that it is possible to believe 'in the truth of historical descriptions'.[54] In contrast to Elton I pointed out the Callinicos position, that facts emerge from theory-inspired historical study, and how recently the debate has focused on whether historical narrative can be considered in and of itself to be a form of explanation.

We should now be in a better position to understand the four main premises of the traditional or reconstructionist school: that history possesses its own epistemology; that historical method consists of the forensic examination of primary sources according to the inferential rules of evidence (comparison, colligation, verification and the impartial interpretation of that evidence); the rejection of general laws in as much as they imply history can be predictive; and finally, that narrative as the medium for historical reconstruction, although it is not an adequate form of explanation, is not an obstacle to the enterprise. In the next two chapters I shall appraise these mainstream premises from the perspective of the deconstructive consciousness.

4   History as deconstruction

INTRODUCTION

The history profession is not starkly divided between deconstructionists and the reconstructionist/constructionist mainstreams, not least
because, as we have seen, there are active debates that cut across all
positions, and most historians presuppose the use of narrative at least
as the vehicle for conveying historical knowledge if not for creating it.
But it is on this very point that there is still a broad division between
those who think self-consciously about the nature and particular role
of narrative in the practice of the craft, what I have designated as the
deconstructive consciousness, and those who view the reconstruction
of the past as primarily a skilled engagement with the evidence and
who think, therefore, that there is little to dispute about its written
form as history. As I have indicated, this division focuses on how content and form relate, specifically the extent to which historical
knowledge and explanation are the function primarily of evidence
placed in context or the aesthetics and structure of narrative discourse.

Conservative reconstructionist historians do not accept empiricism as
only one of several competing modes of knowing the past. They reject
all other methods of historical interpretation, especially those that
smack of an ideology of which they disapprove, e.g. Marxism, cultural
materialism, Hegelianism, bourgeois liberalism, or whatever. Historians
in the mainstreams prefer to view history as primarily a *practice* – the
craft of history.[1] It is perceived as a technique of non-ideological discovery.[2] What is challenged by the deconstructive historical
consciousness is this belief that historical investigation can offer a peculiarly empiricist historical litmus test of knowledge, emphasising instead
the belief that the past is only ever accessible to us as a textual representation – 'the past' translated into 'history'. From a deconstructive

perspective on the significance of language and narrative structure, I will now address each of the four questions in turn.

EPISTEMOLOGY

As a consequence of the post-structuralist challenge to empiricism and the correspondence theory of meaning we are confronted by what, at first blush, appears to be the discomforting notion that there is no access to knowledge except through the murky and dangerous waters of language. Historians as a group respond to this by refusing to explore its implications. In spite of Derrida's and Barthes' warnings, historians generally continue to rely on the commonsense notion that they will locate the knowable external presence to the text in the context . This is the investment the discipline has in referentiality – a referent for each word and consequently a precise meaning to be discovered. The problem is that such a fixation makes it very difficult to view narratives for what they are: meaningful historical explanations *in themselves*, rather than plain *vehicles* with which to explain the past as it actually happened. In order to pursue this we need to know more about how narrative works in epistemological terms.

This opening up of historical analysis to questions of rhetoric is found in the work of Hayden White and other philosophers and historians like F.R. Ankersmit, Hans Kellner, Jörn Rüsen and Keith Jenkins. The deconstructive historical consciousness suggests that history written by working historians should explicitly acknowledge and, when appropriate, explore its emplotted or prefigured form. What is argued for is that the analysis of style, genre and narrative structure, more usually associated with fictional literature, be applied to the understanding of the historian's sources *and* written interpretations. Although this approach emerges from structuralism's early concern with the arbitrary nature of language, history produced within the deconstructive consciousness has a much wider range of concerns. Reconstructionist historians choose, however, to keep both structuralism and historical deconstruction at arm's length by regarding the written form of the past as somehow not especially relevant to the reconstruction and explanation of the past as it actually was. Although they applaud precision in the use of language and recognise its limitations, the importance of language-use in its broadest explanatory sense remains secondary to the discovery of true origins, causal analysis and contextualism.

As I have already indicated, the early seventeenth-century positivist legacy of Francis Bacon has remained the controlling metaphor of twentieth-century historical study even at the practical realist centre. History becomes genuinely problematic only when historians draw untenable inductive inferences, shape history for their ideological/political purposes or, what for a few is worse, dabble in the nether world of hypothesis-making. History should be *like* science to the extent that science is the study of the real world 'out there', is factual not speculative, empirical rather than *a priori*, verifiable, anti-hypothetical, ideologically neutral and, above all, non-impositionalist and objective. Consequently, the fundamental implication of the theories of postmodernism for history – its demise as a legitimate discipline – is unacceptable.

Questioning history as an empirical project ought not, in fact, be a problem for historians. If we accept that there are no master narratives – such as history proper assumes itself to be – then, as Lyotard says, there is no inside track to reality. Questioning the epistemological basis of history, however, cuts deep into the mind of historians. It concerns the objectivity with which the historian deals with sources and then writes up a disinterested interpretation tracing and explaining origins and causes. While most historians would not argue that historical method is scientific, there remains this strong sense of being rationally and objectively in touch with a potentially understandable, causally analysable and truthful past.[3] To argue otherwise is simply to cease to be a historian.

The leading critic of what we might loosely call traditional history is Michel Foucault. In accepting the German philosopher Friedrich Nietzsche's reaction against the certainty of the empiricism of the second half of the nineteenth century, Foucault's attack on history is less directed towards the post-structuralist indeterminacy of language, but rather more against the manner in which historians believe in the recovery of the truth of the past.[4] Foucault challenges the belief that historians can effectively step outside history, capture the context, and be objective – arguing instead that all written history is an act of creation through the narrative impositionalism of the historian as he/she emplots the data, and this act is to some degree the ideological product of the age in which he/she lives.

Foucault's critique of history as a legitimate discipline is paralleled by the French cultural critic Roland Barthes. Building on the distinction between *histoire*, in which events seemingly tell themselves without the intrusion of a narrator, and *discourse*, which is overtly self-conscious and authorial, in his essay 'The Discourse of History' (1967) Barthes contests history's dependence on the correspondence between evidence, the designation of historical facts and the 'reality effect' of 'objective' history as created in the historian's written interpretation.[5] Barthes suggests that written history is only another narrative, effectively collapsing the story discourse distinction.[6] As Barthes' interpreter Stephen Bann comments, the 'rhetorical analysis of historical narrative . . . cannot grant to history, *a priori*, the mythic status which differentiates it from fiction'.[7]

In his defence of narrative in 'The Discourse', Barthes strikes at the very existence of history as an epistemology. History, he notes, is usually 'justified by the principles of "rational" exposition' but he asks 'does this form of narration really differ, in some specific trait, in some indubitably distinctive feature, from imaginary narration, as we find it in the epic, the novel, and the drama?'.[8] He goes on to challenge the authority of the historian based on his/her access to the sources, by emphasising that the real work of history resides in their translation (Barthes describes this as utterance) into a narrative of historical interpretation. Barthes' challenge takes the shape of a critique of the structure of the historian's discourse. The examples he offers include the historian's traditional deployment of lots of detail amid the minutiae of events. In the history of art this is the *trompe l'œil* principle whereby fine detail is intended to create a sense of reality. Barthes' challenge also extends to how historians complicate chronology by compressing time in a few pages, flipping back and forward through the past. Barthes' further probes the historian's unspoken claim to omniscience – the process whereby the historian absents him/herself from the discourse to create the impression of realism through direct access to the referent – from where, as Barthes says,

> there is in consequence a systematic deficiency of any form of sign referring to the sender of the historical message. The history seems to be telling itself all on its own. This feature . . . corresponds in effect to the type of historical discourse labelled as 'objective' (in which the historian never intervenes). . . . On the level of discourse, objectivity – or the deficiency of signs of the utterer – thus appears as a particular form of imaginary projection, the product of what might be called the referential illusion, since in this case the historian is claiming to allow the referent to speak all on its own.[9]

The epistemological status of historical discourse is thus conventionally affirmed and asserted. The historical fact is privileged by being placed in the specially reserved position of a superior claim to truthfulness, as warranted by both a plain language and an independent research methodology and as supported in the notes and references – the scaffolding of proper historical methodology. Barthes goes on to suggest that this illusory correspondence between plain language, historical evidence and historical truth is also to be found in realist novels which similarly appear objective because they too have suppressed the signs of the 'I' in their narrative.

Barthes is claiming that historians play a confidence trick because of the way in which we use the trope of the real – in effect the Elton method – to wring historians out of history and presume to get to the reality of the past. Barthes is suggesting that history is performing an epistemological trick through which the referent is placed in a privileged world of the real beyond arbitrary signification. As he says, 'The historian is not so much a collector of facts as a collector and relator of signifiers; that is to say, he organises them with the purpose of establishing positive meaning.'[10] While most mainstream historians accept an organising role for the historian, they draw the line at this deconstructive vision which holds that there can be no objectivity in selection of material, and that all judgements about what to include or exclude are based on ideology, preferred narrative structures, and the limitations of the signifier–signified–sign relationship. Barthes' deconstructionist point is that the historian deliberately confuses or conflates the signified with the referent, producing a signifier–referent correspondence, hence Barthes' warning that 'in "objective history" the "real" is never more than an unformulated signified, sheltering behind the apparently all-powerful referent. This situation characterises what we might call the *realistic effect*.'[11] This is similar to Foucault's idea that all discourses are at best perspectives that produce *truth effects*. This is not so much anti-referentialism as a recognition of referentialism's boundaries.

Most historians refuse to view the real as only a truth-effect, given the profession's continuing investment in the independence of the discipline and the traditional Western belief in reason and rationality (logocentrism). In so doing we fail to acknowledge that the narrative description of historical facts is integral to our proof of those facts. Barthes comments that by instituting 'narration as the privileged signifier of the real', historical truth emerges as the composite of 'careful attention to narration', and the 'abundance of . . . "concrete details"'. He concludes that 'Narrative structure, which was originally developed within the cauldron of fiction (in myths and the first epics) becomes at once the sign and the proof of reality.'[12] These are concerns that influenced Hayden White, among others, to explore the rhetorical dimension to writing history, and have posed a question mark over narrative structure and the impositions it makes on writing history.[13] Regardless of Barthes' argument that history is at best a fudged-up performative and unavoidably ideological, mainstream historians still insist that they work in a discipline that aspires to a high degree of correspondence with the past as it actually was and that narrative is a vehicle for report rather than the primary (if flawed) medium of explanation. Deconstructionist historians, however, are driven to ask what kind of epistemological status can the sorts of stories historians tell have, and what have they the right to claim, by virtue of their narrative form?[14]

EVIDENCE

There are two related questions raised by deconstructionist history about historical evidence. How can we discover the intentionality in the mind behind the source, and how much reliance can we place on the reconstructionist's contextualisation of events as a form of explanation? It is here that we come across the apparently strange notion of the death of the author/subject. For Barthes, the importance of the author of historical evidence is diminished in as much as he/she is perceived as representative of further texts and ideological positions rather than as the originator of meaning. Evidence does not refer to a recoverable and accurately knowable past reality but represents chains of interpretations, that is, we have no master or transcendent signifiers. In the sense that we as historians cannot know what were the intentions of the author of the source, to suggest that we look to those intentions as a means to interpret the evidence is only to invite yet further textual investigation. This contradicts Lemon's view that narrative's power to explain emerges from its tracking of the historical agent's intentional and intelligible response to their context. Barthes maintains that

> The names of authors or of doctrines have here no substantial value. They indicate neither identities nor causes. It would be frivolous to think that 'Descartes,' 'Leibniz,' 'Rousseau,' 'Hegel,' etc., are names of authors, of the authors of movements or displacements that we thus designate. The indicative value that I attribute to them is first the name of a problem.[15]

The inevitable rejection by empiricists of this position is founded on the belief that the historian and the evidence are separate entities – a further re-stating of the traditional distinction between knower and known – and this gap permits historians to stand back and see the origins of meaning in the evidence.

F.R. Ankersmit describes what he calls the postmodernist historian's perception of evidence as a tile, not to be picked up to see what is underneath it, but as something which the historian steps on in order to move on to other tiles: horizontally instead of vertically.[16] For Hayden

White, this perspective (stepping from tile to tile) has further significance for the constitution of meaning because of what it says about ideology.[17] The real problem with historical evidence for White is not Barthes' unending roundabout of meanings, but the inevitable ideological dimension to the interpretation of evidence.

The idea of historical interpretation being influenced by ideological considerations seems wrong to reconstructionist historians. Elton, for example, rejects any ideological impositionalism of the historian of the kind acknowledged by White because it produces 'uncertainty around historical truth'. The 'true view of the past' emerges instead for Elton from 'the deficiencies of the evidence and the problems it poses, rather than from the alleged transformation of events in the organising mind of the historian'.[18] White opposes this, persevering with the argument that

> there is no such thing as a *single* correct view of any object under study but . . . there are *many* correct views, each requiring its own style of representation. For we should recognise that *what constitutes the facts themselves* is the problem that the historian, like the artist, has tried to solve in the choice of metaphor by which he orders his world, past, present, and future.[19]

Any crossing of the boundary between the observer and that which is to be observed, through the choice of metaphor, thus clearly contravenes one of the most basic 'rules' of traditional historical analysis because it threatens Elton's ideal of objectively dealing with the evidence. Because objectivity is the central metaphor of empiricism, the ideological meshing of historian and his/her sources starkly presents the danger of subjectivity and eventual corruption of history. Even R.G. Collingwood's interventionist historical method, 'that the historian must re-enact the past in his own mind', presupposes a minimum level of objectivity. I have already pointed out how this also prompts the argument that, by a thorough knowledge of the facts, the reconstructionists reject the folly of social science model-making as applied to history, notably the use of social theory and the appeal to covering laws.[20] While the question of subjectivity in dealing with the evidence is at the heart of the long contested issue of covering laws in history, it is also a debate that is important for the deconstructive consciousness. It further opens up the epistemological foundation of narrative as a legitimate type of explanation in distinction to, among other things, overt social theorising.

THEORIES OF HISTORY: CONSTRUCTING THE PAST

To his own question, 'Of what can there be historical knowledge?', Collingwood's reply, 'Of that which can be re-enacted in the historian's mind', remains a problem for many reconstructionists because it is not based upon their method of historical analysis.[21] Collingwood elaborated, 'Of that which is not experience but the mere object of experience, there can be no history.'[22] To overcome the lack of direct experience in historical explanation Collingwoodian historians like E.H. Carr plunge themselves in the evidence and experience the past as best they can – by rethinking it. Although crude empiricists like Geoffrey Elton believe this to be a quite wrong-headed method – believing instead in maintaining the distinction of knower and known – they would generally agree with Collingwood that, whatever method is used, historians must avoid the more grievous error of appealing to a universal explanatory social theory that is usually just a fancy cloak for personal bias or the methodological dead-end of covering law positivism. The framing of laws in the form of a proposition suggesting why an event occurred in order to yield causal connections is taken not to be history.[23] But, as Callinicos suggests from his constructionist Marxist standpoint, the study of how humans relate to their contexts necessitates a social theory. For Callinicos, all history must attempt to discover some pattern in the transformations in human society.

As we have already noted, covering law theory is unpopular among those who judge it to be founded on a model of historical explanation acquired from science. For others, its unpopularity stems from its relegation of the power of narrative to explain the past. Consequently, few historians have employed what Hempel designated in the early 1940s as covering law theory. Some fifty years before, one of the most influential pieces of written history – Frederick Jackson Turner's work on the role of the frontier in American history – illustrates positivism's limited influence. While denying the existence of general laws in history, Turner was largely alone in using them in practice. By borrowing from the social and the natural sciences, Turner became one of the leading historians of his generation by inferring the existence of a general law that applied directly to American historical experience.[24] He argued in his famous lecture before the American Historical Association gathered in Chicago in 1893 that

> The existence of an area of free land, its continuous recession and the advance of American settlement westward explain American development.[25]

For Turner, this law of westward movement accounted for American history. Turner's approach made him one of the leading social scientists of his time. However, the reaction against positivism in historical explanation emerged in the interwar years, led by two more American historians, Carl Becker and Charles Beard. Derived again from a Nietzschean position, but specifically under the influence of Italian historian Benedetto Croce, Beard and Becker challenged any objectivist history that saw itself as above the concerns of the present.[26] Endorsing this relativist line, Becker asserted that 'Historical thinking . . . is a social instrument, helpful in getting the world's work more effectively done.'[27] Most historians by today have accepted relativism at least to the extent that they continue to reject absolutist covering laws, but still refuse to accept that there may be more fiction in history than positivists will admit.[28]

For deconstructionist historians, the rehearsing of these arguments for or against constructionism is a rather meaningless exercise if one entertains doubts about the truth-value of textual evidence and the interpretation built upon it. Debating covering law theory is irrelevant if the whole empiricist model of induction and inductive inference is flawed, because facts neither measure nor produce the kind of historical knowledge that mainstream historians claim. Most mainstream historians ignore the implications of this, preferring instead to concentrate on the sources, endorsing Collingwood's description of the historical method as the objective analysis of sources into their component parts to distinguish which are the more trustworthy. However, Collingwood also acknowledged the role of the historian in construing historical accounts. As he argued, historians know how to do their own work in their own way and should no longer run the risk of being misled by trying to assimilate scientific method into history.[29] The almost universal rejection of positivist constructionism rests, however, on the doubtful belief of most historians that historical explanation is really objective interpretation cast in a narrative form. The deconstructive argument holds instead that our sources are never transcendent signifieds because they have a pre-figured historical status by being already recounted in chronicles, diaries, legends, memories and interpretations, even before another generation of historians go to work on them again.

The deconstructive critique of empiricist representation and referentiality effectively asks: does knowledge emerge through social being and/or language-use? Although as a form of representation, narrative always fails the correspondence test, it remains of crucial importance in the reconstruction/construction of the past. It is worth considering at this point that the effort to find out truth in the past may be less about the rules of evidence, covering laws and even narrative, but is perhaps about the will to gain power. For Foucault there is a fundamental chasm between language and reality. The only reality is found when language produces a meaning. We use language but language also uses us.[30] Consequently, narrative is a discourse, the currency of which is power. That power may well be used to create a usable past for a nation. Narrative may, therefore, be viewed as a discursive formation that exists in the present and is not a simple and uncomplicated reference to the past.[31] The accretion of historical knowledge – 'knowing the past' – often justifies the present, or some preferred version of it, and this is the motivating force that drives the historian as a professional. Accordingly, Foucault argues that all historians, because we are attached to a profession and a discipline, have a vested interest – usually ideologically framed – in maintaining the importance of the myth of the objective search for truth, whether reconstructionist or constructionist in orientation. The worst offenders in Foucault's eyes are liberal bourgeois empiricists who believe that they have a control over their ideology that allows them objective access to the essential past. The point of deconstructionist history is the challenge it throws down to the idea, which reaches its ultimate expression in hard-core constructionism, especially of the statistical variety, that there are essential (true) patterns 'out there' to be discovered in the past.

The deconstructive consciousness assumes that the treatment of the evidence in the historical narrative deals mainly in verisimilitude and coherence rather than objective explanation. This does not mean that we are all extreme relativists. White, for example, rejects extreme scepticism about the epistemological value of narrative, in fact putting it at the centre of what history is really about. 'As thus envisaged, the "content" of the discourse consists as much of its form as it does of whatever information might be extracted from a reading of it.'[32] White concludes that a discourse should be regarded as an 'apparatus for the production of meaning rather than as only a vehicle for the transmission of information about an extrinsic referent'.[33] In acknowledging the cognitive importance of narrative, White does not suggest that it can recover the past as it actually was any more than can positivism. Deconstructionist history's suspicions about referentiality and representation in the reading of sources, and the writing of history, doubts about recovering the intentions of the author, constructionist theorising, and the often hidden agenda of power not only mean questioning the claims of the mainstream, but also attest to the need to address more fully the shortcomings, as well as the potential, of historical narrative as a means of explanation.

HISTORY AS NARRATIVE

The impact of the deconstructive consciousness means not only questioning historical interpretation as an objective avenue to the past as it actually was, but also entails exploring the explanatory or story-telling power of narrative. If historical writing is the analysis of complex, pre-existing chains of interpretation, whereby documents do not guarantee authorial meaning and signifiers create only more signifiers, then discussion of content in history must begin with an understanding of its linguistic and story form. Historians are increasingly encouraged to think not only about researching the past, but also about how to express *and* undertake that research. Thinking about the form will make us think about how to deal with its content. To what extent then is the form of written history as significant as its factual content?

W.H. Dray summarised the various positions that can be held on the importance of narrative to historical explanation, namely that

> history simply *is* narrative; or that it is *essentially* narrative; or that a history must contain *some* narrative elements; or that *one form* of history, at any rate, and perhaps the most important one, narrates. It has been held, too, that it is through narration that historians achieve whatever is specifically historical about historical understanding; or that historical explanations get their distinctive structure by reason of their occurring in the course of historical narratives. It has even been held that narratives can themselves be explanatory in a special way; or that narrative is *per se* a form of explanation, if not indeed *self*-explanatory.[34]

The functioning of narrative is thus a dilemma for historians. Narrative claims to represent the complexities and realities of the past, but because it is a story form it must be the creation of the historian's imagination. Can it therefore entertain any claim to being a true representation of what actually happened? Narrative, Louis Mink suggests, is the product of an 'imaginative construction which cannot defend its claim to truth by any accepted procedure of argument or authentication'.[35] This means that historians unavoidably impose themselves on the past by inventing narratives as they try to explain what the past 'really meant', what the source-text 'really says', what the author's intentions 'really were'.[36]

As we know, for most historians narrative is the unquestioned *form* of history. Although a number of philosophers of history have argued narrative to be the essential and distinguishing feature of history, most practitioners fail to grasp its practical methodological significance, still regarding it as only a casual stylistic property that some essays possess and others do not. Like most things, whether narrative is explanatory or not comes down to how we define it. The debate on it as a legitimate form of historical explanation has produced anti-narrativists, among them philosophers of history Maurice Mandelbaum and Leon Goldstein, who claim that although narrative is an element of historical study, not all history has to be framed in the narrative form, and the discipline has other prior and more important methodological claims. Then there are pro-narrativists like philosophers Frederick A. Olafson, David Carr, William Gallie, Arthur Danto and A.R. Louch who insist there is a strong correspondence between the past as lived, and history as written.[37] Then there are those pro-narrative but determined anti-deconstructionists like J.H. Hexter and Lawrence Stone, who do not accept that language must always fail the correspondence test. Finally, there are those of a broadly defined deconstructive turn like Hayden White, Dominick LaCapra, F.R. Ankersmit, Hans Kellner and David Harlan, who view narrative as the essential but largely misunderstood feature of historical explanation – a misunderstanding that among many other things permits history a claim to a spurious epistemological legitimacy through its favourite metaphor of objectivity.

Maurice Mandelbaum, in observing the general relevance of narrative, suggests that historians write it while keeping their 'eyes on higher things' – the prize of historical truth.[38] Like Arthur Marwick, philosopher of history Leon Goldstein cannot understand the fuss made over history's narrative form, what he calls the superstructure of history. Its real business is research on archival sources, the infra-structure. For Goldstein, history is 'a technical discipline', one that uses methods that are peculiarly its own: 'History is a way of knowing, not a mode of discourse.'[39] He concludes, 'What we know about the historical past we know only through its constitution in historical research.'[40] The deconstructive turn counters this by declaring that the past exists as history only because a narrative or story structure has been imposed by the historian on the evidence.

Because the historical text consists of a narrative that purports to describe and evaluate past reality, what is at issue is the power to explain of story-form narrative. As we have seen, structuralist and post-structuralist literary theory has thrown open the question of how historians employ narrative as a way to fix historical knowledge as unique to itself, and consequently divide history from other kinds of writing.[41] In support of a pro-narrativist position, M.C. Lemon argues that the logic of life is replicated in narrative. As he says, the lesson is that 'there are, "out there", amidst a virtual infinity of occurrences real stories to be truly told and their telling must conform to the logic of narrative explanation'.[42] Lemon's view is shared by Dominick LaCapra, Hayden White and Paul Ricoeur, who maintain that because of its essential narrative form, history cannot be categorised as anything other than a kind of literature, but that this does not devalue its significance or explanatory power. The consequence is, in fact, a recasting of its character and functioning. As Paul Ricoeur says, history must possess an 'irreducibly narrative character' in the same way that human existence does.[43] Its function is to describe the process in which people construe themselves and their culture through the production of language. This emphasis on the cognitive value of narrative does not of course mean that we now suddenly have *the* access to the past as it actually was – we only have *a* story version of it. Narrative can explain the past, but not guarantee that its explanations are truthful.

Deconstructionist historians approach this issue through the following thinking. The past as it actually was, and the individual historical statements composing its narrative, can never coincide precisely. The problem is that we cannot verify the past by the evidence. Evidence is not past reality because our access to it must be through many intermediaries – absence, gaps and silences, the contrived nature of the archive, signifier–referent collapse, the historian's bias and, not least, the structure of the historian's imposed and contrived narrative argument. It is probably best to view historical narratives as propositions about how we *might* represent a past reality, suggestions of *possible* correspondences rather than *the* correspondence. Hayden White endorses philosopher Arthur Danto's view that historical facts are really only events under a description.[44] It follows that, as events under a description, these narrative proposals/suggestions are the result of individual historians' interpretations and compete for acceptance in those terms. History results not from the debate about past reality as such, but from competing narrative proposals about the nature and possible meanings of past events. Of course, once a narrative proposal has achieved a more or less universal acceptance (like 'the Cold War' or 'the Industrial Revolution'), it becomes concretised as past reality. It is no longer a narrative proposal, but has become *the* past. This makes it impossible, in effect, to distinguish between language-use and past reality. It is at this point that empiricism notches up another success.

What is undeniable is that it is historians who construct narratives through which historical knowledge is acquired and disseminated. How is it possible for us to distinguish between the narrative proposals of different historians, between those likely to be *right* and those *wrong*? How can we tell *good* history from *bad* history? This is not too hard to do for reconstructionists. They judge the degree to which the narrative lacks structure, unity and/or coherence in its congruence or correspondence with its contextualised sources. The most convincing historians are those who write narratives possessing this in full measure. Unity and cohesion are found in the intelligible and reasonable relationship established between individual statements and the sources, but even more importantly the narrative *as a whole* possesses an informing structure of argument – the article, essay or book is not waffly or rambling. In 'good history' the informing narrative argument will contain a clear and up-front statement as to how the past actually was – the coherence of form coming from the overarching social theory deployed, or the fact that they have got the story/theory straight according to the evidence.

What is 'good' or 'bad' history for the deconstructionist? Hopefully the narrative in a deconstructionist essay will be coherent and sensible, but it will not be epistemologically self-assured. This lack of certainty arises because of the doubts harboured about correspondences. How can we readily differentiate truth-effect plausibility from fact? How may we disentangle social theory arguments from low-level descriptions of events? How can we unpick ideologically inspired gaps and silences or unravel the collapsed signifier–referent? For every history that aims to get at the past as it actually happened, there is always another version, which, like the first, is by definition another fiction. As to what constitutes good history, then, it is that which is self-reflexive enough to acknowledge its limits, especially aware that the writing of history is far more precarious and speculative than empiricists usually admit. Deconstructionist history openly accepts a dissenting role for the historian as someone who must challenge the established notions of authority within contemporary society by refusing to 'tidy up' the past by ascribing origins and causes with the claim to evidentially certified truth. What does this mean in more practical terms, and what are its implications for history as narrative?

We have now arrived at two conclusions about history: first, all composed, written narratives *are* supported by a philosophy or ideology, often buried so deeply that no amount of conscious historical awareness can eliminate it; and second, because it relates stories about real past events in the evidence, deconstructionist history is not a fictional narrative. But, as a form of representation, all historical narrative proposals are shaped by the conventions of rhetoric and language-use – emplotment, argument and other culturally provided constraints, both material and ideological. This relationship between narrative form and historical content is explored by Hayden White in his study of historical interpretation, which in turn owes much to the investigation of language and representation undertaken by Roland Barthes, Paul Ricoeur and Michel Foucault.[45] For the anti-narrativist White, the essence of history is that it is a literary enterprise, and we 'know the past' through the narrative design we impose on it, which, as Ankersmit agrees, 'acquires a substantiality of its own'.[46] Both White and Ankersmit request that before historians can embrace the true character of historical explanation through a figurative narrative, we must resist the temptation of keeping up our pretence to objectivity, and turn instead to a richer understanding which is to be gained through an appreciation of history as literature. In his 1973 text *Metahistory*, White argued that all history writing is basically a linguistic and poetic act. Facts are not discovered, they are actually sources interpreted according as much to literary as any other criteria. Consequently, if we approach history as literature we may even write better history, as we deploy an additional range of critical apparatuses to the established rules of contextualised evidence. By recognising its literary form we are not constrained to present it as mainstream history would have it done.

Because written history is a literary artifact, White claims that historians share the same formal narrative structures used by writers of realist story literature based on the main categories of figurative language – the tropes – what White calls tropic prefiguration. White uses something like a base-superstructure metaphor himself to explain how this works. Historians construct narratives (stories) to produce explanations employing three superstructural strategies of explanation, viz., explanation by emplotment, explanation by formal argument and explanation by ideological implication. These strategies of explanation are the surface features of the narrative, with White suggesting a deep or infra-structure of consciousness (operating at the level of the tropes) that ultimately determines how historians elect to explain the facts explored in their narratives. Extending the base-superstructure metaphor, White argues that language is not to be located in the economic base of society, nor the social superstructure, but is prior to both.

Next, White carries forward the analysis from the level of rhetoric to that of the historical by borrowing Michel Foucault's concept of the episteme – a way of describing how a culture in each age acquires and uses its knowledge as embedded in figurative language. White suggests that it is possible for historians to interpret the culture of any historical period with reference to its ascendant tropic prefiguration.[47] White proposes that as the tropes organise the deep structures of human thought in de Saussure's sense of constituting meaning through binary opposition – the idea of otherness, or difference in any historical period – tropes lie at the core of every society's and every historian's historical imagination.[48] White has explored the literary theory of tropes as a way of distinguishing the dominant modes of the historical imagination in nineteenth-century Europe, and by extension to the cultural level his model allows the identification of the deep and surface structures of the historical imagination.

I will explore the importance of this view of history in more detail in Chapters 7 and 8, but for the moment it is important to note that the key to this narrative model of cultural change is White's conjecture that ideology and the exercise of power are ultimately settled by the cardinal text, yet operate in the real world of social relationships.[49] In moving from the rhetorical level to that of the material context, White is describing the writing of history as an intertextual and material act, with history as a conforming or dissenting voice. This he attempts to demonstrate in his analysis of E.P. Thompson's *Making of the English Working Class*, claiming that like all history it is a necessarily fabricated work because of its inevitable dependence on the tropic model of historical explanation. Thompson is in the business of metaphorically 'making' the English working class for overtly ideological reasons. According to White, 'The pattern which Thompson discerned in the history of English working class consciousness was perhaps as much imposed upon his data as it was found in them.' But White goes on to make an even more telling point: 'the issue here surely is not whether some pattern was imposed, but the tact exhibited [by Thompson] in the choice of the pattern used to give order to the process being represented'. As White says, the 'planned or intuitive' tropological pattern Thompson selected for the English working class is the movement from a 'naive (metaphorical) to a self-critical (ironic) comprehension of itself'.[50] What is significant for historians in White's analysis of history is his questioning of the relationship between the trope and social and cultural practice. In his work *Mythologies*, Roland Barthes also interprets language as being assembled by one social group to be consumed by another as ideology.[51] With others like the anthropologist Clifford Geertz and cultural critic Michel Foucault, White has constantly reviewed the representational and ideological status of the tropes (metaphor) in forming the social institutions of power and consciousness.[52]

White is fully aware of another central problem raised by his rhetorical approach to the study of history, and that is the fear of extreme interpretative relativism. This can threaten a 'free play' of interpretative fantasy that may take us further from, rather than closer to, the origin and subject of the evidence. White accepts that we have here a division between the historian who wants to 'reconstruct' or 'explain' the past and one who wishes to interpret it or use it as 'the occasion for his own speculations on the present and future'.[53] In following Foucault's logic on the text–context relationship, White does draw a line at the argument of Jacques Derrida that there is only figuration and hence no meaning in and through language.[54] The deconstructive historian need not be trapped in a forlorn snarl of rhetorical relativism. White believes, along with Foucault, that we can actually know many things about the real world despite the limitations of language. But withal there remains his warning about the power of language:

> The use of a technical language or a specific method of analysis, such as, let us say, econometrics or psychoanalysis, does not free the historian from the linguistic determinism to which the conventional narrative historian remains enslaved. On the contrary, commitment to a specific methodology . . . will close off as many perspectives on any given historical field as it opens up.[55]

The charge of rhetorical relativism, with its descent into moral decline and the sink of ideology, is countered by White's claim that all languages – whether the language of supposed objective history, or of the poet – are equally relativistic, and equally limited by the language chosen 'in which to delimit what it is possible to say about the subject under study'.[56] When the historian interprets the past he/she is not inventing it, or producing a fictionalised version that plays with the real events and real lives of the past. The historian is rather imposing a narrative structure that has coherence and unity, endowing the past 'experience of time with meaning'.[57] It is far from a descent into rhetorical relativism (and the moral turpitude, as Saul Friedlander suggests, that would deny events like the Holocaust) to recognise that the past is intervened in when emplotted by historians, or, as Ricoeur puts it, 'the narrative art [that] characteristically links a story to a narrator'.[58] What White is saying is that it is the function of the historian to explore the emplotments that may already exist in the past:

> The meaning of real human lives . . . is the meaning of the plots . . . by which the events that those lives comprise are endowed with the aspect of stories having a discernible beginning, middle, and end. A meaningful life is one that aspires to the coherency of a story with a plot. Historical agents prospectively prefigure their lives as stories with plots.[59]

This daring vision of the historical enterprise necessitates rather than denies the kind of attention to the evidence that all empiricists and contextualists would applaud. The logic of this argument is that we historians, while we tell stories, have little of the imaginative freedom exercised by writers of fiction because we are in the business of the retrospective emplotment of historical events and narratives. While the historical account is a figurative exercise in the sense of being a product of the literary imagination, its relativism remains limited by the nature of the evidence.

CONCLUSION

The deconstructive consciousness raises several fundamental questions about the character of history defined as the reconstruction of the past according to the available sources, and the construction of the past by the imposition of explanatory frameworks. The empiricist argument that our knowledge of the past is derived through the painstaking study and interpretation of fragmentary and partial evidence, and that the sheer professionalism of the working historian will overcome the problems of bias, ideology and the many other obstacles to historical understanding, is countered by the proposal that history is instead a recognition of the intimacy existing between content and form. In other words, we remind ourselves that history is not only about the sifting of evidence and constitution of facts, and that interpretation itself is an act of linguistic and literary creation.

This approach to historical analysis suggests that that which we call 'the historical' cannot be understood in all its fullness by *a priori* logic, positivism, or by the painstaking reconstructionist analysis and constitution of facts alone. Instead we may grasp more of the richness of historical analysis by incorporating into the study of the past the intertextual nature of history as a discourse. The truth found in histories, White suggests, 'resides not only in their fidelity to the facts of given individual or collective lives' but 'most importantly in their faithfulness to that vision of human life informing the poetic'.[60] It is by recognising the expressive and figurative content of historical narrative, 'the content of its form',[61] that the historian contributes to our understanding of the past. This does not mean that we historians only examine the purely figurative or metaphorical level of the discourse of history, but we intervene in the past by actively extrapolating from the literal to the symbolic level of understanding, from the present to the past.

Perhaps the central point about the deconstructive turn is the recognition that narrative upsets the assumed balance between language and reality. Historical language (Ankersmit's narrative proposal) becomes the primary vehicle for understanding. We should abandon the traditional empiricist epistemology in favour of a radical new hermeneutic or interpretative approach to the generation of knowledge about the past. I will elaborate on this significant suggestion later in my more detailed study of Foucault and White. For now I will repeat that we must examine the figurative use to which the historian puts the literal sense of meaning he/she has supposedly discovered in his/her research. This applies not only to the interpretations of historians but also to our sources. Consequently, every history is always something more than the events described. The historian represents the past rather than reclaims it as it really was. It is the deep suspicion, generated by this emphasis upon narrativisation and presentism, that motivates the empiricist critique of the deconstructive consciousness. Deconstructionists, it is claimed, forget the sources, the problems of research, and assume that ideology must unavoidably colour our historical descriptions. It is to this critique of deconstructionist history that I now turn.

5 What is wrong with deconstructionist history?

INTRODUCTION

The idea of meaning being located in a narrative or representation model of historical explanation is, for conservative reconstructionists, as much a constructionist-type imposition as is explanation through social theory. But it is not just hard-core reconstructionist historians who reject so-called postmodern history: a broad group of pro-narrativist practical realists such as Frederick A. Olafson, James Kloppenberg, James Winn, James F. McMillan, Joyce Appleby, Lynn Hunt and Margaret Jacob also seriously doubt the kind of history promoted by the deconstructive consciousness. In a summary of their position, Olafson insists that 'It is not . . . possible to give up all truth claims . . . for historical interpretations.'[1] As I have tried to show, deconstructionist history confronts each of the six principles of traditional empiricist hermeneutics under each of the four headings of epistemology, evidence, social theory and narrative form. The message of the deconstructionive consciousness – that the mainstream still naïvely pursue past reality through their assumption of an objective study of the sources – is rejected by those who argue that this image of what historians do today misconceives and grossly oversimplifies the nature of traditional history. So, from the established perspective, what is wrong with deconstructive history?

EPISTEMOLOGY

In the view of the British historian John Tosh, there is at one extreme of the profession those like G.R. Elton 'who maintain that humility in the face of the evidence and training in the technicalities of research have steadily enlarged the stock of certain historical knowledge',[2] but that methodologically to be a historian means that most ultimately do incline towards Elton's position. Those that do not, like Theodore Zeldin, who insists that no historian can offer more than a personal perspective on the past, are certainly not in the two main tendencies of accepted practice.

As moderates, Appleby, Hunt and Jacob have it that the postmodern dethroning of independent reality perceived as objective historical truth has been a difficult process of discovering 'the clay feet of science'.[3] As reasonable historians of goodwill describing themselves as practical realists, they suggest that the Second World War and subsequent Cold War together produced a substantial scepticism about the verities of science and what constitutes truth. Our present age of uncertainty was also consequent on the mid-twentieth-century Kuhnian–Popperian debate over how science gets at truth. Thomas Kuhn, arguing in favour of so-called paradigmatic shifts whereby science suddenly challenged and transformed its dominant theoretical constructs, seemed to be opening up scientific proof to the influence of social forces.[4] This apparent ending of objective science was denied by Karl Popper, who argued that he was no positivist because truth in science could be grasped only through non-falsifiable logical processes which might yield the covering laws of historical constructionism rather than the messiness of empiricism. Not for Popper the crudities of correspondence theory. The growing acceptance by Appleby, Hunt and Jacob that knowledge may be socially constructed does not mean of course that they accept that all truth is relative or value-laden, nor less that writing about the past in the present (historicity) makes relativism inevitable. In fact, as Appleby, Hunt and Jacob have it, the social reading of knowledge is actually epistemologically advantageous in the search for historical truth. Cautiously they declare that historical objectivity can actually emerge from, as they say, the 'clash of social interests, ideologies, and social conventions within the framework of object-oriented and disciplined knowledge-seeking'. For them, hard-won truth 'however mired in time and language' is still truth in a democratic society.[5]

The postmodern age of which deconstructionism is an attribute is keynoted by an enhanced and unwarranted sense of irony at the presumed disappearance of the certainties of objective knowledge, in which disciplines are viewed as historical cultural practices (meta-narratives) or canons intended not to generate truth and unbiased knowledge, but rather to sustain present or prospective dispensations of dominance and subordination. From the postmodern or deconstructionist perspective objective science is not objective, non-sectarian, universal and transcendent, but it legitimates the present dominant forms of Western civilisation. Lyotard, Foucault, Barthes and Derrida have argued that we are unable to represent reality accurately in language, and that we cannot, therefore, assume that objectivity is feasible, nor should we accept either the correspondence theory of knowledge, or Popper's logical positivism. It follows that the notion of the individual as a potentially autonomous, non-ideological animal is also flawed, and knowledge produced by such a creature must be a fabrication, an assembled invention that disguises the will to power. Hence, the wedge of relativism and scepticism reaches its apogee in postmodernism.

Such a Nietzschean-inspired universe which has no truth, which accepts the failure of representation, and which consequently accepts relativism in moral standards, is rejected by traditional history. Foucault's position is likewise rejected where it means accepting an anti-humanism that itself rejects human agency.[6] By the same token, the traditional paradigm has it that history is quite capable of recognising 'the other', the marginal, the oppressed and the hegemony of bourgeois ideology that sanctions colonialism and Third World exploitation. So, how is it possible to base historical method on the belief that there is no direct access to independent knowledge because there is no clear separation between objectivity and subjectivity, fact and value, and history and fiction and truth can never be more than perspective? Appleby, Hunt and Jacob summarise the deconstructive perspective as assuming that

> Human beings do not achieve a separation from the objects they study; they simply invest them with their own values. Thus along with modern history, the idea of the human being as an autonomous, subjectively willing, rational agent [is] brought into question.[7]

What is being questioned by Appleby, Hunt and Jacob's traditional hermeneutics is the inevitable result of the Saussurean position that if language is built on the arbitrary relationship of signifier and signified, we must doubt the correspondence theory of reality and deny the commonsense notion that the truth is 'out there'. Although the practical realist mainstream can accept, along with deconstructionist historians, that the reality of the past is always mediated through culturally influenced narrative structures, that language is not a transcendent measure of truth and, as another American historian, Linda Gordon, has concluded, that objectivity is 'certainly an issue', deconstructionist relativism is not the only response.[8]

The most rugged rebuttal of the deconstructive turn has undoubtedly come from the British Tudor historian Geoffrey Elton. Elton has strikingly combined his long-standing opposition to constructionism and what he views as E.H. Carr's scepticism, with an equally energetic rebuff to deconstructionist historical analysis. Quoting correspondence theory, Elton insists that historical truth is the product of the independent relationship between knower and known, and historians aspire to reach it, but any failure to achieve it on their part 'does not abolish the truth of the past event'.[9] With regard to the historian seeking truth, the philosopher of history Michael Stanford echoes Elton in claiming that the historian 'is permitted only one attitude – that of impartial observer, unmoved equally by admiration or repugnance. Nor does he presume to dictate the reader's response; he simply relates the facts.'[10]

Arthur Marwick supports Elton's position with his own attack on 'postmodern relativist' Hayden White. Marwick sustains the notion of history as a distinct epistemology by denying White's 'imagined disjunction between what the historian discovers . . . and the writing up of those discoveries'. According to Marwick, White produces a 'rabbit-out-of-the-hat' with his claim that all written history must 'obey the codes of narratives and discourse' and consequently cannot ever be logically demonstrated. Marwick is firm in the argument that history exists independently of the historian and is certainly not written according to White's formal grid or structure of tropes and emplotments. Marwick remains convinced that the historian is not ruled by structures of language to the extent that historical truth can never be known, concluding that '"deconstruction" and "discourse analysis" . . . are no use to historians looking for precise, and in some sense unique, answers to specific questions'.[11]

This staunch Elton–Stanford–Marwick defence of fundamentalist reconstructionist epistemology also finds expression in the mainstream voices of Appleby, Hunt and Jacob in their more nuanced but still ultimate denial of the cognitive value of the written form of history. First they pose the fundamental deconstructionist question of 'how does the historian as author construct his or her text, how is the illusion of authenticity produced, what creates a sense of truthfulness to the facts and a warranty of closeness to past reality (or the "truth-effect" as it is sometimes called)?'. Their answer is that history is unmistakably an independent discipline and not merely a mimetic or ersatz literary genre dependent for its power to explain on the *trompe l'œil* principle. Appleby, Hunt and Jacob regard the deconstructive argument as being productive of not only relativism, but of a relativism 'possibly tinged with cynicism or arrogance' that insults the efforts of people in the past who themselves believed that they were seekers after truth. Finally, without the ability to 'represent reality in any objectively true fashion', they say that we can never expect to explain anything at all.[12]

A further defence of empiricism as the foundation of traditional hermeneutics is offered by American historians like James Winn, Linda

Gordon and especially James T. Kloppenberg.[13] Relativism, or 'intellectual and moral chaos' as Peter Novick described it, is not the only alternative to objectivity. Like Appleby, Hunt and Jacob, James Kloppenberg fortifies reconstructionism by invoking certain arguments of contemporary pragmatic philosophers Richard Rorty and Richard J. Bernstein.[14] Instead of accepting the six key principles of empiricism as inevitable dualisms, Kloppenberg attempts to moderate the absolutism of empiricist objectivism. He does this by suggesting that history can be regarded as epistemologically viable through a 'pragmatic theory of truth [that substitutes] continuing social experimentation for certainty [accompanied by] a historical sensibility' that conceives of all knowledge 'as intrinsically meaningful and rooted in cultural processes that can be known only through interpretation'. This defence of empiricism does away with Derrida's extreme insistence on relativism as the inevitable result of the collapse of objectivity. Consequently, history remains a legitimate epistemology because of its fundamental empiricist deductive–inductive methodology. As Kloppenberg says, articulating the mainstream methodological position,

> Hypotheses – such as historical interpretation – can be checked against all the available evidence and subjected to the most rigorous tests the community of historians can devise. If they are verified provisionally, they stand. If they are disproved, new interpretations must be advanced and subjected to similar testing. The process is imperfect but not random; the results are always tentative but not worthless.[15]

From this perspective (derived from the first two of the six key principles), the duality proposed by deconstructionists of historians as either objectivists (naïve realists) or relativists (sophisticated ironists) loses its validity. Kloppenberg's is not a new response. The American historian Charles Beard (with Carl Becker) argued in the 1930s that history was then a complex process of 'hermeneutics and pragmatic truth-testing, in which knowledge derives from weaving together fact and interpretation to create stories [myths, Becker called them] whose accuracy must therefore always be considered provisional'.[16] Beard accepted as incontrovertible the principle that facts could be acquired objectively, but recognised that absolute truth as a historical generalisation claiming to explain those facts was an unobtainable goal. As he often said, 'We see what is behind our eyes.'[17]

Reconstructionists, ranging from Elton, Stanford, Marwick and Himmelfarb to mainstreamers like Kloppenberg, Appleby, Hunt and Jacob, are thus agreed on defending history as a distinct epistemology.

Where they divide is on the historian's use of models, the deductive method and use of narrative. Hard-liners defend the discipline's inductive methods on the grounds offered by Leon Goldstein that deduction has 'no role at all in the . . . road to historical truth',[18] while practical realists would join the conservatives in their opposition to deconstruction because of their shared belief in the ultimate existence of a knowable reality 'out there' located in the evidence, and which those so inclined can interrogate through their social theorising. It follows that it is how we treat the evidence that in large part determines the response to the deconstructionive consciousness.

EVIDENCE

In the previous chapter I suggested that deconstructionists question the authority of the source in several ways: by maintaining that the intention of the author of the evidence must always remain unknown (the death of the author), by considering the understanding of evidence through its contextualisation to be a doubtful procedure, and by casting doubt on the explanatory power of the practice of *Quellenkritik*. The majority of historians today can be described as practical realists who acknowledge that the actuality of the past is always imperfectly encountered, whether through social theory or narrative impositionalism. Those practical realists in the mainstream tendencies like to argue that today only deconstructionist historians get hot under the collar about endless chains of signification and a reality that is always in an altered state, given its narrated form. They argue that deconstructionist colleagues have erected a straw man in their over-inflation of the issue of crude empiricism – as Marwick has suggested, 'postmodern critics . . . totally misconceive the way in which historians go about their business'.[19] The problem of indeterminate meaning is now openly acknowledged. The only difficulty lies with the deconstructionist refusal to understand that most mainstream practical realist historians today accept their role as being essential to the interpretation of written evidence, rather than demonstrating the failings of empiricism. They point to E.H. Carr, who said almost forty years ago that facts emerge as historical facts only when processed through the mind of the historian. Historians are by definition interpreters and not just facilitators of meaning.

Allowing for the deconstructionist arguments that language clouds rather than clarifies meaning, that there are a multiplicity of meanings in our source texts and that the author of the source is (like the historian also) the creature of multiple cultural discourses and significations does not mean that culture and ideology write history. Even granted these constraints, reconstructionist historians would argue that neither historians nor sources are adrift on a sea of significations nor necessarily subject to the tides of cultural relativism and ideology. No reasonable historian today, or quite possibly ever, has claimed either that empiricism is a system that guarantees the objective discovery of truth, or that there can ever be a hermetic seal between knower and known. As John Tosh has said, the process of creating historical knowledge starts with the questions the historian 'has in mind at the outset of research'.[20] This is natural, normal and nothing to worry about. Marwick adds, 'the technical skills of the historian' lie in sorting out the problems with sources as well as deciphering the 'codes of language' they employ.[21]

The nature of the access to an independent and real past as represented in the evidence has been extensively addressed by C. Behan McCullagh and Frederick A. Olafson. McCullagh holds that the basic yardstick for historians is the commonsense and commonplace assumption that their perceptions 'are caused by roughly similar states of the world . . . an assumption which we all make most of the time, with complete equanimity and success'.[22] Founded on the assumption that the world exists separate to our knowledge of it, historians 'do not construct past reality by attempting to describe it. All that they construct is our knowledge of it, our beliefs about it.'[23] As a result, historians constitute the truth of historical descriptions not by a direct comparison with the reality of the past, because this, it is agreed, is inaccessible, 'but by inferring them from the present evidence'.[24] Deconstructionists are thus presumed consistently to underestimate the sophistication of the inferential method. They miss the genuine sophistication and complexity of historical practice today. Olafson declares that the evidence of the past, as found in the statements of the author(s) of the evidence, is directly referential in so far as the evidence refers to the past. Evidence thus construed does actually signify a referential linguistic event. Inductivism – inference from the sources, or *Quellenkritik* – thus remains the primary defence against the deconstructionist perspective. Of course, inductive inference can be wrong if based on false or non-verifiable evidence. Consequently the reasonable historian always distinguishes what he/she *believes* to be true about the past, and what may *actually* be true. Such a belief is inevitably founded upon some idea about what the world of the past was like and how it was ordered. This initial thought is the start of the process for the construction of historical facts.

This, the most popular vision of the use of evidence in history, is derived from E.H. Carr in his highly influential 1961 book *What is History?*. By following the logic of R.G. Collingwood (a historian scorned for his relativism by Marwick and Elton), Carr set about answering the question 'What is a historical fact?'. He argued that historical facts are derived through 'an *a priori* decision of the historian'. It is the manner in which the historian arranges the facts derived from the evidence, as determined by his/her prior knowledge of the context, that creates historical meaning. Using Carr's analogy, a fact is like a sack: it will not stand up until you put something in it.[25] The something is a question addressed to the evidence. However we describe it, historians quite legitimately impose on the past through their knowledge-based interrogation of it. As Carr insists, and mainstream historians would agree, 'The facts speak only when the historian calls on them: it is he who decides to which facts to give the floor, and in what order or context.'[26] In *The Idea of History*, his earlier study of the creation of historical meaning, Collingwood suggested that the historian arranges the information available about the past in the light of the context, which he described as a 'web of imaginative construction'.[27] Facts are constituted when they are verified by comparison and placed in a meaningful relation to each other in the overall historical context.

As Carr describes the derivation of the historical fact, 'Its status . . . will turn on a question of interpretation. This element of interpretation enters into every fact of history.' He concludes, much to the vexation of Elton, that the 'historian is necessarily selective. The belief in a hard core of historical facts existing objectively and independently of the interpretation of the historian is a preposterous fallacy, but one that is very hard to eradicate.'[28] Since the 1960s Carr's arguments have constituted the dominant paradigm for moderate reconstructionist historians because he pulls back from the abyss of relativism to which his own logic, and that of Collingwood's, directs him. In the end Carr rebuffs Collingwood's excessive insistence on the formative role of the historian, and replaces it with an image of the historian who, in acknowledging the dialogue between past events and future trends, believes that a sort of objectivity can be achieved. This is not then the absolutism of the crude Eltonian reconstructionist, but a workable or pragmatic objectivity based upon a degree of self-reflexivity – a position fully endorsed by Appleby, Hunt and Jacob.[29]

Facts remain, then, a contested terrain, and it is not something new that deconstructionists have discovered. There are, of course, some hard-core empiricists like Peter Gay, who would deny Carr's relativist conclusion while accepting that his thinking, 'the historian's mental set or secret emotions', rather than producing distorting interpretations, may actually provide a clear view of the past.[30] As Gay says, 'To equate motive with distortion . . . is demonstrably illegitimate', especially if the motive drives 'the inquirer toward the efficient comprehension of the outside world. The need that generates inquiry may be sublimated into disinterestedness. Even empathy, the very emotion that the modern historian is ceaselessly enjoined to cultivate, has its objective component.' Gay concludes, in support of what Novick calls the 'hyperobjectivist position', that although the rhetoric of history is different to that of science, 'this does not entail the expulsion of history from the family of the sciences. It simply makes the historian's science special, with its own way of telling the truth.'[31] In this fashion Gay provides perhaps the ultimate denial of the deconstructive turn – interventionist historians can write objective history.

The motivation behind the work of the historian is found in the questions they ask of the evidence, and it is not, as deconstructionists would have it, automatically to be associated with ideological self-indulgence. Deconstructionist worries about motivation and inference from the sources have little strength as long as historians do not preconceive patterns of interpretation and order facts to fit those preconceptions. As McCullagh remarks, the fact that historians can locate more than one pattern in the same evidence does not mean that those patterns cannot represent reality. Indeed, taking up Hayden White's specific argument that there are many correct views of any object under study, McCullagh regards this as old news and quite unproblematic, arguing that in virtually every case past events are 'capable of several different true descriptions'.[32] Like most other practical realists, McCullagh is eager to challenge the deconstructive belief that historians are incapable of writing down even a reasonably truthful narrative representation of the past. He thinks that they can because their narratives are based on a close scrutiny of the evidence.

Hence historians do not deny that the process of translating the evidence of the past into the facts of history involves making initial *a priori* interpretative decisions – that is part of the winnowing process as Carr calls it.[33] This is right and as it should be. Although deconstructionists like Dominick LaCapra can bemoan fact fetishism, this again is old news. Almost half a century ago, Carr described the 'fetishism of facts' as a nineteenth-century fashion, not one that modern historians need concern themselves about. Deconstructionism, along with Elton's conservative reconstructionism, underestimate the sophisticated nature of mainstream historians today in their dealings with the evidence in context. As John Tosh explains, they 'seek to reconstruct or re-create it – to show how life was experienced as well as how it may be understood –

and this requires an imaginative engagement with the mentality and atmosphere of the past'. Moreover, 'the evaluation of documentary sources depends on a reconstruction of the thought behind them', and before anything else can be achieved 'the historian must first try to enter the mental world of those who created the sources'.[34] It is up to the historian to turn sources into history. Sources are useful only when they are processed like raw materials into the evidence from which historical facts are created.

As Collingwood suggested, evidence does not constitute an off-the-shelf or ready-made historical knowledge that can simply be swallowed and then disgorged by the historian. Source materials become useful as historical facts only when the historian has applied to them the range of contextualised knowledge he/she already possesses. It is not good enough to rely upon the correspondence theory of historical proof, as deconstructionists appear to believe historians do. The process of historical interpretation based on the evidence is far more sophisticated than the simple description of sources that deconstructionist historians like to assume occurs. Neither do most historians accept a Popperian scientific model of explanation any more than they accept being trapped in ideology. The post-Kuhnian relativist and deconstructionist preoccupation with the failings of empiricism and the illusory character of objectivism are largely irrelevant because they address issues with which historians have long been familiar and with which inferential historical methodology, if properly applied with an appropriate sense of practical realism, presents few genuine or insoluble problems.

From what I have said so far it should be clear how moderate or practical realist reconstructionists work: through a complex deductive–inductive process that recognises history to be the product of a dialogue between historian and source. It is generally understood that this relationship involves hypothesis-framing, to the extent at least of establishing preliminary interpretations or conceptualisations based on knowledge of the context as well as familiarity with the sources. These initial thoughts are the essential first step when addressing a problem and/or new evidence. This is not a definition of constructionism because such thoughts have not reached the same level of activity as that of social theorists, identified by Elton as 'adherents of theory [who] do not allow facts to disturb them but instead try to deride the whole notion that there are facts independent of the observer'.[35] For mainstreamers it is the bellicosity of such a conservative position that gives the arguments of deconstruction more credence than they deserve and that denies the importance of much highly valued constructionist history. Most practical realists would argue that the volume and range of history presently are testament to its vitality, and the 'linguistic turn' and the influence of post-structuralist thought, which a voluble minority of historians fear as a threat to the discipline, has instead given it a new lease of life as the 'new cultural history'. It seems that history has little to fear from post-modernism, which is really only a diversion from the main agenda.

THEORIES OF HISTORY: CONSTRUCTING THE PAST

It seems clear that the line drawn between reconstructionist and constructionist historians in their employment of *a priori* or deductive method is for practical realists a narrow one, but the debate over where that line is drawn has distinct implications for deconstructionist history. In an influential presidential speech before the American Historical Association in 1910, the social science-inspired American historian of the frontier, Frederick Jackson Turner, warned his audience that

> The economic historian is in danger of making his analysis and his statement of a law on the basis of present conditions and then passing to history for justificatory appendixes to his conclusions. . . .The historian . . . may doubt . . . whether the past should serve merely as the 'illustration' by which to confirm the law deduced from the common experience by *a priori* reasoning tested by statistics.[36]

Heeding this sort of warning, Geoffrey Elton not only jettisons covering laws but imagines something worse: an ardent pro-narrativist-inspired merger of speculative philosophy with a degraded empiricism. Mainstreamers generally consider that this is not the terrain on which to enjoin battle with the deconstructionists.

As I have suggested, although Elton is dismissive of all theory, in his conservative call to arms he reserves his most trenchant criticism for deconstructionism, which he describes as 'the conviction that since history has to be written the only kind worth having operates within the framework of a general theory of language', an idea that, along with various other kinds of constructionist impositionalism, undermines 'claims to rational, independent and impartial investigation'.[37] What he calls 'the endeavours to use literary theory to destroy the reality of the past' can only do serious harm, like all other forms of constructionist theory, to the historian's first duty which is to reconstruct the past as objectively and independently as possible.[38] All that theory in history does, Elton maintains, is to turn the historian into its slave:

> The theory directs the selection of evidence and infuses predestined meaning into it. All questions are so framed as to produce support

for the theory, and all answers are predetermined by it. Historians captured by theory may tell you that they test their constructs by empirical research, but they do nothing of the sort; they use empirical research to prove the truth of the framework, never to disprove it. . . . Adherents of theory do not allow facts to disturb them but instead try to deride the whole notion that there are facts independent of the observer.[39]

Marxists, in a brief alliance with deconstructionist historians, reject the logocentrism of the conservative bourgeois reconstructionist version of a past 'reality'. But Marxists eventually turn their guns on deconstructionism because it fails to acknowledge that texts, like beliefs and ideas, are read and understood in the real world. For Marxists, the deconstructive consciousness fails because it de-materialises reality. Marxists view deconstructionism as just another version of idealism that de-couples human beings from their economic and social context. Texts have authors, even deconstructionist history has authors, and the intentionality of those authors can be seen in what they do, and read, and write in the material world of recoverable structure and pattern.

There are other fundamentalist reconstructionists apart from Elton who are concerned about both the constructionist and deconstructionist challenge to the Rankean paradigm. Their disquiet is well put by the American social historian Gertrude Himmelfarb:

All historians, new and old . . . have something to worry about – not only the fragmentation of history but the deconstruction of history – and not only on the part of avowed deconstructionists but on the part of social historians who unwittingly contribute to the same result.[40]

For Himmelfarb, deconstructionism is merely a more pernicious version of constructionism:

Although deconstruction, as a conscious, systematic philosophy, has been most prominent among intellectual historians, the mode of thought it represents, even its distinct vocabulary, is permeating all aspects of the new constructionist history. Historians now freely use such words as 'invent,' 'imagine,' 'create' (not 're-create'), and 'construct' (not 'reconstruct') to describe the process of historical interpretation, and then proceed to support some novel interpretation by a series of 'possibles,' 'might have beens,' and 'could have beens.'[41]

For Himmelfarb, deconstructionism and constructionism are two sides of the same relativist coin. She reasons that the New History's 'increased use of quantification, models and other social science techniques' has produced not greater objectivity but 'an increased sense of relativism and subjectivism'. Marxism is her regular target, but various other kinds of social theorising are also threatening history:

> It is not only political history that the new historian denies or belittles. It is reason itself. . . . This rationality is now consciously denied or unconsciously undermined by every manner of new history: . . . by anthropological history . . .; by psychoanalytic history . . .; by *engagé* (and *enragé*) history . . .; by the new history of every description asking questions of the past that the past did not ask of herself, for which the evidence is sparse and unreliable and to which the answers are necessarily speculative, subjective, and dubious.[42]

Such comments have been held to be ill-directed by Lawrence Stone, who suggests that Himmelfarb should not divide the mainstream historical world at a time when the greater threat to rationality is not from constructionist New History but from 'philosophy, linguistics, semiotics, and deconstructionism'.[43]

Stone had already declared his own anti-constructionist and deconstructionist position in the late 1970s when he claimed to have detected evidence 'of an undercurrent which is sucking up many prominent "new historians" back again into some form of narrative'. He continued:

> In some countries and institutions it has been unhealthy that the 'new historians' have had things so much their own way in the last thirty years; and it will be equally unhealthy if the new trend, if trend it be, achieves similar domination here and there.[44]

While disclaiming any attempt to make value judgements on the new trends, Stone explored the nature of 'scientific history' – translated as constructionist Marxism, *Annales*, cliometrics and 'other "scientific" explanations of historical change' which 'have risen to favour for a while and then gone out of fashion'. Stone had both French structuralism and Parsonian functionalism in mind. Instead of explaining the past, Stone concluded that all these trends did was to usher in 'historical revisionism with a vengeance' as a result of their focusing on 'the material conditions of the masses' and relegating the major historical movements associated with the elite. As he said, 'In this new model of history such movements as the Renaissance, the Reformation, the Enlightenment and the rise of the modern state simply disappeared.' He finished with the thought that 'This curious blindness was the result of a firm belief that these matters were all parts of . . . a mere superficial superstructure.' The revival of narrative was due to 'widespread disillusionment with the economic determinist model of historical explanation' and in particular with the *Annaliste* relegation of social and intellectual developments. For Stone the way to reverse this process was through a revival of narrative which would spin 'a single web of meaning'.[45]

The description 'revival of narrative' describes Stone's effort to move historical methodology away from what he saw as its constructionist economic monocausal determinism by groups of new historians no longer constrained by a 'specific methodology, structural, collective and statistical'. By 'narrative', Stone was referring to a 'cluster of changes in the nature of historical discourse'[46] which, in the 1970s, witnessed 'a quite sudden growth of interest in feelings, emotions, behaviour patterns, values, and states of mind'. To this end he evidenced the work of narrative-inspired sociological theorists E.E. Evans-Pritchard, Norbert Elias, Clifford Geertz, and political theorists J.G.A. Pocock and Quentin Skinner, whose ideas had been utilised by historians. For Stone, this 'movement to narrative by the "new historians"' spelled the end of the attempt 'to produce a coherent scientific explanation of change in the past'.[47] It has to be pointed out, however, that for Stone 'narrative' as a term was a particularly bad shorthand to describe what was, in effect, a broad cultural reorientation among historians, especially because in the 1980s the issue of narrative structure developed along more specific deconstructionist lines.

In a 1991 issue of *Past and Present*, Stone criticised the latest postmodern trends in history which 'brought seriously into question' its subject-matter, data and its mechanisms of explanation.[48] Stone isolated three distinct threats from the constructionist and/or deconstructionist camps: 'The first threat comes from linguistics, building up from Saussure to Derrida, and climaxing in deconstruction . . . The second . . . cultural and symbolic anthropology. . . . The third . . . from New Historicism.'[49] Stone maintained that together they challenged history's basic empiricist principles. Stone elaborated on what he took to be the essence of history today. Rather than the positivism of the nineteenth century which deconstructionists fondly believed was still the dominant practice, Stone established what for him were the key mainstream beliefs: that history should be written in 'plain English, avoiding jargon and obfuscation'; that 'historical truth is unattainable, and that any conclusions are provisional and hypothetical, always liable to be overturned by new data or better theories'; that we should accept that historians have bias and would do well, like E.H. Carr, to study the historian 'before we read history'; that the documents, because of their inherent textual limitations and our difficulties with authorial intentions, should be 'scrutinised with care, taking into account . . . the nature of the document, and the context in which it was written'; and finally, that historians do know that 'perceptions and representatives of reality are often very different from, and sometimes just as historically important as, reality itself'.[50] Here again a moderate reconstructionist–contextualist is pointing out how deconstruction actually misrepresents the empiricist case. Quoting Joyce Appleby (in an echo of E.H. Carr), Stone asserts that 'a text is merely a passive agent in the hands of its author. It is human beings who play with words; words don't play with themselves.'[51]

Stone spoke for many historians when he said that his disagreement with postmodernist history was when it claimed

> that truth is unknowable, . . . that there is no reality out there which is anything but a subjective creation of the historian; in other words that it is language that creates meaning which in turn creates our image of the real. This destroys the difference between fact and fiction, and makes entirely nugatory the dirty and tedious archival work of the historian to dig 'facts' out of texts. It is only at this extreme point that historians have any need to express anxiety. But since nearly everyone . . . seems to be retreating from this position, there is now at last a common platform upon which we can all, without too much discomfort, take our stand.[52]

Stone here is making sense to most historians, few of whom insist on the absolutism of the text. But to accept intertextuality, a historicist reading of the past, or an impositionalist and mediatory role for the historian, is not to wave a white flag in the face of the deconstructionist onslaught. A compromise with the deconstructionist critique is offered by the historian of France Gabrielle M. Spiegel when she says that

> If one of the major moves in post-structuralist thought has been to displace the controlling metaphor of historical evidence from one of reflection to one of mediation (that is, has been a shift from the notion that texts and documents transparently reflect past realities, as positivism believed, to one in which the past is captured in the mediated form preserved for us in language), then we need to think carefully about how we understand mediation and how that understanding affects our practice.[53]

If by mediation we mean acknowledging the historical and social creation of a text as well as the need to evaluate it 'as a literary artefact composed of language' which demands 'literary (formal) analysis', then reconstructionists and constructionists can both capture the reality of the past, accept the referentiality of language, and at the same time see texts 'as material embodiments of situated language-use'. In other words, historians can view texts as the material embodiments of the various uses of language, which reflects the 'inseparability of material and discursive practices and the need to preserve a sense of their mutual . . . interdependence in the production of meaning'. Spiegel calls this practical realist compromise with deconstruction 'the social logic of the text'.[54]

Less charitable to the deconstructive consciousness is John Tosh in his support for the moderates in their attempt to compromise the two mainstream approaches. He maintains that significant advances in historical understanding are

> more likely to be achieved when a historian puts forward a clearly formulated hypothesis which can be tested against the evidence. The answers may not correspond to the hypothesis which must then be discarded or modified, but merely to ask new questions has the important effect of alerting historians to unfamiliar aspects of familiar problems and to unsuspected data in well-worked sources.[55]

All historical study is selective and, as Tosh would have it, 'therefore presupposes a hypothesis or theory, however incoherent it may be'. Because this process of hypothesis-making goes beyond the evidence, it is legitimate for historians to use 'a flash of insight or an imaginative leap, often the bolder the better'.[56] None of this, of course, is an endorsement of the deconstructive emphasis on the cognitive functioning of narrative. For mainstream constructionist historians, this Collingwood–Carr approach provides a more sympathetic definition of history than positivism, and one which seems a reasoned and legitimate riposte to the deconstructive stress on the linguistic turn.

HISTORY AS NARRATIVE

In the early 1970s, A.J.P. Taylor suggested that we historians 'should not be ashamed to admit that history is at bottom simply a form of storytelling. . . . There is no escaping the fact that the original task of the historian is to answer the child's question: "What happened next?".'[57] Like E.H. Carr, Taylor believed that historians impose a pattern on events in the shape of a dialogue. Between the events

> and the historian there is a constant interplay. The historian tries to impose on events some kind of rational pattern: how they happened and why they happened. No historian starts with a blank mind as a

jury is supposed to do. He does not go to documents or archives with a childlike innocence . . . and wait patiently until they dictate conclusions to him. Quite the contrary. His picture, his version of events is formed before he begins to write or even to research. . . . When a historian is working on his subject, the events or statistical data or whatever he is using change under his hand all the time and his ideas about these events change with them.[58]

Although he clearly accepted the impositionalism of the historian, Taylor did not directly address the issue of narrative structure as a form of historical understanding. The closest he came to this was his claim that history 'just like historical fiction is an exercise in creative imagination'. Taylor's rider was, of course, that we historians are constrained 'by the limits of our knowledge' and by the historian pushing himself 'backwards into time' or empathising with the past. Nevertheless, Taylor was astute enough to recognise, along with Karl Marx, that when historians write history, 'our version, being set into words, is itself false'. He concluded: 'We are trying to stop something that never stands still. Once written, our version too will move.'[59] What Taylor was referring to was the perpetual revisionism that goes on in historical interpretation, but he was getting close to articulating the main inhibiting factor acting on historians attempting to understand the past – its organisation as a narrative which has the best 'fit' to the truth of what actually happened – what the historian Robert Berkhofer calls *the* or *a* Great Story.[60] Taylor recognised that it is narrative that bridges the interpretative or cognitive gap between the historian and the evidence – *a* history and *the* past. Pushing the argument further, do historians – mainstream or deconstructionist – all simply offer up a narrative of the past, or discover its innate narrativised character? As Berkhofer says, can we get beyond an imposed Great Story to the reality itself – the real story?

If we prioritise language before the content of history, the issue of relativism emerges with our choice of emplotment rather than with matters ideological. In 1995, the American Historical Association published the updated third edition of its *Guide to Historical Literature*. In its first section Richard T. Vann addressed theory and practice in contemporary historical study, noting the recent greater consciousness about the role of narrative in the constitution of historical meaning. Vann recognised that the focus of interest in history 'has largely shifted from preoccupation with causation, explanation, determinism, and moral judgements to the language historians use and the stories they tell'.[61] He accepted that in the past thirty years the most influential book on historical method has been Hayden White's *Metahistory*. But in Vann's view, White unfortunately presumed 'to show that historical events could support *any number* of narratives – even narratives of quite different sorts'. Instead of dealing with empirical data ordered via social theory, history for White is created through poetic, emplotment, ideological and moral decisions. According to Vann, this 'raised the spectre of relativism in a new way, forcing historians to confront the problem of comparing possible narratives, each of which might be composed entirely of true statements'. As a result, the new-found freedom of narrative was bought at the cost of no longer being able 'to discredit alternate narratives by an appeal to the evidence'. This, in Vann's opinion, is not a price most historians are willing to pay, hence the antipathy with which much of White's narrativist deconstructionism has been received.[62]

While most historians agree with Collingwood that, although we cannot ever know historical truth, we are happy to accept 'the obvious fact that we can and do substitute one narrative for another', this is clearly not done on the deconstructive or relativist grounds offered by Hayden White. As Collingwood says, it is done 'not on the grounds of personal preference but on wholly objective grounds, grounds whose cogency anyone would have to admit if he looked into them, while yet fully aware that our own narrative is not the whole truth and is certainly in some particulars untrue'.[63] McCullagh agrees with Taylor (and Collingwood in this instance) that historians cannot get away from language and words:

> almost all descriptions of the world use language [but this] . . . does not prevent their being true or false. In the case of literal descriptions, they are true if one of their possible sets of truth conditions corresponds to what actually happened; and to say that they are true is to assert that such a correspondence exists, that the world was as it is described.[64]

This position rejects the Whitean model of historical interpretation founded on generic plot configurations, arguing that it is unlikely that, for example, the 1944 Warsaw Uprising could be interpreted *equally* well as romance, farce *or* tragedy.[65]

This seems to be the position adopted by most mainstream historians. As the American historian David Carroll has said of the impact of Hayden White's *Metahistory*:

> it would be fair to say that the history profession as a whole has refused to take seriously any approach to history that has the

appearance of being too 'literary' or rhetorical. Historians have for the most part ignored or simply rejected the critical possibilities opened up by White's . . . work . . . influenced by critical strategies associated with poststructuralist and deconstructionist theories of discourse and textuality.[66]

But, having said that, Carroll agrees with the French historian Philippe Carrard that more and more historians are (or they should be) aware of the literary or poetic as *an* important dimension or characteristic of history-writing. The main lesson for mainstream historians today is to understand that 'the goal of objective history is impossible to realise in language'.[67] Neither crude empiricism nor positivism are the routes to follow in the attempt to overcome the rhetorical and figural character of language and textuality. For Carroll, this recognition is not, however, a sell-out of history to the deconstructionists, but is a simple acknowledgement of history's 'epistemological and ideological assumptions and limitations, on the one hand, and its formal, rhetorical operations, effects, and contradictions, on the other'.[68]

This pro-narrative but anti-deconstructionist position is endorsed by moderate reconstructionists like Appleby, Hunt and Jacob, who, with their 'new theory of objectivity', assume truth comes from the conflict of ideas 'among diverse groups of truth-seekers'. Our pragmatic access to this truth is through 'the validity of each reconstruction' which depends 'upon the accuracy and completeness of the observations, not . . . perspective'.[69] They argue that 'To deny the writing of history objective validity because of the historian's essential creative effort is to remain attached to a nineteenth-century understanding of the production of knowledge.' While rejecting the postmodernist collapse of subject and object and the deconstructive consciousnesses caricature of history as little removed from nineteenth-century positivism, with McCullagh and Carroll, Appleby, Hunt and Jacob fully accept the constraints of language in the pursuit of truth. They recognise the poor fit between what happened in the past and the historian's narrative reconstruction of it.

How does this poor fit look in practice? Historians, as Arthur Danto has suggested, use narrative sentences to refer to events occurring over time.[70] Such a process requires using narrative to explain the causal connections between events as the end product of the study of the sources and their interpretative contextualisation. For deconstructionists like White this process is flawed because the historian cannot capture the past faithfully in language or as narrative, and the search for truth is replaced by the truth-effects of the explanatory narrative devices of figuration and style, emplotment, argument and ideological statement. Another philosopher of history, Andrew P. Norman, rejects White's anti-narrative analysis of history, arguing instead that while narrative is the essential explanatory device for historians, its figurative nature does not mean that it cannot at the same time be literal, claiming that 'there is nothing contradictory in this'.[71] In other words, language in its narrative form is not a desperate illusion but is sufficiently in touch with past reality to make the search for historical understanding viable.

Appleby, Hunt and Jacob accept this view, and that the historian constantly makes literary choices in describing *and* evaluating the past which 'has a very strong influence on the way that evidence and arguments are presented'. As they say, form and technique are deliberately selected by the historian to implement arguments and make them convincing. Their text *Telling the Truth About History* was, they frankly admit, written from a position intended to

> go beyond the current negative or ironic judgements about history's role. We as historians . . . [have made] our own aesthetic choices, just as others have chosen comedy, romance, or irony for their writings. We are emphasising the human need for self-understanding through a coherent narrative of the past and the need for admittedly partial, objective explanations of how the past has worked. In this sense, we have renounced an ironic stance.[72]

In a rebuttal of Hayden White's conception of the unavoidable literariness of history, these three appreciate that what they have written requires 'aesthetic or literary choices because they involve ways of organising a narrative', but they are sure that 'history is more than a branch of letters to be judged only in terms of its literary merit'. They construe their history, written in part as a result of their literary choices, as being 'political, social and epistemological' rather than conforming to a classic literary emplotment type. In a summary of their moderate practical realist reconstructionist position they conclude that these literary choices

> are political and social because they reflect beliefs in a certain kind of community of historians and society of Americans. They are epistemological because they reflect positions on what can be known and how it can be known. With diligence and good faith they may also be at moments reasonably, if partially, true accounts of the . . . past.[73]

As practical realist historians they accept that 'social reality is culturally constructed and discursively construed in the first instance' and that 'discursive or linguistic models throw into doubt the once absolutist forms of conventional historical explanation', and in this fashion they open up the way 'to new forms of historical investigation', noting that 'Foucault's own work is perhaps the best known example of such a new form with direct historical relevance'.[74] Their attempt to meet the deconstructionists halfway, to the extent of not 'rejecting out of hand everything put forward by the postmodernists', has its limits however. Postmodernism has not convinced them, as it has not most historians, of the validity of 'linguistic determinism . . . the reduction of the social and natural world to language and context to text'. They continue: 'If historians give up the analogies of levels (the Annals school) or base-superstructure (Marxism), must they also give up social theory and causal language altogether?'[75] In other words, they do not accept that deconstructionism has cast genuine doubt on the power of narrative to explain. This defence of realist narrative history has united both practical realist reconstructionists and constructionists as they accept the narrative impositionalism of the historian as an important dimension of historical analysis.

Many constructionists do still, of course, deny any explanatory power to narrative, arguing instead that non-narrative history is the only genuine history. Stanford, for example, maintains that narrative, defined as the description of events in their original or naturally occurring time sequence, cannot be analytical. Regardless of whether every narrative (whether historical or fictional) requires heroes and the tracing of emplotted change over time, many constructionists remain far more interested in mapping themes and structures that can quite legitimately lack any sense, as Eric Hobsbawm said, of 'directional or oriented change'.[76] Most constructionists do, of course, have a sense of change over time, as well as having preferred ideas about the direction in which their description and evaluation of events takes them and their reader (their history possesses a teleology). What this means is that they believe in empirically derived facts, and the need for a narrative description of their meaning, while not accepting that such a description has a cognitive power. As post-Marxist constructionist philosopher Alasdair MacIntyre has argued, it will not do to exempt stories from the criterion of truth: 'It matters enormously that our histories be true.'[77]

So, while some Marxists may accept narrative as the vehicle for carrying historical analysis they would not agree that it provides the *real* meaning of the past. Marxist Alex Callinicos accordingly rejects White's version of the role of narrative in historical analysis as anti-realist and ideologically loaded. Conceiving history as a fictive historical representation, where meaning ultimately derives from how it is written rather than according to the factual anchor of objectively discoverable and describable real events, suggests to Callinicos that White has a sceptical and relativist (that is a postmodern) North Atlantic bourgeois liberal agenda! White is thus not equipped to tell fact from fiction or, as Callinicos says, able to distance himself from 'nationalist historical mythologies', by which he means White's treatment particularly of events like the Holocaust. In Callinicos's view, as well as that of other non-Marxist critics, White's formalism and relativism make him incapable of distinguishing truth from interpretation, and fact from fiction.[78]

Most constructionists, however, still tend towards the view of narrative held by R.G. Collingwood in *The Idea of History*. It is simply not good enough, in his apt phrase, to 'scissors-and-paste' evidence to produce, through a process of compilation, historical accounts.[79] For Collingwood, this 'pre-scientific form of history' is inadequate because it does not permit the historian to challenge the authority of the sources. In effect it creates historians who only practise a passive kind of inductivism (similar to the crude reconstructionist position). The genuine historical method is a process of question and answer, challenge and interrogation through the application to the evidence of testable theory. In other words, historical facts emerge from what Carr would claim was an interpretative dialogue involving some form of social/political categories of analysis. The evidence becomes a source of questions not answers, and history is an interrogation of the past through the emplotment of an appropriate social theory. Facts are as much constructions as anything else in history. For constructionists, then, neither a conservative empiricism lacking in theory, nor a radical deconstructionism that denies social theory but relies on a flawed narrative, can prise open the reality of the past.

CONCLUSION

Moderates in both the constructionist and reconstructionist mainstreams accept that language-use – whether writing *the* or *a* story of the past – directly influences historical understanding. But this does not mean that history is just another kind of fictional literature. Accepting this would mean agreeing that history is epistemologically no different to poetry, drama or television scripts. Practical realists reject the claim of deconstructionists that because a gap exists between interpretation and the facts, narrative must fill it as the constitutor of historical meaning. If historians continue to accept that their enterprise is about the study of the contextualised evidence and the valid use of social theory that purports to explain the links between events, then to claim, as deconstructionists do, that history as a text is analogous to fiction, is both dishonest and bad logic. Thus the historian James A. Winn, following in the Collingwood–Carr tradition, maintains that deconstructionists and new historicists 'tend to flog extremely dead horses' when they accuse historians of operating on assumptions that include believing that history is knowable, that words mirror reality and that historians insist on seeing the facts of history objectively. Few mainstream historians today work from these principles in pursuit of 'the illusory Holy Grail of objective truth' but strive only to ground 'an inevitably subjective interpretation on the best collection of material facts we can gather'.[80]

What we might summarise then as the Collingwood–Carr-inspired moderate response to deconstructionism is a far more telling and reasoned response than that of Elton and Marwick, who continue to bluster about empiricism and its six principles. The deconstructive contention that primary sources cannot provide access to historical truth because of the essential unknowability of past reality is not at all convincing, given that all the available evidence demonstrates the opposite. As Appleby, Hunt and Jacob hold:

> Assuming a tolerance for a degree of indeterminacy, scholars in the practical realist camp are encouraged to get out of bed in the morning and head for the archives, because there they can uncover evidence, touch lives long passed, and 'see' patterns in events that otherwise might remain inexplicable.[81]

Historians today recognise that the act of describing an observation does not necessarily invalidate the truthfulness of that description. Equally, the historian is not a free agent, like a sculptor who can take the clay of evidence and shape it however he/she likes. All this adds up to a historical relativism that has always been there, and historians who have been living long before the deconstructionists moved into the neighbourhood and pointed it out as an unacceptable practice. It is now necessary, in the interests of community well-being, to examine the complaints of those deconstructionist newcomers about their neighbours in greater detail.

6 What is wrong with reconstructionist/constructionist history?

INTRODUCTION

In the last thirty years historical explanation in a positivist mode has been rejected in favour of that of narrative.[1] I have suggested how, apart from the diehards, most reconstructionist and constructionist historians have become aware of this development. Although most mainstreamers may still not yet accept that narrative is *the* peculiar form of historical explanation – imposed stories – all accept narrative as the *dominant* form of historical reporting, while maintaining that the six principles that form the bedrock of empiricist hermeneutics remain fundamental to the study of the past. Practical realists, while acknowledging the culturally provided nature of knowledge, still insist on the sanctity of the source (evidence) as offering an adequate correspondence to what actually happened in the past. While they accept that figuration exists in the representation of historical knowledge, they will not deny the ultimate legitimacy of empiricist epistemology. For historians of the deconstructive turn this is the flaw in their argument. History, rather than being a projection of the content of the past, is a projection of its form. In this chapter I will address the implications of this for the established empiricist paradigm through the four headings of history as a separate epistemology, historical evidence, the historian and social theory, and the significance of narrative to historical explanation.

EPISTEMOLOGY

Most historians today are at least aware of the doubts held by a number of colleagues about history as a discrete empiricist discipline. Joan W. Scott, for example, in invoking the thinking of Michel Foucault, has argued that by 'history' she means not what happened, not what 'truth' there is 'out there' to be discovered and transmitted, but what we know about the past, what the rules and conventions are that govern the production and acceptance of the knowledge we designate as history.

She continues, 'history is not purely referential but is rather constructed by historians'. With such issues as the linguistic turn and the exploration of gender in mind, she insists that history's 'standards of inclusion and exclusion, measures of importance, and rules of evaluation are not objective criteria but politically produced conventions'. She directly challenges the attempts by the 'guardians of orthodoxy' to maintain the 'unquestioned predominance for their point of view by insisting that only they represent "truth," or "science," or "objectivity," or "tradition," or "history-as-it-has-always-been-written"'.[2] In this fashion Scott throws down the gauntlet to the supporters of the traditional paradigm. Empiricism is less a convincing and timeless foundation for the discovery of historical knowledge through its dependence on the relationship of the word and the world, than an increasingly threadbare disguise for a rigid, exclusive and conservative ideological vision of what constitutes history as a modernist epistemology.

The majority of historians still accept the six points of the empiricist charter, while seeking to relegate history's cognitive literary dimension. But not all philosophers of history accept the six empiricist tenets while still not accepting the deconstructionist position. Leon Goldstein, for example, seriously doubts McCullagh's justifications for empiricism, especially what he sees as its three fundamental assumptions: first, the world exists independent of our beliefs about it; second, our perceptions can provide an accurate impression of that reality; and third, the historian's rules of inference and contextualisation are a reliable way of arriving at new truths about reality. For Goldstein the first assumption is frankly meaningless, the second has no relevance to history at all, and the third does not exist in so far as there are no explicit rules of historical inference that can produce proof positive. All the inferential method can do is provide indications of a possible or, what may be more accurate, plausible past based on the evidence.

Beyond Goldstein's critique of empiricism the main thrust of deconstructionist history remains centred on the consequences of writing history. Hayden White, supported by other philosophers interested in narrative like Kellner, Rüsen, Carr and Ankersmit, has declared that historical explanation does not emerge naturally from the documents. History possesses no objective research method, the results of which are then written up in a detached manner. In written history there is never certainty of meaning. The *meanings* of history are to be found not, as Kellner argues, in the traditional primary documents, but in the structures of figurative representation. As Kellner insists, all history is 'part of a story, an explicit or implicit narrative',[3] and it is up to the historian to emplot the events referenced in the documents.

This means construing history as an aesthetic and poetic act rather than an empirical one, and it means accepting that writing history generates a particular kind of *historical* truth rather than *the* truth. Most mainstreamers still assume that the written medium is essentially transparent, and that it is time-wasting to explore narrative as a cognitive device. Like scientists, they prefer to draw attention to the reaction rather than the retort. It fell to philosopher of history Perez Zagorin to summarise this iron law of empiricist historiography: 'In history language is very largely subservient to the historian's effort to convey in the fullest, clearest, and most sensitive way an understanding or knowledge of something in the past.'[4] It is in these terms that most historians maintain the fiction of history as non-fiction. Most prefer not to think too deeply about the form in which they report their findings and even less about the possible range of things they could say about (emplot) the evidence.

In responding to this it is worth reminding ourselves that the arch-empiricist Leopold Von Ranke's emphasis on research into the sources did not stop him recognising that research must result in an 'acceptable story'. As Ranke said:

> History is distinguished from all other sciences in that it is also an art. History is a science in collecting, finding, penetrating; it is an art because it recreates and portrays that which it has found and recognised. Other sciences are satisfied simply with recording what has been found; history requires the ability to recreate.[5]

Mainstream historians do not follow up this argument, that history may be conceived of as both art and science, and do not remain alert to the power of language to shape meaning and create understanding. In spite of the power of language it is usually overlooked because the established paradigm characterises what historians do and believe according to criteria other than the aesthetic. As we know, in the twentieth century this has produced the view that history is epistemologically concerned with finding out *the* truth and objectively confirming the validity of historical knowledge.

But this mainstream opinion has not gone wholly unchallenged. If not in the terms used by Von Ranke, empiricist-inspired objectivity has long been under intermittent attack from so-called relativists. In the 1930s Collingwood and the American historians Charles Beard and Carl Becker argued that historical objectivity was a myth. As Collingwood pointed out, history must have a purpose, and who else can discover that purpose but the historian? For Collingwood, the historian uses evidence to isolate the intent behind actions, hence his/her empathic approach. Gathering pace since the 1970s, the new wave of deconstructionism – inspired in part by the postmodern surge and what Ankersmit describes as its narrativist philosophy – rather than taking up these early Collingwoodian notions to challenge the reconstructionist consensus, has instead chosen to emphasise the structures of narrative employed by the historian, which unavoidably implicates him/her in what he/she creates. But the upshot for both Collingwood and postmodern historians is that we cannot divorce ourselves from what we observe. All historical interpretation is, therefore, provisional, relative and constructed. Deconstruction, as a historical method, is the de-layering of these constructed meanings and interpretations.

This peeling-back process seeks out that which is repressed in the text (primary or secondary) – not only what is hidden from the naïve reader but also what is hidden from the intentions of author(s). The deconstructive historian seeks out that which is present in the text that runs against the grain of what, at first blush, it appears to assert. This self-conscious reflexivity seeks out that which is avoided and suppressed as well as that which is openly de-legitimised and denied. We must constantly seek out that which, in the name of objectivity and rationality, the text is indifferent to – what many historians call 'the other'. The rationalist objectivity of Western culture in the twentieth century has visited death and destruction upon itself and other cultures on a hitherto unimagined scale in the repression of 'the other' – Jews, Serbs, Croats, women, the poor, lesbians, immigrants, aboriginals, gays and many other members of marginalised and persecuted groups. In challenging the six points of the empiricist charter, the deconstructive consciousness does not reject rationality or reason *per se*, but instead suggests that its exercise does not always result in rightness or will lead to truth. The deconstructive position does not reject historical reality but questions our access to it, our apprehension of it and, therefore, its meaning. Deconstructionist history argues that there is always more than a single truth. Finally, deconstructionist history does not declare that there is no hierarchy of value, but declares instead that all are capable of making different and legitimate value judgements about what is right and wrong.

Commentators like F.R. Ankersmit, Peter Novick and David A.

Hollinger have recently argued that the commonsense empiricist model for deriving historical knowledge, as founded on the belief in historical objectivity, has been substantially damaged.[6] This is not because of an intentional conspiracy to attack history as a discipline, but is the result of the general postmodernist recognition that the notion of scientific objectivity, as a measure of truth and a constitutor of knowledge, and which somehow exists outside social experience, is an assumption, and a doubtful one at that. Other philosophers of history, apart from Leon Goldstein, have cast doubt on the nature of empiricism as the basis for historical understanding. The British philosopher of history Mark Bevir recently reiterated the telling point that our accounts of our experiences rely as much upon our organising categories as on the experience itself. As Bevir said:

> This does not mean that our categories determine what experiences we have . . . but it does mean that our categories influence the way we experience the sensations we have. We make sense of the sensations objects force on us using our categories. Because our experiences embody theoretical assumptions, our experience cannot be pure, and this means that our experiences cannot provide unvarnished data for determining the truth or falsity of our theories.[7]

I read Bevir as saying that empiricism is faulty as a method of acquiring knowledge because our understanding of that knowledge is always influenced by our 'theoretical assumptions'. From their different traditions, both Collingwood (how can we interpret the textual evidence so as to locate the intent behind human action?) and Derrida (how can we interpret texts at all?) have contributed to the deconstructive consciousness which, as we have just noted, emphasises an awareness of the importance of the impositionalism of the historian as well as the orchestration of narrative in the creation of historical knowledge. At the millennium, under the impact of our postmodern condition, we are experiencing a re-definition of the philosophy of knowledge and historical study because we are now facing foursquare the issue of the mismatch between words and things. When historians say that they are confronting the past, they are actually confronting language. Language, like memory, can recollect, but it can never be reality.

On practical as well as formal epistemological grounds, the new cultural history accepts that change and continuity in the past may be explained as a function of the discourse of the historian as much as by the raw evidence or record of the realities of past everyday life. The explanations for cultural formation in the late nineteenth century in both America and Europe are not only derived from the written experience of political, religious or factory life, or of urban or rural living conditions (real events under a description narrativised), or the discourse of dominant and subordinate groups represented in the voices of race, community, class and gender. This record and these voices are interpreted by the historian through the structure of narrative he/she selects and through which understanding is achieved. Historical interpretation means the past translated through narrative.[8] The growing dialogue between history and literary criticism expands the natural horizon of the relationship between cultural change and our historical knowledge of it. It also seriously questions history as an epistemology distinct from its cultural practice and contamination by society's needs, demands and power structures.

Our discussions so far have been framed as basic epistemological questions about history as a form of knowledge. Do we really expect historians to reconstruct the past as it actually was? Perhaps it is better to view history as a kind of literature written in the name of seeking truth? Can we, ultimately, believe in the past only because of the substantial amount of agreement among historians about what happened through the creation of historical facts? How do deconstructionist historians derive so-called historical facts, and what degree of reliability can we place on them? Can history ever be objective?

EVIDENCE

In his book *Child Loving: The Erotic Child and Victorian Culture*, James R. Kincaid says that he is 'less interested in reconstructing the past than in examining what our methods of reconstruction might tell us about our own policies' in the present.[9] Annoying to hard-core reconstructionists, Kincaid's position is indicative of the deconstructive attitude towards sources and method. Rather than accepting sources as relics of past truth, and empiricism as the only authoritative methodology capable of accessing their truths, Kincaid extends the horizons of the study of the past by recognising its presentism. Such a mode of analysis permits the kind of sophisticated reading of sources undertaken by other historians like Carol Douglas Sparks. As a historian of the imperialisation of Native American women, Sparks' deconstructive consciousness reveals how her Anglo sources are racially skewed as images and signs of Indian women. As she says:

> Deconstruction of these signs, or symbols of cultural significance, not only reveals the gender-coded fabric of nineteenth-century American colonialism and its patriarchal environmental ethos, but

also peels back layers of Orientalist imagery to uncover the historically 'real' women beneath.

Sparks qualified this insight by rejecting the popular version of
Derrida's famous invocation that there are only texts not contexts,
maintaining that 'Textual analysis provides a useful tool in deconstructing such colonial imagery', while reminding us that 'this exegesis
must be firmly rooted in a broader historical context which incorporates
political, social, economic, and intellectual factors'. For Sparks, deconstruction allows her to burrow beneath the 'factual content' of Anglo
texts like letters, poems, memoirs, newspaper articles and even military
and scientific reports to expose their 'fictive origins': the reality created
by their colonial authors 'drawn from their immediate surroundings,
but filtered through their experiences and expectations. Often, Anglo-
American "fact" dramatically conflicted with the reality of Others.'[10] In
other words, figuration once deconstructed can reveal much about the
alternative and different layers of historical meaning to be invoked by
the historian.

The work of Kincaid and Sparks alerts us to the misleading character of the reconstructionist metaphor which likens our textual sources
to rock strata. The meaning of our sources cannot be chipped away at
until we reach their *real* meaning. As another deconstructively conscious historian, Roger Chartier, pointed out, texts do not conceal
their meaning 'like an ore its mineral'. Instead a text 'is the product of
a reading and is a construction on the part of its reader'. The reader,
whether the consumer of another historian's writing or as the historian
him/herself, reading a source does not occupy the position of the text's
author by knowing his/her intentionality, but is likely to be inventing
a meaning different to that intended.[11] Taking up McCullagh's definition of interpretation that we came across in Chapter 3, the
interpretation of a text involves an inevitable recombination of source,
context (the text existing intertextually with others), as well as the
author's intentionality. This can produce a multiplicity of legitimate
meanings and interpretations rather than necessarily lead to the true
meaning.[12]

The sanctity of the sources is defended by the British philosopher of
history Mark Bevir, who declares: 'good history depends solely on accurate and reasonable evidence, not on adopting a particular method'.[13]
We are always thrown back on the evidence. It may well be that Peter
Burke's deconstructionist suggestion has merit, that while serving the
available evidence it might be possible to make events in history more
intelligible by following the novelistic method of telling the (hi)story

from a multiplicity of viewpoints, rather than just that of the presumed omniscient historian – what he calls heteroglossia.[14] Spiegel's pessimistic conclusion, however, is that if texts can be expected to reflect not reality but only other texts, 'then historical study can scarcely be distinguished from literary study, and the "past" dissolves into literature'. Spiegel rejects what she takes to be deconstructionist extremism, preferring to retain a belief in a knowable past reality while still acknowledging history as a written discourse. Spiegel does this by deploying the compromise of 'mediation'.[15] If past reality cannot be reflected (but is assumed to exist) then maybe it can be mediated, whereby texts do not transparently reflect the past but capture it in 'the mediated form preserved for us in language'. In other words, Spiegel accepts that texts, defined as extended discourses or cultural practices, create meaning as between the real social world and our discursive knowledge of it. The language of the text is the murky medium through which we understand the past.

Spiegel eventually, but seemingly with a strong reluctance, accepts that language constructs the object rather than mediates or represents it. This is, of course, a reiteration of the common observation of the social construction of reality in, and through, language. As she describes it, rather than being extrinsic to both reality and interpretation, mediation in language is intrinsic to the existence and operation of the reality it creates, and all that this entails for the distribution and use of power in society. Consequently, when researching sources we are actually studying already mediated discourses, composed of complex codes of metaphoric meanings and understandings about how society works, intentions, and the role of history in it. We are not reading some pure reality of unclouded meaning – facts as linguistic fragments of truth or historical reality – even less are we reading a text written out of the cultural flow.

Historians might, as a consequence, do well to conceive of evidence – texts and their intertextuality – as being ultimately determined by forces that are a highly complex mix of the cultural, the metaphoric and the narrativist. To put it more simply, past cultural change may be mediated through the written discourse(s) of not only historians, but also past historical agents whose voices exist intertextually within their own linguistically mediated social, political and economic imagination and situation. For all we know, it may be that *the past as it actually happened* did so according to a discoverable narrative emplotment which itself mediates the principles on which knowledge and meaning are created and policed. The interesting question then arises of whether we can discover *the* dominant form of figuration and historical emplotment, which in turn will lead us to a fuller understanding of the arguments, rationalisations and ideological benchmarks held within our sources.

Historians, as Hayden White points out, have to use language as they undertake this task, thus employing the same poor conductor of meaning as their sources. What this double bind does is remind the deconstructionist historian that we must not confuse either written history or evidence with the past. Historical interpretation ought not then attempt to recover *the lost true meaning* in the sources – the historian like a down-at-heel inebriate sorting through the debris of a dustbin in search of the unbroken, and full, bottle. In accepting 'the use of deconstructive strategies in reading historical texts', Spiegel allows that they are 'powerful tools of analysis in uncovering and dismantling the ways in which texts perform elaborate ideological mystifications'. A fuller understanding of the past might then be achieved by establishing a historical context 'from *other* sources'. Saying this, in effect, reveals her undiminished reconstructionist urge to infer the existence of *the real* historical context *within* which she can deconstruct texts. Her rationale for this is the provision of a complex strategy of research that will interrogate text and context and thereby reach into the past for its meaning. In the end, the incipient reconstructionism in Spiegel's argument emerges as she confesses to accepting the past as 'a once material existence', although it is 'now silenced', while her embryonic deconstructive consciousness surfaces briefly with her claim that the past is now 'extant only as sign' and one that draws to itself 'chains of conflicting interpretations' among those historians hovering over its relics. Spiegel thus tries to compromise the incommensurable. The deconstructive consciousness always doubts the correspondence between the source and any presumed past, a position Spiegel always tries to avoid.

More convincing is the American historian David Harlan's plain challenge to the traditional understanding of what to do with evidence. Taking up a position derived from the German philosopher Hans-Georg Gadamer, Harlan maintains that historians can never strip the evidence of its accumulated meanings, nor by placing it in its context expect to rediscover its original author's meaning. Evidence can never be 'severed from the interpretation through which it has been passed down to us'.[16] It means realising that the historian is not able to place him/herself in an all-knowing, all-seeing situation, but rather contrives and frames, and is in turn controlled by, those discourses as power dispensations, which predominate in any historical epoch or personal context. Reconstructionism cannot reproduce the original meaning, even when the effort is made by historians like Gabrielle Spiegel to harness it to a deconstructive awareness. Deconstructionist history is not reconstructionism looking over its shoulder. As Harlan points out:

> if recent developments in literary criticism and the philosophy of language have indeed undermined belief in a stable and determinable past, denied the possibility of recovering authorial intention, and challenged the plausibility of historical representation, then contextualist-minded historians should stop insisting that every historian's 'first order of business' must be to do what now seems undoable. Historians should simply drop the question of what counts as legitimate history and accept the fact that, like every other discipline in the humanities, they do not have, and are not likely to have, a formalised, widely accepted set of research procedures, and that nothing helpful or interesting is likely to come from attempts to define one. If we ask, 'what is historical writing?' the answer can only be, 'there is this kind of historical writing, and that kind, and then again that kind.'[17]

Although talking about intellectual history, his words encompass all history, which

> is concerned not with dead authors, but with living books, not with a return of earlier writers to their historical contexts but with a reading of historical works in new and unexpected contexts, not with reconstructing the past but with providing the critical medium in which valuable works from the past might *survive* their past – might survive their past in order to tell us about our present. For only through such telling can we ever hope to see ourselves and our history anew.[18]

Harlan thus offers what is the clearest of statements in defence of the deconstructive approach to history. History is open to many ways of studying the past other than the belief that we can accurately reflect it. The study of history usually tells us as much about the historian's constructed narrative in the here and now as it does about past reality.

THEORIES OF HISTORY: CONSTRUCTING THE PAST

What does this deconstructive threat to the authenticity or purity of the evidence mean for the constructionist historian? It means a vigorous rebuttal. For hard-headed Marxist constructionist Alex Callinicos it necessitates reiterating the well-worn argument that the historian saturated in the sources is well equipped to formulate hypotheses that can be verified through future siftings of the evidence. I have already noted his suggestion that all history is theoretical. As he says, most mainstreamers 'draw (albeit in most cases tacitly) on theories about the nature and transformation of human society'. He quotes Marxism, the *Annales* school and the New Economic History of the 1970s as examples of the 'self-conscious pursuit of a research programme in history'. What this means is that the historian deliberately, and promiscuously at times, deploys various kinds of social theory to 'clarify issues that have arisen in her research, or even to define its objective'.[19] This does not, he insists, mean that history is reduced to hypothesis-testing by reference to some general or covering law.

Callinicos, in his argument against deconstructionism, claims three things: first, that it fails to acknowledge the materiality of history; second, that deconstructionism is flawed because it does not accept that genuine historical understanding relies on conceptualisation to explain causality, and that neither tropes nor emplotment on their own can adequately explain anything; and finally, that deconstructionism fails to give due respect to the critical examination of the primary sources (*Quellenkritik*). The upshot is what Callinicos calls a 'displacement' from the true nature of historical inquiry (that accepts a past reality to which documents give access) to 'the process of historical representation itself', which is the extent to which our historical descriptions can ever correspond to what actually happened in the past.

Deconstructionists in reply turn to other (non-Marxist) attempts to explore the nature of constructionism, notably those of the philosopher Paul Ricoeur and historians Philippe Carrard and Robert Berkhofer. Ricoeur points out that constructionists still have to depend on narrative to explain the past, and that their analysis must eventually be configured as an emplotment.[20] Carrard also notes how what he calls New History (which I have designated here as constructionism) has signally failed to eliminate narrative as the model with which to organise its reports. As he says, 'it is the plot that . . . provides a forceful answer to one of the central questions these [constructionist] texts are asking: How did we get where we are now?'[21] The *Annalistes*, for example, have been quite unable to avoid the structuring effects of narrative in their writing of the past. While they have conceptualised and re-conceptualised the past over several generations, they have been wholly unable to dismiss the power of language to effect meaning. Berkhofer accepts that while so-called non-narrative histories transmit the cognitive effects of realism, by their aping of science they still cannot escape the conventional devices of literature.[22] Eventually even Callinicos admits that facts 'are themselves discursive constructs'.[23]

While defenders of constructionism attack deconstructionist historians, it is not the advocates of the deconstructive turn who have created the doubts about the correspondence between the referent and its discursive signifier. Such ambiguity would exist without the deconstructive consciousness pointing it out. Equally, narrative remains as the basic vehicle for historical understanding and explanation, and its tropes and emplotments will still be employed in writing history even though, as White says, it cannot give access to *the* truth. While it is possible to argue the constructionist position, that historical facts are arrived at by questioning the evidence using an *a priori* theoretical construct, this does not, as some Marxist constructionists claim, reduce history-writing to the level of *mere* narrative as if it were a secondary issue of historical presentation. Deconstructionist history does not, however, criticise constructionism on the Elton ground that it pre-judges the past, or is reductionist, or for that matter determinist, but rather argues that its results still have to be written down and understood as narratives.

As we know, although Lawrence Stone misconceived the meaning of narrative in his 1979 article 'The Revival of Narrative', he did point to the key non-Marxist trends in constructionist methodology then comprising anthropological, ethnographical and structural history. When moved to repeat the exercise in the early 1990s, he appeared to have a problem not with the re-emergence (and explanatory failings) of descriptive story-telling, but with the growing authority of the deconstructive or linguistic turn itself. As he said, he parted company with those historians 'bedazzled by the lures of "discourse" [when they extended their arguments] about the autonomy of "discourse" to the point of making it a historical factor in its own right', thus allowing it to get in the way of explaining historical change according to the 'more complex interactions of material conditions, culture, ideology and power'.[24] This is actually a rather good defence of the mainstream constructionist position. Stone went on to say:

> As for the use of symbolic and social anthropology, influenced largely by my friend Clifford Geertz, I can only repeat what I have said before. It has already had, and is continuing to have, a stunning effect upon historical scholarship.

Stone then catalogued the constructionist historians he had in mind like Robert Darnton, Natalie Zemon Davis, Carlo Ginzburg, Emmanuel Le Roy Ladurie, etc. Next he quoted Simon Schama's book *Dead Certainties* as an illustration of the blurring of 'archival fact and pure fiction'.[25] In effect, Stone overstated the case while failing to appreciate the complexity of the deconstructive consciousness which now increasingly inflects the work of the very historians he notes, particularly

Davis. At the time of writing, it would be of interest to know Stone's opinion of Schama's fascinating 1995 text *Landscape and Memory* which explores the relationship between landscape and history. What Schama calls the 'cultural psychology of nature' may not be much to Stone's liking as a form of history that is intensely personal and impositionalist in character.[26]

Since the 1970s, cultural historians using psychological, cultural and anthropological models of cultural analysis have blurred and blended imperceptibly into the structuralist, post-structuralist and linguistic-inspired analysis of the poetics of culture using the textual metaphor. Influenced by Michel Foucault, what had hitherto been regarded as hard, objective social facts like race, gender and class (derived by *Quellenkritik* means) are now generally seen as culturally provided or socially constituted. The constructionist notion of social theory providing facts that reproduce the reality of historical life is now revised to offer access to the *possible* rather than the *real* nature of society. This can be achieved at least equally as well by viewing society as a text in which events are presented as a complex series of discursive representations, metaphors, symbols, icons, signs and rituals – all to be emplotted by the historian as cultural critic. It is not very much of an insight to say that emplotment is part of a mix of pre-figuration, social theory, ideological positioning and empirical investigation. Facts as well as emplotment remain propositional for constructionist historians.

In his 1985 collection of articles *Islands of History* the cultural historian Marshal Sahlins attempted to embed the idea of history as a text into historical explanation by deploying a structuralist-inspired methodology which he called structural historical anthropology.[27] The significance of Sahlins' book lies in its attempt to wed constructionism to a recognition of the relativism of history. Sahlins argued that history is culturally determined and that language plays a highly significant role in that determination as well as its later interpretation. This text is a leading example of those that lead us to the conclusion that the linguistic turn and the influence of post-structuralism have clearly manifested themselves in the shape of the new cultural history.

The new cultural history, while being methodologically in debt to structural anthropology, has also been liberated by Barthes, Derrida and Foucault, among others. For Foucault and Derrida the methods of the social sciences are quite inadequate, based as they are on an outdated positivism, which they denounce as 'logocentrism', or on the idea that there is a fixed meaning (or explanation/cause) existing independently of language. No matter how complex and sophisticated are constructionist models of past social reality, the nature of the representation of their conclusions is now contested, but not only by the deconstructionive consciousness. The constructionist philosopher Peter Burke has proposed that historians examine the product of a marriage of narrative and constructionism by

> making a narrative thick enough to deal not only with the sequence of events and the conscious intentions of the actors in these events, but also with the structures – institutions, modes of thought, and so on – whether these structures act as brake on events or as an accelerator.

He asks tantalisingly, 'What would such a narrative be like?'[28]

HISTORY AS NARRATIVE

Burke believes that narrative can be a reliable vehicle for historical analysis if it can convey an understanding of wholesale changes in social structures and institutions as well as single events. Burke insists that narrative can be a medium for social theory by pointing to novelists like Leo Tolstoy and Shimizaki Toson. As he says, 'it is likely that historians can learn something from the narrative techniques of such novelists . . . but not enough to solve all their literary problems'.[29] Historians cannot, as Burke points out, invent people, places or events and so must turn to 'real' people, places and events, but he concludes that historians will have to 'develop their own "fictional techniques" for their "factual works"'.[30] Highlighting what he calls the micronarrative producing microhistory, which is the telling of the story of the lives of ordinary people, he cites Natalie Zemon Davis's *The Return of Martin Guerre* as illustrative.[31] In this instance Davis recounts the history of an impostor who arrives in a sixteenth-century French village to claim the missing Martin Guerre's life, wife and property. Davis deliberately employs the micronarrative and fictional techniques to illustrate broader structural issues and the sweep of French peasant life. As she says, the intention was to mix old and new cultural history. Such stories, like Geertz's thick narratives, can thus illuminate big social structural change and continuity. The process of illumination is dependent, however, on the power of the historian to use her subject-matter, argument and, above all, her consciousness of the deconstructive power of figurative language. As Burke points out, historians in the 1990s have become ever more inventive in the way in which they employ the powers of narrative to invest the past with life.

The vision of history as primarily an empirical and analytically founded problem-solving epistemology is thus an ever diminishing one. The American philosopher of history Allan Megill points out in support of Carrard that, even in the positivist world of the sciences, explanation commonly depends on the use of metaphor and description, or 'recounting' as he prefers to call it. He defines recounting as the provision of historical answers on the model of 'telling a tale . . . a tale for the truth of which' is attested to by evidence and argument. For Megill, both recounting and explanation are to be found in the historian's narrative mode of exposition. Megill and Carrard are making the same point as Lemon, Gallie, Mink, White, Ankersmit, and all the other narrativists, that while narrative is by its nature explanatory, this does not mean that it is any more independent of the author or more truthful than other kinds of explanation. We may make the point more tellingly by appropriating Simon Schama's reference to the Yosemite National Monument in the USA. As he says, we like to imagine the park as empty of people even though the very act of painting or photographing it 'presupposes our presence, and along with us all the heavy cultural backpacks that we lug with us on the trail'.[32] By extension it is the same with history. We may wish to imagine history as empty of historians, a temporal wilderness, but every interpretation represents a historian backpacking through the past – the observer inside what he/she observes. Maybe we have reached the point where we are no longer explorers but settlers?

While the idea of narrative as a report is generally accepted then, as a mode of explanation I have suggested that it is far from universally accepted. The American historian and methodologist James A. Henretta maintains that many social historians remain 'sceptical of the interpretive range and power of the narrative mode of presentation' because of its 'often impressionistic' use of evidence, and its not being 'amenable to quantitative or conceptual types of analysis'. Nevertheless, even Henretta judges narratives to 'embody a phenomenological perspective, and for that reason have been widely adopted by historians working in the pragmatic tradition'. He continues that 'By placing as much (or more) emphasis upon the subjective perceptions of the actors as upon the objective circumstances of existence, narratives underscore the importance of human agency.' He concludes that 'historians who adopt a chronological framework establish a basic congruence between the lives of their subjects and those of their audience'. Henretta believes that narrative is, therefore, important for the presentation of the findings of research, 'not primarily because of the absence of "jargon" but because its mode of cognition approximates the reality of everyday life'.[33]

In a footnote to his piece Henretta adds a significant gloss to this process:

> Although some degree of artifice enters into the construction of a narrative – in that the author already knows the outcome of the story and therefore provides a false sense of open-endedness – artifice alone does not constitute a major objection.[34]

From the deconstructive perspective, of course, this is an issue rather more important than Henretta suggests. The impositionalism of the historian may indeed make itself manifest as a matter of artifice in constructing the narrative, but impositionalism operates at a much deeper level *because* of the narrative structure of history. As Ankersmit reminds us, the metaphorical (or tropological) nature of historical understanding emerges from the historian's 'constitution of a linguistic object', what he calls the narrative substance and White designates as the secondary referent. Historical interpretation is immanently metaphoric because the historical narrative, while it is usually intended to be *like* the past, is, of course, nothing more than the historian's surrogate *for* the past. I am arguing that all historical narratives are representations of cultural memories rather than mimes. Historical interpretation is nothing more than a re-presentation of those memories: an artifice, true, but one with a rather more substantive result than Henretta would have us believe.[35] This is a key deconstructive insight not to be dismissed in a footnote.

To extend this deconstructive argument we might note F.R. Ankersmit's judgement that 'History is no longer the reconstruction of what has happened to us in the various phases of our lives, but a continuous playing with the memory of this.' The point, as he says, is that our 'memory has priority over what is remembered'.[36] That memory is our written history. The inspiration behind mainstream history is an ultimately unfulfilled craving. It is, as Ankersmit describes it, 'the desire to discover a past reality and reconstruct it scientifically', but these days it is 'no longer the historian's unquestioned task'. Ankersmit concludes that it is time for us to 'think about the past, rather than investigate it'. This wish can be filled in substantial part by acknowledging the tropic and figurative frontiers in history writing rather than by gorging on empirical science alone.

In the production of historical knowledge, neither naïve reconstructionist empiricism nor constructionist deductive or statistical probability methodology can efface the impositionalism of the historian and the constant issue of textualisation in the evidence of the past, or in our rewriting of it as narrative history. It is impossible to avoid intervening in the past because of our translation of its traces into usable historical facts, akin to mixing colours and producing shapes on a canvas. This impositionalism emerges not only as we compare, verify and contextualise events, but also in subsequent narrative descriptions that possess the reality- or truth-effects produced through emplotting. If this vision is acknowledged, the disputes over the status and character of historical study could, with goodwill on all sides, disappear. When the defenders of the empirical paradigm accept history as a form of literature – a narrative possessing ineluctably rhetorical, poetic and metaphorical elements – they may come to recognise that this does not automatically diminish history's explanatory authority, or reduce their professional status. The fact that figurative language may have nothing to do with past reality (because it is an allegorical or analogical description of it) puts us in no worse a situation than does inference from contextualised evidence. Historians can still study a narrativised past and seek to explain it. Many practical realists do now accept the poetic aspect of history – but as only one among many of the determining features influencing writing about the past. But, to place its poetic nature at the heart of the enterprise would, I suggest, strengthen history as a discipline, rather than reduce it to some weaker project closer to literature. Although most historians would still not accept the past as a lived experience as being an *essentially* literary undertaking, whereby its content is understood *primarily* through its narrative form by people at the time, as well as by historians later, the deconstructionist vision would elevate form beyond the level of mere style.

As it was for Collingwood, and many historians of the deconstructive turn today would still agree, the primary business of history is to study the thinking 'that goes on in the historian's mind', and we may well find ourselves accepting that what goes through the historian's mind constitutes the logic of the historical method.[37] Essential to this process is the historian's self-reflexivity in understanding not only the surface reality-effects produced through style and figuration, but also the deeper, and possibly determining, tropological structures identified by Hayden White and Michel Foucault. What seems increasingly clear to more and more historians today, as it did to Collingwood over half a century ago, is that, on basic epistemological and linguistic grounds, the ideal of the heroic model of science – the goal of objective history – is impossible to achieve, and at best we can produce only an objectivity effect.[38]

Hayden White's suggestion that historical method resides in the selection of *a* story of a particular kind rather than discovering *the* story that faithfully reflects what actually happened paradoxically reinforces the strength of the argument of Paul Ricoeur and David Carr that we live in a narrativised culture. Although White remains unconvinced by the argument of David Carr, that it is possible to objectively discover *the* true story located in the sources, it seems unexceptionable to argue that our everyday lived experience *and* history are both saturated by narrative. This is not to repeat the modernist mistake of a foundationalism to which we can turn for objective certainty, in this case by replacing empiricism with narrative. Simply acknowledging the role of narrative in explaining our past and presenting it to others is not a new kind of essentialism but an opening up of the past to new ways of describing it. Moreover, in the view of Lemon it is still possible to maintain objectivity rather than just project an objectivity effect.

Lemon insists, opposing White, that it remains possible to explain what happened in the past objectively despite the inevitable process of selection and emplotting of events, when the narrator-historian provides enough information to make the *whole* process intelligible. Not unexpectedly leaping between events, so that they appear strangely or spuriously unconnected, constitutes for Lemon an objective account of what happened. Such a connected narrative allows us to analyse and explain beyond simple cause and effect because its structure permits alternative interpretations. Saying that after President John F. Kennedy was provided with evidence of offensive Russian missiles in Cuba he *then* established a naval blockade is rather less causally deterministic than saying that *because* of the evidence of offensive missiles he set up the blockade. This allows for the possibility of alternative policies being open to Kennedy. Lemon's argument is that narrative explanation more faithfully mediates the possibility of human choice or agency which he assumes is more realistic than the historian conjecturing a form of, in this case, a strategic Cold War determinism. We may ask where does postmodern history fit into this? After all, such a definition of narrative is not too far removed from that of the traditional paradigm – narrative can reveal empirical truths.

Deconstructively aware historians are at liberty to conclude several things about what we write and read as history. We could, as Lemon has argued, regard it as the truthful/accurate representation of human agency/choice in history. We could, like Hayden White, view historical narrative as just a defence for a bourgeois-inspired ideological preference for human agency. We could view the historical text as sharing with the novel the important characteristic of authorial intrusion (of the imaginative historian), or as possessing no original author at all by assuming that how the narrative is framed depends upon the successive historians through whose hands (and minds) the text has passed. We may choose not to trust the language of our sources to correspond to past reality, and decide that we cannot reinsert our evidence into a discoverable real past. We may seriously question the distinction between fact and fiction in as much as both are the product of interpretative strategies and the emplotment of events. Although the fundamental structure of factual and fictional narrative always remains the same – as Lemon points out 'this happened, *then* that' – this will not tell us much about how the historian readily deals with the content. Lemon repeats the question asked over a number of years by Hayden White: Can the narrative *form* in itself determine its *content*? Put differently, can the form of the historical narrative, however constituted by the historian, ever conform to the real narrative of the past as it was actually experienced? Can we retell *the* story?

To suggest, as Hayden White does, that the past cannot ever be truthfully accessed, because 'the meaning of the story' is directly influenced 'by the mode of emplotment chosen to make of the story told a *story of a particular kind*', offends the strong empiricist sense of the historian's impartial observer status in not pre-figuring the outcome of the story (or *analysis* as the empiricist would have it). For the inured empiricist the imposition of a narrative structure through the choice of a particular kind of plot structure – tragedy, romance, farce or whatever – brutalises the essential nature of the historical enterprise. Most mainstream reconstructionists, as we are by now only too well aware, are concerned with the correspondence between the event and their report, the source and an accurate corresponding statement about it. White's further heresy, that the choice of emplotment implies an *unavoidable* ideological or philosophical commitment on the part of the historian, is the ultimate slur on the integrity of empiricists everywhere, given that historical narratives should never be seen primarily as ideological forms. It is scandalous to those who believe in the reconstruction of the past as it actually was that writing history might be collapsed into ideology. For deconstructionist historians, on the other hand, the task is to explore the lived narratives of the past, their tropic structures and explanatory strategies which also include the nature of the social theory/laws involved and the ideological implications that are likely to follow/precede.

CONCLUSION

The deconstructive consciousness, in accepting the non-referential nature of language, unavoidably raises doubts about the traditional reconstructionist/constructionist paradigms in several important ways.

When language is viewed as constitutive of *a* meaning, rather than somehow naturalistically reflecting *real* meaning, it follows that the historical narrative cannot generate fixed, absolute or *truthful* understanding. In addition, although we recognise the impositionalism of the historian constantly and necessarily intervening in the past, we may reasonably ask if it is possible to recover authorial intent in either an original source or an interpretation. If the historical context cannot promote *the* real meaning of *the* past, then we are forced to seek *a* meaning in the intertextual realm of the recoded and resignified evidence *and* the historical interpretation it generates. Both the source and its commentary remain ineluctably interpretative, and the traditional, empiricist-founded, reconstructionist/contextualist paradigm that insists on history as craft serves merely to disguise its poetic nature. Instead, the deconstructive consciousness accepts history as what it might have been rather than what it actually was. When, as a historian, I turn to the traces of the past, I cannot reclaim their real meaning – all I have is the tale I choose to bring forth from the sources which are impregnated with the previous readings that I, and other historians, have of them.

History is first and foremost a literary enterprise. Its cognitive function derives from the complex interpretative structure of narrative defined as a set of proposals or suggestions about past events. Narrative explanation is quite unlike the constructionist version of historical change based on the belief in a functioning deterministic or causal law(s). Constituting a narrative explanation requires the ordering, selection and omission of events and occurrences, and by our study of how the historian does this it ought to be possible to reveal something of his/her rationale or motive for producing this or that choice of narrative. Deconstruction starts by revealing how traditional historians conflate representation and referentiality. None of this precludes the deconstructively aware historian from believing that a past once existed. What it does mean is that he/she will write about a past within a self-conscious framework. It means accepting an impositionalism generated through the historian's dialogue with sources that do not necessarily correspond to the past and acknowledging that they are not projections of what actually happened because they are non-referential.

Narrative – the writing of the past – has at least one major dimension remaining to be explored. It is to Michel Foucault and Hayden White that I shall turn in the next two chapters to direct our attention both to the rhetorical structure of history as the written form of the past and to one important implication that the past itself may be understood as conforming to the structure of narrative. If indeed the past is a narrative, from where does it derive, how does it work, and does the very idea further challenge history as an objective practice? Do we find the past itself generated as a narrative by people in the course of their lives, or is it entirely imposed by the historian as he/she fabricates and orders his/her sources into a chosen form? These questions will be addressed in the next two chapters.

7 Michel Foucault and history

INTRODUCTION

In this chapter I shall examine from the deconstructive perspective Foucault's contribution to the study of the past, which has been to question the very nature of history as a distinctive epistemology by replacing its empiricist-inspired inductive/deductive method with narrative interpretation as the primary form of knowing and telling. Foucault's anti-logocentric stance maintains that there is no unmediated access for the human mind to a genuinely knowable original and truthful reality.[1] Our only door to experience (past, present or future) is through the primary medium of language as a signifying process normally constituted within a framework for the exercise of power, legitimacy and illegitimacy. Derived from Nietzsche, this is a fundamental shift from empiricism, because it entertains the impossibility of knowing anything objectively, given that objectivity itself is a historical and cultural construct.

Foucault is thus regarded by the majority of conservative as well as mainstream historians as anti-historical. This is not merely because of his refusal to privilege the modernist conception of scientific truth and traditional categories of evidentially derived analysis, although his rejection of the teleological and progressive assumptions of positivism carves him out for particular suspicion;[2] it is also because of his denial of linear historical causality between events and epochs (or epistemes as he calls them), favouring instead a history based upon the discontinuities between dominant figurative structures operating in human consciousness. Such thinking is profoundly unappealing to the Anglo-American tradition. Foucault is further viewed with suspicion because of his doubts about the historian's capacity to represent any version of the past accurately. The Nietzschean and post-structuralist lineage of Foucault is revealed in his interest in what he sees as history's dubious quest for the origin of truth which is a part of the great myth of Western culture. Equally annoying for empiricists is his insistence – flowing from his historical methodology – that there cannot be any distinction between what philosophers of history think and practitioners do. It is only when all history is self-reflexively engaged with its own philosophy, and specifically the question of where our knowledge comes from and how it is used (the framework of power), that we can confront the questions he raises. Ultimately, as he says, the past construed as history is an endless process of interpretation by the historian as an act of imagination, and our categories of analysis, assumptions, models and figurative style all themselves become a part of the history we are trying to unravel.

EPISTEMOLOGY

In his 1966 text, *The Order of Things: An Archaeology of the Human Sciences*, Foucault states what he believes to be the central epistemological issue for history.[3] He addresses how Western culture has organised knowledge, and historical knowledge in particular. In assessing the impact of discourse and social/cultural practice on the way in which people in the past and historians order experience and memory, he asks the inevitable structuralist question: What is the impact of language on history and experience when language is an arbitrary system of socially constructed signifier/signified/sign relationships between the word and world?

In practical terms this means that when Western thought first acknowledged that such master concepts as 'man', 'society' and 'culture' refer not to things (referents) but to linguistic constructs, then the human sciences all founded on reason, rationality, knowing, certainty and inductive inference also became, in effect, the prisoners of the historical figurative modes of discourse in which they were composed.[4] Foucault's archaeological dig into the human sciences (especially the disciplines of medicine and history) lays open the figurative and narrative strategies that authorise their conceptualisations, to reveal what Hayden White calls the deep structure of their linguistic protocols – the tropes. It is the historical succession of the tropes that constrain discursive practice, and condition the character of each age (episteme) in terms of the creation and policing of knowledge. This indicates the endless character of the interpretative process resulting from the situation whereby we can never scratch back far enough to find the original truth. This, for Foucault, is the essence of what we might now call the postmodern condition.

Specifically, in his studies of madness and medicine, Foucault examined the 'archive' or evidence of the ensemble of discourses (verbal or written narrative statements) that constitute knowledge in any given historical epoch (episteme). Foucault claims that historians should examine the linguistic basis (i.e. narrative statements) that *constitute* history, rather than correspond to, or unproblematically represent, the real world of things – that is, to abandon the search for original meaning. What could become an arid linguistic or narrative determinism is, however, modified by his acceptance of the culturally determined discursive practices that provide the form in which our linguistically based knowledge is produced. This shape or form is generated by the connection between what historical actors say and do within the confines of what society allows or rationalises to be true/false, right/wrong, legitimate/illegitimate. This is the idea of the social construction of reality, and also what Foucault describes as the power/knowledge equation. So far as he is concerned, knowledge, comprised as disciplines, become controlling entities in our lives as they suppress and allow, exclude and include that which is not and that which is permissible. So, there cannot be one history but there must be any number of histories of exclusion (the marginalised or 'other'), inclusion (the accepted as normal) and transgression (normal becoming abnormal).

The archive is taken by Foucault to be the body of narrativised evidence representing and signifying the episteme in which it was generated, but which is, of course, encountered by historians within our own historical epoch or episteme. Such source material cannot be interpreted empirically in and for itself as an unproblematic point of origin. Historical evidence is to be understood not only for that to which it refers (events as interpreted by historians), but as a vehicle by which we can grasp the deeper and more fundamental organisation of the linguistic mechanisms underpinning the creation and constitution of historical knowledge. History must recast itself as a literary and ideologically self-conscious process of thought. The epistemological significance of Foucault's vision of history as a gateway to the human consciousness, as Gilles Deleuze claims, is not found in or through the work of the traditional historian because Foucault's interest lies in seeking out the underlying structures, principles and 'conditions governing everything that has mental existence', in this case 'statements and the system of language'.[5] Because the human consciousness works by manipulating signs and metaphor, it follows that our understanding of the past works this way as well. This will never produce essential truths, only reveal the constant interplay of linguistic or narrative interpretation.

Foucault, like White, accepts the Nietzschean position (precursor to post-structuralism and deconstructionist history) that language as the figurative power of the human consciousness is constitutive of both history's empirical content, as well as the concepts/categories used by historians to order and explain its data.[6] Following on from this complex position of linguistic relativism (on the one hand) and determinism (on the other), Foucault confronts each of the six points of the reconstructionist charter. Today, many historians who acknowledge the significance of the conventions of language-use and the notion of history as a discourse – writing the past becomes the cultural practice of history – accept (wittingly or unwittingly) Foucault's argument that historical interpretation is beyond the touching simplicities of the mainstream paradigms. Foucault confronts the empiricist charter by arguing that history is never objective because it cannot be independent of the historian and his/her own time or cultural context, and it is the power of language to create meaning rather than to discover the true direction that history has taken that is important. As a result, to be honest to him/herself and his/her reader, the historian must avoid any claims to an empiricist-guaranteed disinterested objectivity located beyond the cultural frontier in which he/she lives.

The reasoning behind this position is Foucault's sustained attack on the reconstructionist belief in the adequate representation of reality through the narrative form. Not only is objectivity a myth, but more significantly we should recognise the sheer impossibility of the modernist theory of referentiality between word(s) and thing(s), statement(s) and evidence(s). In all this his main concern is to de-mythify history's claim to represent the reality of the past, and through it, its further assertion that explanation can in some way be complete, or reasonable, or realistic. As Michael Roth points out, this becomes clear when those possessing power make an appeal to history to rationalise their hold on power.[7] The legitimating authority of history is also used by those trying to gain power. Both the dominant and subordinate view history in the same modernist fashion – claiming it as a rational statement of truth – so as to deploy it for their own ideological ends.

Like Nietzsche, Foucault has come to accept that all modernist history's claims are ultimately spurious. In his important essay 'Nietzsche, Genealogy, History' published in 1971, he is particularly scornful of the efforts of naïve empiricists to locate *the* historical truth which they believe to be 'timeless and essential'. He argues instead that because history is fabricated and we are implicated in it, we are wrong to conclude that somehow we can stand outside history, or, what is worse, that it is the essential requirement of our discipline.[8] As he says, historians take 'unusual pains to erase the elements in their work which reveal their grounding in a particular time and place'. He concurs with Nietzsche that history should be 'explicit in its perspective' and should acknowledge that its 'perception is slanted, being a deliberate appraisal, affirmation, or negation'. This impositionalism of the historian is not merely noted by Foucault, but celebrated. To be effective, the act of writing history must be interventionist and reconceived so that it may openly reach the 'lingering and poisonous traces' of the past 'in order to prescribe the best antidote'. It follows that this new history should not be given over 'to discrete effacement before the objects it observes' and should not 'submit itself to their processes [nor] does it seek laws, since it gives equal weight to its own sight and to its objects'.[9] This vision of postmodern history not only rejects the fable of the correspondence theory, which maintains that the 'truth' is 'out there', but also dismisses the reconstructionist belief in a transparent narrative that permits *the* historical truth to emerge as if it existed beyond its description. Hence Foucault dismisses the crude myths that flow from this general position: brute factualism, disinterested historians, objectivity, progress, stability, continuity, certainty, roots, and the demarcation between history, ideology, fiction and perspective. He rejects, in his own words, empiricism's will to truth.

In these terms Foucault attempts the de-thronement of both major traditions of relating theory, interpretation and evidence around the axis of *the* reality of *the* past. In typically robust language he puts 'proper' historians in their place by claiming that as 'the demagogue is obliged to invoke truth, laws of essences, and eternal necessity, the historian must invoke objectivity, the accuracy of facts, and the permanence of the past'.[10] So far as Foucault is concerned there is no undisputed content in the past, hence the need for greater self-consciousness among historians about the nature of our debates. In *The Order of Things* and *The Archaeology of Knowledge*[11] his contribution to history is to provide histories based upon three basic and successive conceptions of what he is trying to do. Initially he uses the designation 'archaeology', then later he employs the term 'genealogy', and finally 'problematization'. The basic trademark of his historical method – which he calls his genealogy – describes how each unconnected and discontinuous historical epoch unilaterally imposes an intellectual order on the generation and utilisation of knowledge.

History is no longer defined then by the established categories of analysis – economic structures, competing nationalisms, political and cultural revolutions, the march and opposition of ideas, great men and women, periods of excess and ages of equipoise, republics and monarchies, empires and dynasties, famines and plagues – but instead by how societies interpret, imagine, create, control, regulate and dispose of knowledge, especially through the claims of disciplines to truth, authority and certainty. Events do not dictate history: history dictates events. This radical conception translates into Foucault's practical conception of an epistemic imposition on the past. This imposition provides the intellectual culture in which society, ideology, technology and all human behaviour exists. The particular field that Foucault selected in which to mount this challenge to traditional history is his study of how the treatment of the insane (a medical discourse) is related to its social context (as it becomes a social practice), which he examined in his early 1960s texts *The Birth of the Clinic: An Archaeology of Medical Perception* and *Madness and Civilization: A History of Insanity in the Age of Reason*.[12] So, how does Foucault's conception of history work in practice? How does he challenge the established and still dominant epistemological paradigm?

Foucault argues that people unconsciously organise and create knowledge as discourses and practices within each of the four distinctive historical ages or epistemes that existed between the sixteenth and twentieth centuries. Each episteme was constituted out of the abstractions of thought (concepts) that characterised the various disciplines, fields or branches of knowledge (by disciplines he meant the law, economics, biology, history, etc.) in Western thought. It is the function of his genealogy to unearth these epistemes and to locate the epistemological principles or concepts upon which the various fields or branches of knowledge that compose them were and are built. Foucault notes three fundamental branches of knowledge – life (biological discourse), wealth creation (socio-economic discourse) and language (cultural discourse). The concepts that these branches of knowledge employ provide the questions with which they interrogate their data and thus create knowledge.

Foucault argues that each of the disciplines is undergirded by shared trans-disciplinary mental attitudes towards the conditions of thought through which we organise all our knowledge. These orientations are commonly referred to as our mental or intellectual senses of difference, resemblance and representation. It is this that leads him to the formulation of each episteme as an assemblage of concepts that fix and define knowledge within its own epoch. These trans-disciplinary attitudes or conditions of thought are, of course, displayed in the pre-figurative tropes and narrative strategies we employ as historians, and which characterise each epoch's dominant form of narrative representation. Each age thus possesses its characteristic and dominant tropic signature. All thought is contingent, therefore, on its origin in the tropic deep structure of the mind. In this particular, Foucault is no different to any other traditional historian trying to find the basis or origin to history. The key difference is his insistence that epistemologically such a task of finding objective historical truth is going to be futile because of the collapse of the distinction between knower and known. As he willingly and I suspect somewhat pessimistically admitted, his own method is, of course, subject to this collapse. But it is a collapse that the mainstream traditions deny. Unsurprisingly perhaps, the main feature of his own discourse on the status of history is found in his reiteration of a key deconstructive principle with which we are now familiar, the contention that the discourse of history exists within, rather than outside of, our culture and society.

The crude empiricist insistence that an accurate and accessible reality exists beyond the realm of interpretation is thus dismissed by Foucault through his rejection of the belief that evidence corresponds with the truth of what happened in the past. As we know, a true historical statement is defined by empiricists as a proposition that corresponds or conforms to the available and verifiable evidence, and in its turn this determines the nature of the objectively written history text. Deconstructionist and other cultural historians, following Foucault, prefer to explore the failure of the correspondence theory, especially in the relationship between evidence and context, knower and known – referred to as the intertextuality of written history – and a central problem to which I now turn.

EVIDENCE

In spite of his assault on the epistemology of traditional history, like all historians (including deconstructionist historians) Foucault accepts the need to study the evidence in the archive. The essential proviso is that history's facts are understood primarily as the epistemic discursive creations both of people in the past *and* of the historian, written as the relationship the historian believes exists between words and things in any episteme he/she studies. This means that his/her understanding of the data results from, and can only be revealed in, his/her composed or invented narrative which itself is ultimately a function of the tropic structure of his/her own age. Because historical data are viewed then as representations of events, not the events themselves, it follows then that Foucault believes that historical meaning derives neither from the objective historical contextualisation of evidence (discovering correspondences) nor from discovering the intentionality of the author (hence the death of the author).

Evidence, in the form of documents, is not to be seen as reconstructable traces of the past that are amenable to established inferential hermeneutics. History is the record not of what actually happened, but of what historians tell us happened after they have organised the data according to their own version of social reality. The reconstructionist dependence on the empiricist process of inductive inference – from the evidence to secure the truth of the past – is a counterfeit undertaking. The tropic determination of the episteme does not relegate the importance of evidence, but inevitably places it in a secondary role to the functioning of language – narrative form over content. Evidence, rather than being the point of departure, is history's point of arrival. Metaphor is the point of departure.

Foucault views the evidence of the material world as the yield of the discursive practice of the episteme. This means that evidence as events under a description cannot generate brute facts conceived and understood as non-discursive relics, or bits of unmediated past reality. Foucault goes so far as to suggest that the concept of the empirical fact is nothing more than a naïve discourse of nineteenth-century science. This means that how historians treat the evidence depends on the dominant linguistic protocol (or trope) of the epistemic archive they are working with *and* within. So, while we must continue to study the available evidence, it should be interpreted *at its most fundamental level* as a mediation of the episteme's conditioning narrative structures. It is the knowledge of those structures that forms the cognitive dimension of the deconstructionist historian's linguistic turn, and informs the very nature of his/her historical enterprise. It is in this respect that I mean that all history has within it an irreducible element of philosophical self-reflexivity.

This recognition of the past as a written text *also* provides the platform upon which we may deconstruct the historian's own explanatory narrative. This point is now frequently made. Both the cultural critic Antony Easthope and social historian Patrick Joyce have flown the flag for this argument. They contend (in Foucauldian fashion) that because we historians are *in* history just as much as anyone else, it is impossible for us to disentangle representation from content. As Joyce says, first interpreting then quoting Easthope:

> For a fact to be accurate or not there does not have to be a relation of correspondence . . . between discourse and the real. If the epistemological debate is not resolvable, then there is no problem about

discriminating accurate from inaccurate data, and tenable from untenable arguments. We do this all the time, widely different protocols obtaining in different areas. None the less, these protocols are themselves the product of history, logic turning out on inspection to depend on 'consensus and social construction (rhetoric)'.[13]

This once more raises the issue of socially constructed power relationships and their representation in language, the connection between the will to truth and what Foucault calls the will to power.

Foucault argues that because evidence is always presented to us as the product of pre-packaged figurative codes, its character is dependent on how people in the past and historians now choose to interpret an event as either in conformity or conflict with accepted notions of human nature and/or cultural practice (sense of difference/similarity). In any given culture, at any given time, there are dispensations of power, by which some behaviour patterns are likely to be forbidden while others are encouraged. These taboos or approvals, usually given a moral gloss or rationale, are constructed for social and political purposes that have to do with social power and its uses. As such, these cultural practices defined as thought and behaviour, either of which is forbidden or allowed, immoral and moral, are produced by an arbitrary system of cultural encodation. This encodation, operating in narrative of course, is classified according to the polarities our metaphoric pre-figuration generates – our sense of difference giving meaning to objects understood as a continuity or as a contiguity (often viewed as a discontinuity), with an arbitrarily defined human nature as its measure. As we shall see in the next chapter, White agrees with Foucault that each episteme is almost certainly locked within a specific mode of discourse that allows our access to the 'reality' in the evidence through our encodation of sameness, similarity, resemblance or difference. It is such encodations – representing ideological or social power considerations – that effectively create our sense of social reality.

It ought not now be too difficult to see how short is the step from the interpretation of evidence to the making of moral judgements, ideological positioning and the functioning of power dispensations of dominance and subordinance in society. Defining historical interpretation as the recoding of the signifier and signified relationship – retroping through similarity or difference – prompted Foucault to instance the treatment of the insane in Western European culture from the Renaissance. This was one of the best examples he could find of the exercise of social power and arbitrariness in cultural encodation. He dissected the functional nature and formation of such linguistic encodation that resulted in the different ways in which the insane have been viewed and treated in each of the four epistemes. The point is that while historians may care to arrange evidence chronologically, the interpretation of any patterns *found* are not what actually happened, but are representations of the figurative encoding process we have mentally captured and which surfaces in our narratives. No historian can escape the moral or ethical consequences of the arbitrary signi-fier–signified process. We are all imprisoned in the present as we narrate the past. This is the historian's perennial double-bind. In Foucault's terminology, to be effective, history must acknowledge that it results from the perspective of present linguistically encoded power structures. It is this that gives history its dissenting or, for that matter, status quo reinforcing nature in the here and now.

This emphasis on our state of involuntary historical presentism per-mits us to understand how the encoding process is founded on the dispensations of power among dominant and subordinate groups. As Hayden White describes it, the writing of a historical narrative must always bear the imprint, in both its form and content, of the 'shaping influences of language *and* cultural self-interest' (my italics).[14] What we learn, so far as our evidence is concerned, is that as historians we can rework its meanings only in the light of our immediate cultural experi-ences, and the ways in which that experience in part writes the past for us. The central lesson of Foucault's genealogy is that we now have a vision of history, a postmodernist history if you will, directed by the recognition of the cognitive authority of form, and that all our attempts to obtain truthful representations are conditioned by linguistic and social perspectives. Consequently, no knowledge of the past can be objective, and the world of the past cannot exist independently of our representation of it in the present.

In his texts *Discipline and Punish* and the first volume of *History of Sexuality* Foucault selects from the archive the discursive historical construction of the social encodation of power over the human body – in prisons, mental institutions and sexual practices. Foucault reads the evidence for the changes it represents in the cultural attitudes towards the control of human beings and which mediated the epistemic and epistemological shifts in the construction of meaning in epistemic nar-rative forms. These two texts reveal much about Foucault's historical methodology, in particular his incorporation of issues of power into the process of writing and constituting history. As a professionalised disci-pline, history's traditional function has been to organise the truthful understanding of the past. However, as we undertake the act of writing history – whether as recovery, discovery, reconstruction, construction or deconstruction – we are creating the discipline and the past. Foucault acknowledges this by claiming that the historian's discursive practices constitute various subject positions that people in the past as well as historians may occupy.

Because each historical epoch or episteme is primarily defined by the ways in which knowledge is generated and used – according to the figurative process of distinguishing similarities and differences between objects – language, ideology, power and the writing of history are, therefore, inextricably bound together *in* history. While mainstream historians study evidence in order to wring out its true meaning, to deconstruct means to seek out its multiple messages and through the exercise of our imagination create possible ranges of meanings about referents. Hence, deconstructionist historians must always draw philosophical attention to their narrative messages that possess all the ambiguities and possibilities of their evidential content and epistemic form.

THEORIES OF HISTORY: CONSTRUCTING THE PAST

From the outset of his career Foucault had ambitions to undercut the logocentrist or Cartesian notion that knowledge derives from the way in which we, as human beings, take ourselves as the object as well as the founding subject of that knowledge. His aim was to challenge our Western cultural reliance on the transcendental signified of the clinical empirical method, the rules of inductive inference, the correspondence theory of truth and reliable knowledge, historical objectivity, progress and disinterested analysis. As the *Annaliste* Roger Chartier has suggested after reading Foucault on the treatment of the insane, 'Madness, medicine, and the state are not categories that can be conceptualised in terms of universals', rather they are categories of analysis, which are discursive objects that are founded in the historical context – precisely in the episteme.[15] Foucault is thus offering both a speculative and analytical philosophy of history that offers a particular process of knowledge creation – the epistemic – as the foundation to our understanding of historical change and meaning. It is the conception of the episteme that is likely to have the greatest resonance for constructionist historians.

Despite his later strong anti-positivist, anti-empirical, anti-inferential and historicist method, the young Foucault initially fell under the influence of the *Annales* school. This stimulated what turned out to be his life-long constructionist desire to discover the rules regulating collective cultural practices. Upon reading Nietzsche, however, he turned from speculating on social theory explanations of the history of how people experienced the material world, to studying the rhetorical world of language in which they, as well as social theories themselves, existed. It was his early constructionist-inspired focus that produced his speculative and analytical historical model of the episteme. In *The Archaeology of Knowledge* Foucault offers the following definition of the episteme:

> something like a world-view, a slice of history common to all branches of knowledge, which imposes on each one the same norms and postulates, a general stage of reason, a certain structure of thought that the men of a particular period cannot escape – a great body of legislation written once and for all by some anonymous hand.[16]

This great body of legislation constituting the principles or concepts controlled by this anonymous hand are elaborated in *The Order of Things*, where he demonstrates how our lives conform to the concepts inherent in what he calls the 'empiricities' or evidence located in the three key human branches of knowledge noted above: life (or biological discourse), labour (socio-economic discourse) and language (cultural discourse). Given his later aversion to social science constructionism, Foucault is, in effect, claiming to have discovered in the evidence of the three empiricities the four distinct epochs or epistemes, or stages of reason, his 'certain structure of thought' that effectively constitute the epochal fields or branches of knowledge. We should be aware that the notion of the episteme is not new with Foucault, having been previously elaborated by the Italian philosopher Giambattista Vico in the eighteenth century. Foucault's view of history has basically the same premise that fired Vico – we can only be certain about that which Man has created. I shall return to Vico in the next section, but for the moment it is necessary to be aware of Foucault's position that natural science must always remain ultimately unknown to us, whereas because we have created them, the human sciences afford our only chance of genuine knowing. Thus knowledge and history emerge from our own social constructions – in this instance Foucault's notion of the epistemic/figurative basis of historical experience.

In his elaboration of the episteme, the point where he most radically departs from traditional constructionist stage-theory history is his non-constructionist assumption that the four epistemes do not grow organically out of each other, nor do they occur as revolutions in thought through some version of a dialectical process as they come into conflict. Instead they spontaneously appear in parallel to each other, filling in the spaces suddenly vacated by other conditions of knowledge. In this fashion we see an archipelago of branches of knowledge constituting epistemes rather than a peninsula linked by bridges of causality – clashing classes, industrial revolutions, frontier experiences, catastrophic famines, scientific discoveries, individuals bent on world domination, information revolutions, or whatever else most historians take to link historical epochs. In the language of structuralism, Foucauldian history does not evolve diachronically, but is best understood synchronically, as an explosive discursive structure. While he doubts our access to reality through language (though it is the only means we have) and, therefore, doubts the possibility of a genuine knowledge about reality, even Foucault is forced still to work from the reconstructionist assumption that the nature of history, in his case the creative existence of the episteme, is indeed 'out there'. Foucault's understanding of the four epistemes depends on knowing how language has developed and functioned in each to create and convey knowledge. Unfortunately, because we cannot escape our own episteme, we can never know what constitutes historical change, for that is what happens catastrophically between epistemes. All we can do is map the past cataclysmic train of epistemes but, naturally, only from our own episteme – the postmodern – which regulates how we undertake that mapping exercise.

The first episteme, from the Middle Ages to the late sixteenth century (the Renaissance), characterises knowledge according to the dominant cultural/linguistic or narrative protocol of resemblance or similitude, where closely connected objects were viewed as part of what contemporaries called the Great Chain of Being. As the range of comparison (and the search for hidden links between objects) widened into analogy, a natural sympathy between objects was (arbitrarily) assumed – hence the notion of a linked chain. In the second episteme, from the seventeenth to the eighteenth centuries (the Classical), knowledge was generated according to a linguistic protocol representing a clear sense of differentness. In this age, objects were understood and explained by people distinguishing them from each other so as to create meaningful comparison (like history discriminated from science); thus in this second age the formation of knowledge for Foucault is dominated by contiguity and continuity. This second episteme is thus dedicated to the stability of classification and measurement, and particularly the idea that order can be imposed on the real world primarily through the vehicle of a transparent language.

The third episteme, from the end of the eighteenth century to the early twentieth (the Modern or Anthropological), did not evolve out of the Classical, any more than the Classical did out of the Renaissance.

The epistemological breaks between epistemes, those unforeseen and catastrophic switches in the grounding of knowledge, are witnessed in the spontaneous emergence of the third episteme. Its preoccupation was with Man as the central subject (and object) of reality. This preoccupation is, for Foucault, best understood through the invention of the discipline of history through its typical modernist definition as the understanding of social change over time, as historians cast origins and development in the trope of differential succession. Foucault perceives the Modern episteme as creating a basic epistemological paradox for humanity: Man as the product of his lived social experience, and also the constitutor of knowledge by the invocation of deductive knowledge. Such an epistemic tension cannot last for too long, and eventually the invention (Man as both an empirical and deductive animal) will almost certainly disappear as the idea of Man as a foundation of thought dims into obscurity, and knowledge (and consequently Man as a subject of knowledge) is recognised as nothing more than an epistemic creation, and so we witness the deaths of certainty, history and Man as a knowing animal. Needless to say, such apocalyptic visions do not impress empiricists.

The legacy of the Modern or Anthropological episteme in the invention of the academic discipline of reconstructionist history is accompanied by the naïve assumption of transparency in language and the belief that narrative can objectively correspond with what actually happened in the past. Taken together, these beliefs produced the predominant nineteenth- and twentieth-century conception of history as an empiricist epistemology. From this standpoint, history, as understood and practised by the mainstream, is but a vestigial remain of a previous conceptual epoch. Foucault's provocation to this version of what history is and does has been in part responsible for history's present status crisis. It is this intellectual space in which this crisis of modernist history exists that evidences the shift to the fourth episteme.

The present episteme, the fourth (the postmodern), if it has not already occurred, is in process of creation as the twentieth century closes. Because Foucault is at great pains to insist that the episteme is defined by the basal shifts that occur in the nature of language, and use to which it is put, he argues that we come to understand history (defined as the mapping of catastrophic epistemic change) by examining not its content, but rather the form or structure of the language in which that content is re-presented by people in the past *and* the historian. In his study of cultural change he noted the nature of power situated in discourse but refused to trace the workings of power back to what mainstream historians would assume, in government, imperial centres, or class struggles. Instead he sought them out in narrativised emotions and instinct – specifically in the three empiricities of labour, life and language. From the study of these empiricities Foucault concludes that historical facts as well as constructionist theories (his own included of course) can only exist as discursive entities, the products not of the process of inductive inference, nor less the rules of evidence, and even less the correspondence theory, but as imposed linguistic or, to be more precise, narrative processes.

HISTORY AS NARRATIVE

Foucault maintains that at the deep level of the human mind there is a homology or parallel between the discursive construction of the three empiricities and the epistemic organisation of knowledge. We know the world in which we live only to the extent that we prefigure and narrate it to ourselves. History may, or may not, be merely *a* story we tell ourselves for various social or power purposes, but equally it is possible to conceive of it as a retelling of *the* emplotment of the lived past itself – history construed by people at the time through the dominant epistemic figurative trope. Apart from confirmed anti-narrativists like Hayden White (who believes that there is no actual narrative in the past to be discovered and retold), in reading Foucault we are reminded of the distant voices of philosophers of history like W.B. Gallie who claimed that it is the referent that turns *a* narrative into *the* story. As we now know, Foucault's version of history depends on it being understood as a language system of arbitrary socially constructed relationships between words and things, and through this process we create and live out our own narratives. In his definition of the episteme, Foucault places great significance on language in the constitution of knowledge (knowledge of our own lives and the world in which we live). In a further elaboration of his definition he says:

> By *episteme*, we mean, in fact, the total set of relations that unite, at a given period, the discursive practices that give rise to epistemological figures, sciences, and possibly formalised systems; the way in which . . . each of these discursive formations . . . are situated and operate.[17]

Language accordingly shapes differently the dominant modes of thinking in different epochs. Although we cannot ever know if thought is indeed the product of different discursive or linguistic (tropic) formations, it is possible to imagine that the central role in creating meaning may be given to the discursive practices that constitute branches of

knowledge like history. However, as Foucault attempted to demonstrate, in each of the four epistemes the functioning of language is
different. In the Modern Age the representative accuracy of language
was questioned, with language becoming an object like any other, and
with Foucault accepting the modernist conception that language cannot
carry the weight of expectation that it will transparently represent the
true order of things or correspond to the past as it actually was.
Language has become just one more thing in a world of things. It possesses no inside track to reality. Its use by historians does not guarantee
the accurate representation of all other things. All it can offer is the possibility of emplotment (telling), and through it some kind of
understanding (knowing). Foucault, like White, but unlike Gallie, cannot then tell *the* story, only *a* story. It is this modernist denial of the
representational character of language that forms part of postmodernism's inevitable inclination towards uncertainty of knowing, and its
desire to deny history's traditional foundations.

This opacity of language not only makes it impossible to reconstruct
the past as it actually was (or emplotted as it actually was?), but it may
also account for the discontinuity between epistemes. This is because
the branches of knowledge in each epoch are generated by using modes
of representation based on different narrative conceptions of the relationship between the word and the world (our sense of difference). So,
as imaginative historians of the linguistic or deconstructive turn, we
may examine the textualised evidence, and characterise the dominant
form of narrative emplotment in each episteme. We may dig into past
epistemes to distinguish how events therein (cast as Foucault's empiricities of life, labour and language) were explained by people to
themselves at the time through that age's dominant and subordinate
narrative structures. We may then seek to understand how, in each episteme, the meanings invested by people at the time in life, labour and
language changed according to the ebb and flow of unconscious tropic
forces operating beneath the level of their own explicit myth-making,
empiricism or social theorising. The undertow of tropically inspired
epistemic rules that moved the thinking of people in the past – intellec-
tuals, politicians, reformers, or whatever – would, of course, remain
unknown to them. These tropic rules are, however, the fundamental
codes that constitute the structure of narrative, the 'total set of relations
that unite, at a given period, the discursive practices that give rise to
epistemological figures, sciences, and possibly formalised systems' noted
by Foucault.

At another point, Foucault claims that the episteme is constituted as
'the totality of relations that can be discovered, for a given period,

between the sciences when one analyses them at the level of discursive regularities',[18] emphasising the notion of the episteme as the mental infrastructure of all the human (non-scientific) branches of knowledge, the tropic historical *a priori* that can be revealed and constituted only in narrative representation. By definition then, because of its narrative form, written history cannot avoid the use of the four primary figurative tropes: metaphor, metonymy, synecdoche and irony. Today many critics, if not yet the majority of historians, believe that we have entered into an age (the fourth episteme) in which we cast the narrative of our lives predominantly in the ironic trope – the dominant trope of the postmodern episteme. Even some mainstream empiricists ask ironically how is it that the social reality of the past can really be known to us – or indeed be represented accurately in narrative? This book, for example, could probably have only been written at this particular time. We know that Hayden White holds that relating text and context requires the historian to employ strategies of explanation that openly acknowledge the defining tropes, emplotments and imposed formal arguments, all of which carry, as Foucault has identified, moral/ideological/power implications. If we follow Foucault, we are led to how the cultural signature of each episteme works through the way in which similitude, difference and comparison are characterised. Altogether this means that historical explanation employs the tropes, not just as stylistic figures of speech, but as pre-figurative strategies of explanation in their expression of whole–part, part–whole relationships. I am suggesting, therefore, that the troping processes of metonymy, synecdoche and irony are the cultural signatures of pre-modern, modern and postmodern understanding.

Foucault's linkage of epistemes with dominant tropes, however, is not really a modernist (or postmodern) invention. Indeed, the basic idea of the episteme and the tropic foundation of knowledge originated in the Renaissance episteme with the Genoese historian-philosopher Giambattista Vico. In his treatise *The New Science* (completed between 1725 and 1744), Vico explored more fully than ever before the extent to which language (as trope and narrative) represents things in the world, and also constitutes our understanding of the relationships presumed to exist between them. This notion was by definition lost in the Modern episteme when the modernist myths of rationality and science were decoupled from the cognitive power of language and rhetoric. The consequence, as White says, was to obscure 'to science itself an awareness of its own "poetic" nature'.[19] Science, with modernist history aping its methods and sharing its mythology, assumed that it too could stand outside language and discover the truth of the past.

Vico rejected such Cartesian certainty and Enlightenment rationality by emphasising the socially constituted nature of knowledge (Vico subscribed to the opinion of *verum ipsum factum*, that the true and the manufactured are the same). The modernist corollary to the view that science is certain because it is man-made is science's own absolute conviction that truth must emerge from experimentation by Man in the physical world with the aid of the calculus of mathematics. Because of the modernist preference for historical inductivism, and constructionist deductivism, historians have failed, as Vico suggested at the time and Foucault subsequently accepted, to appreciate fully the fragility of the written form of the past and the ideologically bourgeois nature of the Enlightenment project. For Foucault, following what he understands to be the logic of Vico, historians must be willing to suspend their belief in objective proof in historical knowing, and instead accept a presentism and impositionalism that mediates and represents moral positions in the world. Vico suggested that when historians write the past as a text they unavoidably impose the present as its context. To try to avoid what they perceive as this particular problem, mainstream historians accept the Collingwood–Carr empathic approach to historical understanding. Deconstructionist historians, following Foucault, have instead found an opportunity here for further insights into the formative role of language in the constitution of the past – rethinking the past unavoidably means rethinking history.

Study of the four primary tropes provides an opportunity to familiarise ourselves with, as White puts it, the stages or cycles through which consciousness 'passes in its efforts to know the world' but which ultimately always fails 'to know it fully'.[20] Such failure of knowing, which Foucault also accepts, ought not stop us from writing the past. We should, however, write it reflexively, aware of the power of narrative to shape us ideologically as well as recognising that the past we are construing in narrative is not reality. As many commentators since Vico have pointed out, but particularly Michel Foucault, language is the primary vehicle for ideological dominance and opposition. Specifically, the deconstruction of the past hinges on our understanding of, as Algerian Marxist Louis Althusser describes it, the ideologically interpellative functioning of language – the capability of language operating at the ideological level to place people in less powerful or subject positions. Althusser maintains that the mass of people are constituted and located in situations of ideological subordinance because of the ideological state apparatuses working through the media and other communication systems which are epistemically determined.[21] Because knowledge is power, and the limit and the form of our knowledge is determined by the language we use to express that knowledge, how we deploy language must give effect to what we think of as constituting value, authority and legitimacy.

Put at its plainest, the tropes that prefigure (determine?) historical writing, as well as our understanding of the epistemic rules generating knowledge, are ideologically saturated. For the historian who wishes to locate the dominant trope, this means seeking out, in both evidence and in his/her historical imagination, the relationship between form and content. We should understand that the reality of the past (presumed to exist) is a textually generated and ideologically tainted reality-effect. By this I mean that *written* history must grasp the nature and significance of the troping process in the past as both a lived and written experience. Just as the tropes were the foundation of Vico's stage theory of history (metaphor represents the age of gods, metonymy the age of heroes, synecdoche the age of men and irony the age of decadence and decline), so for Foucault there is a tropic foundation to each of the epistemes. Not surprisingly we might view post-structuralism and deconstruction themselves as postmodern empiricities, each in their own way rejecting man-centred modernist history, both evidencing the present status crisis in history.

CONCLUSION

In 1984 Mark Poster could claim, with some accuracy, that the main reason for what he called the incoherence of historical writing is 'the absence of theoretical reflection by the practitioners of social history'.[22] While this is no longer the case, by and large the mainstream are, however, still recognisable by their wilful disregard of Foucault's work. They deny Foucault's insight that it is the role of the historian to locate and explore the archive's discursive and non-discursive practices within an episteme, so he/she may present to the reader the narrative transformations generated, and how they may have directly conditioned events, actions and beliefs in the past. While Foucault may or may not be the first deconstructive or postmodern historian, he is qualified to bear the title if only because he points to the epistemological break between the Modernist Age and our own. It may be that the title is more deserved because of his refashioning of history as a form that does not rely on the inductive inference or imputation of causality, origins, certainty and truth. Consequent upon this rejection of empiricist foundationalism we can rethink the nature and purpose of historical evidence as an archive of discursive and non-discursive practice, recognising that its utility resides in what it ultimately tells us about the organisation of knowledge according to criteria other than the correspondence theory of knowledge.

This new view of the nature of history seemingly flings philosophy into the face of practitioners: as Elton said, bringing it out of the scullery into the drawing room. Historians after Foucault are increasingly coming to terms with their study of the past, and the past itself, as composed narratives. It is in line with this new consciousness that Hayden White has established his own contribution to the writing of history. His assertion, following Foucault, is that while narrative as a form of cognition and representation is unavoidable, it is also infuriatingly recalcitrant. However, if history as a discipline is not to be confused with the past – a central plank of White's programme – then its possible realities can be accessed only through the conceptual powers of historians as constrained by linguistic structures and categories. It is to White's narrative model of historical explanation that we now turn.

8 Hayden White and deconstructionist history

INTRODUCTION

Historians who normally reject the idea that the form in which their research is written up creates historical meaning, do so on the assumption that the language used to write *about* the past can correspond to *the* past as a narrative. This is a view rejected by Hayden White (along with others like Louis Mink, F.R. Ankersmit and Paul Ricoeur). White's analysis of how historians, as they describe and evaluate past events, effectively invent the past is probably the most radical development in historical methodology in the last thirty years. It has forced other philosophers and historians to address the issue of the correspondence or homology between narrative form and lived experience. For White, because the past is invented or imagined rather than found, history the first time around does not conform or correspond to a pre-existing narrative or story. White does not dispute that the past existed, and he is not anti-referentialist, but his answer to the question I posed at the outset, asking whether the past pre-exists as a story told by people in the past to explain their lives to themselves, is to argue that we impose stories on the past for a variety of reasons which are explanatory, ideological and political. Narratives are not detached vehicles for transmitting past realities, nor less can historians discover *the* true narrative of the past in the evidence of human intentions and beliefs.

Historians within the two main tendencies believe in recoverable author-intentionality, truth, causes, origins, an adequate correspondence between words and the world, and insist that history emerges from the ultimate freedom of people in the past to act, think and make rational choices (or explicable irrational ones) not absolutely constrained by material conditions like class. From this ideologically conservative position they insist that there is a genuine, empiricist-founded history methodology. However, some seem to want it both ways by insisting on this set of beliefs about method, yet nevertheless wishing to claim that 'there is nothing much to say about historical explanation; nothing that cannot be said about explanation in everyday life'.[1] This inconsistency ignores the twentieth-century debate whereby analytical philosophers have argued over the proposition that language is the primary state in which knowledge is produced and understood, and that the structure of the historical text *as a whole*, rather than just its micro-level of individual statement about intentions, may be cognitive, that is, create meaning.

We may, of course, choose to challenge White and ask again to what extent is the historical narrative actually homologous to the past – can history recover *the* story of the past, or do we merely impose *a* story? This would be a different correspondence to that imagined by empiricists – what I will call a narrative correspondence – the extent to which our story matches *the* story of the past not via empiricism, but via a study of past dominant/subordinate rhetorical structures. The recovery or match is, in the way of things, itself subject to the structure of narrative that permeates written history today. In this chapter I will address this issue and White's rejection of the idea of the historian's discovery of *the* story. As F.R. Ankersmit has suggested, not until relatively recently has the historical text 'as a whole' ever been 'the topic of philosophical investigation'.[2] This is regrettable, given that history is the literary activity most suited to this level of textual analysis. It is at this level that we address what is perhaps the central question for White and all those interested in the role of narrative in history: does life itself have a narrative structure and is it recoverable? If it does, and is, then history as it is written must not be viewed as either the report of an objective empiricist research programme or a subjective piece of literature, but as *a* representation of past life and culture.

EPISTEMOLOGY

The recalcitrant nature of the signifier–signified relationship, the unfixing of referentiality and empiricist correspondence, the decline in covering law constructionism, and Foucault's exploration of the relationship between the past and narrative form, have prompted the examination of the complex ideological, explicatory and emplotted structure of history as a form of explanation. So it is that we view history as a literary artifact rather than as the unalloyed product of contextualised sources, or a reconstruction of *the* empirically derived and accurate experience, or the construction of a social theory. Like Foucault, Hayden White places his emphasis in the writing of history upon discursive practices and determining tropes, offering a formal model which, when taken with Foucault's vision, allows historians to relate the structures of narrative representation to the nature of historical change.

In epistemological terms, White's engagement with Foucault's notion of the episteme, together with his own formal narrative model of tropically engineered historical explanation, raise important questions about the past as a textual product. White's model of historical writing and understanding is now well known.[3] Briefly, White offers a model of historical narrative in which its form is taken to prefigure the historian's understanding of the meaning of the content of the past. White's key text is *Metahistory*, published in the early 1970s. In it he demonstrated how a historical narrative endows itself *and* the past with meaning. For most historians a clear literary style in their historical explanation is taken as a measure of narrative's irrelevance to understanding. When it comes down to it, why study the lens rather than the object of study beyond it?

White, however, forces us to confront the fundamental issues. Does language act in opposition to our assumption of reality because it is only through language that we can apprehend that reality? (Yet, because of its figurative character, it must always fabricate that reality.) Does the prison house of language mean that we can never escape to truth? Does the form of our historical reconstruction directly condition or constitute our interpretation? How do we impose our own narrative structures on the past? White has not been alone in considering these questions. As a hermeneutic issue the functioning of narrative has been addressed by many historians. Frederick A. Olafson, for example, has pointed out not just the significance of the historian's understanding of the language of the primary sources, but its importance in framing and answering our questions. Through language we historians are central to the process of creating historical understanding.[4] White takes this up in arguing against the maintaining of a language–world distinction. While it is certainly important for historians within the mainstream tendencies to claim adequacy in the representation of the past, White disputes this empiricist investment directly.

As I have already indicated, White's historical method works from the general assumption that written history is unarguably a literary enterprise and we cannot gain access to what the past was about other than through it. It follows that we understand the past through the narrative form we devise to organise it. History at every level, therefore, is a text possessing an imposed or invented meaning. The deconstructive historian's function remains that of interpretation, but an interpretation viewed as the translation or rendition of one text (the past) into a new narrative version which is another text of the historian's own invention (written history). This textual rendering of the past is, as we are aware, steered by the four master tropes of resignification – metaphor, metonymy, synecdoche and/or irony. Because there is no necessary correspondence between words and things, or language and past reality, the historical text can be linked only to other historical texts and derive its meaning from those other texts. This is the argument that history gains its meaning intertextually, and while it reveals the full import of Derrida's play on the concept of *différance*, it also emphasises the insight of Foucault that the past may itself be regarded as a text. Of course, none of this stops the reconstructionist in his/her tracks – nor should it. As White points out, history defined as a verbal model can still be 'offered by the historian as a representation and explanation of "what *really* happened" in the past' if that is his/her wish. Neither White nor the deconstructionive consciousness is embargoing the evaluation of the past's content as such; they are only questioning the empiricist claims to an ultimate referentiality and knowing history.

It is White's contention that to understand what the past was about we must impose a narrative upon it; hence our knowledge of the past is through a poetic act. This is the element of fiction in all historical accounts, and it is this part that is so abused through the neglect of historians. Chosen by the historian, and constituting the fictional dimension to historical understanding, narrative offers a subtle rendering of pastness. The fictional element emerges both when empiricists claim to be representing *the* story as it actually happened and when the deconstructionist choice of emplotment is taken to represent *a* story of pastness. It follows, if White is correct, and people in the past do not actually live stories (that is, they do not impose emplotments of a particular kind on their lives and times in order to make sense of them), that the reconstructionist argument that they have discovered *the* reality of the past in *their* story is undermined in as much as there is no story in the past to be discovered. White insists that the past as history is not *the* story – it is the fictional invention of historians as we try to recount what the past was about. As he says:

> Historical situations are not *inherently* tragic, comic, or romantic. They may all be inherently ironic, but they need not be emplotted that way. All the historian needs to do to transform a tragic into a comic situation is to shift his point of view or change the scope of his perceptions. Anyway, we only think of situations as tragic or comic because these concepts are part of our generally cultural and specifically literary heritage. *How* a given historical situation is to be

configured depends on the historian's subtlety in matching up a specific plot structure with the set of historical events that he wishes to endow with a meaning of a particular kind.[5]

At another point White is adamant that 'No one *lives* a story' and thus all emplotments are imposed later by historians.[6] We do not, of course, have to agree with White. History viewed as an essentially literary endeavour may not preclude the possibility that people living in the past did indeed explain their lives to themselves as narratives as construed within their particular episteme. It follows that there may be some kind of narrative correspondence possible between past events *as lived* and their *history* as emplotted later by historians, but it could also mean there are a variety of stories, or possible emplotments, in the past that are *generally* constrained by the deep narrative structure of the episteme. Indeed, as White asks, is there an analogy between 'the dynamics of metaphorical transformations in language and the transformations of both consciousness and society'?[7] This suggests that stages in history may well coincide, in some more or less determinist relationship, with their ascendant figurative tropes, with the variations from metaphoric to metonymic, and synecdochic to ironic expressions of thought associated with the fundamental cultural transitions in Western society since the Renaissance. Are there, in effect, emplotments to be recovered from the past?

If indeed emplotment is tropically determined, and if Foucault is correct in his analysis of epistemic historical change, then White is in a bind. As Robert Berkhofer points out, if White's flow of tropes (following Foucault's sequence of epistemes) do forecast or prefigure the aesthetic and level of emplotment, the cognitive level of argument, and their joint ideological implications in historical accounts, then past events can only be construed as poetic acts independent of the real content of the past.[8] That the tropic process directs the historian's own figurative understanding of the past and people in the past may be seen in recent applications of White's model to America's modern historical development.[9] The use of White's rhetorical constructionism does not mean that we cannot study what the past was about, but means that we must recognise the severe limits of empiricism. Of course, as we deconstruct the past, we can deconstruct each other's rendering of it. One of the radical benefits of deconstructionist history is its breaking down of the barriers between its own form and the content of the past. As we deconstruct the past we deconstruct the history we write about it. Hence, you or I could deconstruct this book, or White's *Metahistory*. Indeed, at the conclusion to *Metahistory* White himself suggests such a course – as he says, the formalism of his model may reflect the present/emergent ironic stage of human history in which the book was written. So, as we deconstruct the past we inevitably deconstruct the discipline.

White concludes that historians are at liberty to exercise their imaginations and view Foucault's four epistemes as essentially sequential periods in which dominant tropes serve to organise knowledge, and we may choose to argue that the structure of narrative at any time or in any place provides the cognitive conditions influencing how people narrated the meaning of their lives to themselves.[10] White's formal model does not entertain such speculations, being epistemologically narrower and sticking to the issue of how, and in what ways, historians shape and contour the past through the linguistic, literary and specifically figurative forms available. White's model does not resolve the question of whether there is only one fundamental reading or emplotment of the past available to be discovered by historians. White is concerned not with *the* reality of the past as guaranteed by empiricism, but with the emplotment of the impositionalist historian, generating Barthes' reality effect. As I have suggested, White's formal model does not stop us from studying the content of the past, what the past was about, but it casts such a study in a radically different light. It opens up a new vision of how to treat the past at its most basic cultural level, that is, at the level of narrative.

EVIDENCE

White maintains that the attempt to rediscover or reconstruct the *original* intentions of the author and, therefore, the meaning of the evidence is always more difficult than the forensic problems associated with the empirical/inferential method suggest. Beyond the simplest level of the individual referential statement (that President Madison was 5 feet, 4 inches tall), it is the constitution of historical facts as a totality that *creates* their meaning, rather than the discovery or recovery of the essential/original and intentional meaning as constituted by the original author. I have argued that all traces of the past are mediated because they are categorised or ordered (narrativised) in some way both in the past and now – a hermeneutic or interpretative circle. This means that as we invent an emplotment to transform individual events or statements into historical facts, in its turn the emplotment becomes more than the sum of its parts, and as both White and Ankersmit argue, it is the prefigured emplotment that initially defines the selection of evidence as well as its interpretation.

As White says, when historians attempt to explain the facts of the French Revolution or decline of the Roman Empire:

What is at issue . . . is not What are the facts? but rather, How are the facts to be described in order to sanction one mode of explaining them rather than another? Some historians will insist that history cannot become a science until it finds the technical terminology. . . . Such is the recommendation of Marxists, Positivists, Cliometricians, and so on. Others will continue to insist that the integrity of historiography depends on the use of ordinary language. . . . These latter suppose that ordinary language is a safeguard against ideological deformations of the *facts*. What they fail to recognise is that ordinary language itself has its own forms of terminological determinism, represented by the figures of speech without which discourse itself is impossible.[11]

So, as we use language we are subject to its figurative demands, but we always inject more of ourselves into our partnership with language. White notes that 'most historical sequences can be emplotted in a number of different ways, so as to provide different interpretations of those events and to endow them with different meanings'.[12] The input of the historian, therefore, is his/her ability to develop the figurative or metaphorical nature of the narrative as a form of explanation – to expand the nature of his/her historical imagination.

Most historians accept that even if we could revisit and reproduce the past as it actually was, we would still be interpreting it in our own time and place, and most likely for our own ideological purposes. No one today, apart from the ever-diminishing band of naïve empiricists, seriously supports the view that historians objectively recover the past to discover the truth. In place of naïve empiricism I would argue that we now have a situation whereby, in practice, most historians seek *their* truth in the past. No matter how pristine is their technical recovery of the past in the contextualising and creation of historical facts, I would contend that it is always going to be imposed upon by an ideologically aligned *and* rhetorically constructionist historian. When we interpret the evidence we contribute to a presumed centre of 'truth' by adding our interpretation to the weight of existing interpretations. The meaning of historical facts so created, in effect, changes as historical interpretations are continually revisited and the meaninglessness of the past has a fresh order imposed upon it through the disciplining of history. The traditional disciplining or domestication of the past through constant historical revisionism empties the past of what White calls the sublime: the inherent uncertainty of inexplicable change. The deconstructive consciousness willingly acknowledges the sublime nature of the past – its literal meaninglessness, its lack of centre, and its consequent lack of truth – while mainstreamers still insist on asking what was the past really like and, through dint of professional archival research, still believe they can get ever closer to its truthful reality. The fact that *the* truth differs for Marxists, post-colonial liberals, feminists, the revisionist right, post-structuralists, or whomever, should warn us of the impossibility of ever getting at *the* truth.[13] Perhaps we could now accept that the old distinctions between history and rhetoric, evaluation and fiction were at best only a vogue of the Enlightenment and its nineteenth-century positivist legacy, the benefits of which were considerably over-rated?

The denial of the sublime – the What might have been? – in the headstrong desire for absolute understanding operates most crudely in the attempt to extract the real, but hidden, intentionality of the author from the evidence. It is in rejecting this improbable process of discovery that White is at his most insightful. If the past possesses a fictive narrative structure, or if it is quite meaningless, then the reconstructionist insistence on the reality of a historicised context that will allow the recovery of a stable, ordered, preordained and original meaning to emerge from the evidence is destroyed. For White, the effective lack of original meaning – which by definition cannot be recovered by reconstructionist contextualism – is important, especially today, because he believes it is crucial that history should not be categorised and closed off for political and ideological purposes by the left, right or centre. Hence his emphasis that our act of organising the evidence as we narrativise it immediately and effectively closes off any access either to the genuine or, for that matter, to other alternative meanings of an event or thought. When we have decided that we know what it means – then that is what it means.

If the original textualised evidence cannot be trusted to signify what the original author intended, then no amount of forensic analysis can recover what was left out, or de-invent what was invented when the evidence was first created. The element of the sublime that White so welcomes is lost if we fail to understand the nature of evidence. This is a major threat to the reconstructionist mainstream because of the powerful desire of the Rankean will to know what actually happened. I would tend to agree with White that if the historian cannot know *the* story presumed to be embedded in the evidence, it is because there are probably an infinite number of stories told in the past and about the past. What the historian must do is locate the different types of stories that the evidence will support, which may then be reasonably brought forth as a coherent emplotment informed by the pre-generic plot structure or culturally provided myths that allow the configuring of the facts as a story of a particular kind. The historian may well be convincing, plausible or telling good rather than bad history when the story rendered appeals to the same stock of myths and ideological and methodological preferences shared by the reader. This gives the account or interpretation, as White says, 'the odour of meaning or significance' and provides history with its sense of realism.[14] What I think White is highlighting is how this realism is the result of the aesthetic and ethical choices made by the historian, even though it is claimed by those with reconstructionist or constructionist inclinations to be the result of years of painstaking, massively in-depth and clinical archival research and interpretation. It should, of course, be possible to have both.

As we know, the reconstructionist paradigm of *Quellenkritik* is intended to provide for the reader not just a verisimilitudinous rendering of what happened – the odour of meaning – but *the* legitimate and accurate evaluation of human actions and events. But, as F.R. Ankersmit argues, the historical narrative 'resembles a belvedere: after having climbed the staircase of its individual statements, one surveys an area exceeding by far the area on which the staircase was built'.[15] In White's judgement it is literally from or at this point of view that each historian prefigures his/her interpretative (re)textualisation of the past, by selecting between the several universal tropological strategies, emplotments, arguments with their ideological implications in order to frame the perspective and invest the evidence with meaning but not the truth. History thus conceived is more like a painting than a forensic reconstruction – an aesthetic appreciation of a past world rather than the recovery of its lost reality from the sources composed of individual statements about past reality. Ankersmit's contention that we historians never employ all the possible range of referential statements available to us about the past means that we select – like colours from a palette – those to be used according to our emplotment decisions (that is, those that we judged to be significant). As he says, 'The results of historical research are expressed in statements' that can be shown to be more or less true, in that they correspond to other statements with the same referent saying the same things about it; but while narrative interpretations are indeed sets of statements, clearly this does not mean that the historian's imposed interpretative narrative structure of interpretation is truthful (or false). Of course, rhetorical constructionism itself, as a linguistic entity, is not immune to the charge that it is also a representation, and thus no more truthful, or likely to be true, than is empiricism. Ankersmit concludes that while individual statements (evidence) may correspond to the past in the sense of possessing referentiality, when they are collated as narrative interpretations they can then 'only *apply* to the past' and do not *'correspond* or *refer* to it'.[16]

The act of interpreting the evidence is not then dictated primarily by the atomistic content of the past, as reconstructionists would argue; nor less does interpretation emerge as jigsawed evidence fits together to provide the real picture or design. For White the evidence exists in a pre-jigsawed state, a condition that requires the historian to cut and shape it into a narrative explanation. Historical facts do not ordain interpretations; only plot structures do that. Hence, from White's standpoint, evidence is not inherently tragic, comic, satiric or romantic, and Marx's famous aphorism that history occurs the first time around as tragedy and the second time as farce can only be taken to mean that history is written by human beings, and the act of narrative interpretation takes history out of an unknowable past reality and into the present, rather than transmitting us back to the past. This act of creation – literally and metaphorically – constitutes *a* plausible historical text rather than *the* past.

Deconstructionist historians do not automatically doubt the truth of individual referential statements, nor do they claim that it is impossible to demonstrate that certain events did or did not happen, that people were not short or tall, that decisions were or were not made, or that millions of Jews in the early part of the twentieth century were murdered by the German Nazi regime. But the deconstructive emphasis is upon the procedure for creating historical knowledge when we deal with the evidence. We are aware that we take simple verifiable statements, which we compose into a narrative so that they become meaningful (not necessarily the same as truthful). This operation is of the historian's imaginative/fictive power. Having suggested that the past is created as history by an imposed tropically inspired structure, White nevertheless entertains the thought that it is insufficient for the historian merely to learn the language in which the evidence is written, because the historian should penetrate the *modes of thought* mediated in the tropes. This act of penetration is not one of discovery, but one of active narrative constructionism on the part of the historian. This is not an engagement of exploration and discovery, but an act of creation.

Convinced as he is that the past has no inherent emplotment, the fiction of factual representation, as White describes it, resides in the process of impositionalism. As he says:

Confronted with the chaos of facts the historian must carve them up for narrative purposes. In short, historical facts, originally constituted as data by the historian, must be constituted a second time as elements of a verbal structure which is always written for a specific . . . purpose.[17]

It follows that disputes in history depend rarely on facts, but on what they mean, and their meaning is determined by the tropic mode of their narrative construction – the product of the narrative turn. So, if history is a primarily narrative construction, what, for White, can be the role of the historian's social theory?

THEORIES OF HISTORY: CONSTRUCTING THE PAST

As White says:

> To raise the question of the nature of narrative is to invite reflection on the very nature of culture. . . . So natural is the impulse to narrate, so inevitable is the form of narrative for any report on the way things really happened, that narrativity could appear problematical only in a culture in which it was absent. . . .[18]

White's rhetorical constructionist theory of the work of history is built on this insight. He attempts not only to identify the underlying structure of the historical text but, like Foucault, to understand the linguistic forces acting to create the past itself – the modes of thought. He maintains that historical interpretation 'might be regarded as what Foucault has called a formalisation of the linguistic mode in which the phenomenal field was originally prepared'.[19] White is confirming here that knowledge is construed through the prefigurative tropes and the troping process. How does the troping process relate to constructionism?

Plainly, White's emphasis on history as a form of literature defines it as a kind of constructionism. White's link of the prefigurative power of the tropes to Foucault's conception of the episteme offers the possibility of an original and provocative explanatory linguistic model of historical change. This model, which White describes as a tropological reduction, but which I prefer to call a rhetorical construction, has so far been applied in a relatively limited way by historians. The reason is three-fold: first, there is a general suspicion of both Foucault and White because their work questions history as a distinctively empiricist epistemology; second, and flowing from this, we have the professional investment in the existence of history as a distinct profession; and finally, and perhaps most tellingly, there is a deep antipathy to any model of historical change predicated upon the existence of dominant (and subordinate) tropic prefigurative bases to knowledge – a reconstructionist suspicion of constructionism welded to the irrational fear that somehow literature will steal the soul of history. For most in the mainstream what is taken as linguistic determinism is productive of empirical uncertainty, and encourages a dangerous moral relativism, if not outright nihilism. Any attempt to recover the sublime via rhetorical constructionism is a reckless attack aimed at the very heart of the empiricist enterprise.

What White is proposing, following Foucault, is that historians, in writing history, in effect work out a tropically inspired construction. Contrary to this there is the belief – especially popular among Marxist constructionist historians – that historical experience is redeemable as it actually was only with the intervention of non-linguistic, experience-based social theorising. The term constructionism as I employ it in this book refers to history resulting from the imposition of social theory strategies, models, or covering laws of explanation on the past. As we know, constructionism, especially sociological and anthropological varieties, questions reconstructionist historical inference at the individual event level, preferring the general level of explanation covering many individual events. The use of such historical models has tended to reinforce the notion that historians are able to stand apart from the past, maintaining the gap between knower and known.[20] White holds that no historian can maintain such a separation between themselves and their data because historical narrative will always compromise this distinction

Philippe Carrard's submission that even the constructionist New History relies upon narrative through which to report the results of its hypothesis testing has important implications. It argues that the most complex application of social theory still depends largely on story-telling 'to make sense of the world'. He concludes that no amount of scientific apparatus can disguise the fact that constructionism's analytical component 'is still framed by a plot, and this plot retains essential cognitive functions'.[21] Not only this of course, but, as White and Foucault insist, the organisation of data into structures is deceptive at the most fundamental level. Not only is it not an accurate replication of historical events and lost lives, but our impositions are also likely to be instruments for the exercise of power – the obvious examples being self-interest in order to maintain history as a professional discipline, or to write the sort of history that will marginalise and/or exclude minorities, or constitute colonialist and nationalist versions of reality, or, if the historian so wishes, to do the opposite of all these. If narrative's ability to disrupt as well as establish such power arrangements is recognised, then this can liberate rather than constrain our construction of the past. At its most basic it should remind us never to confuse written history with referentiality because history is at best analogous to the (a?) past.

The theory of history-writing-interpretation constructed by White is, therefore, a formal model of historical explanation that insists on history as a figurative construction. Every metaphor the historian uses is itself nothing more nor less than a tropic model deployed to re-present reality, as when Frederick Jackson Turner likened the advance of the American frontier in the nineteenth century to several tides and waves. This description carried with it what was presumably Turner's deliberate intention to create in the reader's mind the sense of an eternal, pre-ordained and unstoppable natural process. In this particular instance Turner's referential signifier was tides or waves of nation-building.[22] As White maintains, all historians act constructively when they compose the past. As he says, if we all

> treated the historian's text as what it manifestly was, namely a rhetorical composition, one would be able to see not only that historians effectively constructed the subject of their discourse in and by writing, but that ultimately, what they actually wrote was less a report of what they had found in their research than of what they had imagined the object of their original interest to consist of. That is why I spoke in *Metahistory* of 'the historical imagination' in nineteenth century Europe and envisioned a 'poetics of history' as an alternative to the various 'theories' of history then circulating.[23]

In claiming that historical explanation is a form of rhetorical constructionism, White rejects some of the more extravagant claims for social theory history. He is especially critical of the Marxian variety which assumes it has discovered in the evidence *the* actual truth of the past – *the* narrative, *the* story – in class-constructed economic determinism. Neither is White, as I read him, suggesting that his rhetorical constructionist model is to be viewed as a kind of bourgeois or ironic linguistic determinism or, for that matter, that historians are merely the instrument of their narratives. What White is doing is far more complex, for he is inviting us instead to explore language as the element in which everyone (including historians) exists and through which we all make sense of our past, present and future. In addition, he reminds us that our evaluation, interpretation and representation of the events and occurrences of the past should be, as he says, judged 'to be "relative" to the time, place and cultural conditions of its formulation'.[24] This kind of contextualism or historicism rests uneasily on the shoulders of most social theory constructionists. Although many constructionists today are more open to the variety of methodological approaches to history than are naïve realists, still very few think about how their construction of the past is changed as they write their narratives. This lacuna bears further examination. Before the application of social theory or hypotheses to the data of the past, White holds that we should address the prefigurative or tropic modes in which covering laws, theories and arguments are composed and offered. Following the logic of White's model this means that literary form, constructed as emplotment, precedes theory and argument, and that all elements or strategies of historical explanation are determined by Foucault's dominant epistemic tropic structures.

All six points of the empiricist reconstructionist–constructionist charter are confounded by White's argument that before the historian can bring to bear on the evidence 'the conceptual apparatus he will use to represent and explain it' he must first 'prefigure the field – that is to say, constitute it as an object of mental perception'.[25] This is White's striking comment on the process of history-writing as a narrative imposition by the historian. His formal model offers the most satisfying theory of how historical narrative works for the historian. His model is predicated on the belief that to raise the question of 'the rhetoric of historical discourse is to raise the problem of the nature of description and analysis', and in this connection he notes the French cultural anthropologist Claude Lévi-Strauss's comment on traditional history, that in effect it has no method 'uniquely its own, nor indeed any unique subject matter'. The important point that White makes here is that historical writing

must be analysed primarily as a kind of prose discourse before its claims to objectivity and truthfulness can be tested. This means subjecting any historical discourse to a *rhetorical* analysis, so as to disclose the poetical understructure of what is meant to pass for a modest prose representation of reality.[26]

White is saying that written history should be categorised primarily according to the way in which it describes its object of study rather than the empirically derived explanatory mechanisms of analysis it applies to the evidence (collection, colligation, comparison and verification). Historical writing explains because of the way it is put together – the content of the form. To understand fully the role of narrative in the writing of the past, and its aesthetic, cognitive and moral content, it is necessary briefly to outline White's formal model of the historical imagination which in turn may give us a significant insight into the character of historical explanation.[27]

HISTORY AS NARRATIVE

White's model is best viewed as a grid of relationships, or elective affinities as he calls them, between the levels or strategies of historical explanation that every historian utilises in reconstituting the past:

Trope	Emplotment	Argument	Ideological implication
Metaphor	Romantic	Formist	Anarchism
Metonymy	Tragic	Mechanistic	Radicalism
Synecdoche	Comic	Organicist	Conservatism
Irony	Satiric	Contextualist	Liberalism[28]

Following the four main kinds of trope, which act as the foundation for all historical interpretation, are four kinds of explanation in three tiers, namely four emplotments, associated with four types of argument and four ideological positions. The historian may emplot his/her narrative in one of the four modalities available – the romantic, tragic, comic or satiric. These then influence his/her appeal to one of four modes of argument – formist, mechanistic, organicist or contextualist; and finally, his/her selection of plot and argument has ideological implications that negotiate the union of the prior aesthetic and cognitive strategies of explanation. The ideological implications are anarchism, radicalism, conservatism or liberalism.

As an aid to understanding how history is written, this model is best summarised by White in *Metahistory*:

These affinities are not to be taken as *necessary* combinations of the modes of a given historian. On the contrary, the dialectical tension which characterises the work of every master historian usually arises from an effort to wed a mode of emplotment with a mode of argument or of ideological implication which is inconsonant with it. For example . . . Michelet tried to combine a Romantic emplotment and a Formist argument with an ideology that is explicitly Liberal. So, too, Burckhardt used a Satirical emplotment and a Contextualist argument in the service of an ideological position that is explicitly Conservative and ultimately Reactionary. Hegel emplotted on two levels – Tragic on the microcosmic, Comic on the macrocosmic – both of which are justified by appeal to a mode of argument that is Organicist, with the result that one can derive either Radical or Conservative ideological implications from a reading of his work.[29]

Clearly then, although the model must inevitably be laid out formally, it is not rigid or absolute in the relationships it offers. But, like Foucault, White is claiming that all three surface tiers of narrative are under-pinned by their tropic or figurative structure, which is (to remind ourselves) the process we engage in as we describe to ourselves and others the relationships presumed to exist between objects, texts, events and contexts. This is the metahistorical level of the model to which White refers as that set of presuppositions which 'is nothing but the web of commitments which the historian makes in the course of his inter-pretation on the aesthetic, cognitive, and ethical levels'.[30] This basic level of consciousness is 'that of language itself, which, in areas of study such as history, can be said to operate tropologically' in order to prefigure 'a field of perception in a particular modality of relation-ships'.[31] In other words, this troping process creates an imagined context through which, for illustration, metonymic (part-to-whole) or synecdochic (whole-to-part) relationships are established between events and things. Because history is literature it can apprehend its data only through the dictates of its narrative form; the figure(s) of speech we impose on the data act to sanction the very nature of our historical understanding. The tropes, as representational models, thus preshape our descriptions of the data, preceding and prefiguring the emplot-ment, argument and ideological levels of our historical narratives.

Troping means using metaphors to imply meaning and explain events by altering our perceptions, forcing us to look again at objects and con-cepts from the perspective of something different – signification and resignification. Each of the four tropes is defined according to its par-ticular rhetorical and, therefore, explanatory function. We relate events and human actions not according to some wholly extrinsic situation, but through language, and specifically how language operates in relat-ing parts to wholes and vice versa. As White says:

> Irony, Metonymy, and Synecdoche are kinds of Metaphor, but they differ from one another in the kinds of *reductions* or *intergrations* [*sic*] they effect on the literal level of their meanings and by the kinds of illuminations they aim at on the figurative level. Metaphor is essentially *representational*, Metonymy is *reductionist*, Synecdoche is *integrative*, and Irony is *negational*.[32]

Following Vico, White takes this troping process to constitute the inescapable prefigurative act of historians and all those who write nar-ratives. White, like Foucault, is suggesting that the mechanism of writing history operates at the subterranean level of language and human consciousness – the prefigurative act being divined in and through 'the dominant tropological mode in which it is cast'.[33] Even if the aim remains the stated attempt to recapture what actually happened in the past, even then we must first 'prefigure as a possible object of knowledge the whole series of events reported in the documents'.[34] This kind of contextualisation is not just a narrative version of empiricism (which endorses the link between statement and referent), it is rather a means of understanding that precedes empiricism as well as all other philosophies of history. The result is that as historians we do not objectively report the past, we create it as we deploy language to define the concepts used – not merely to identify our objects of study, but also to characterise the kind of relationships (troping) we see (imagine) between them. History is validated not solely by the appeal to past reality, but also by how that reality is written. As one commentator wrote recently, history after White cannot be judged as if it were itself outside history – some natural object of reality.[35]

For White, the important point is that in metaphor, metonymy, synecdoche and irony

> language provides us with models of the direction that thought itself might take in its effort to provide meaning to areas of experience not already regarded as being cognitively secured by either common sense, tradition, or science. And we can see that in a field of study such as history 'interpretation' might be regarded as what Foucault has called a 'formalisation' of the linguistic mode in which the phenomenal field was originally prepared. . . .[36]

Metaphor thus identifies thought as representational in which the similarities between objects are stressed, metonymy signifies by reducing an object to a part or parts; synecdoche works the other way by integrating objects, emphasising their similarities or essences, and to trope ironically is to negate literal meaning.

If we use the example of Frederick Jackson Turner's history of the American frontier to illustrate the troping process, one of his claims is that the 'free land' of the frontier possessed the power to assimilate or Americanise pioneering settlers. Read as a metaphor, 'free land' is defined as 'the line of most rapid Americanisation'. If read as a metonym, Americanisation is reduced to its most significant part, namely the existence of 'free land'. If read as a synecdoche, 'free land' signifies the essence of Americanisation. If read ironically, 'free land', stated as the literal truth of the Americanisation process, would be negated by the context created by the historian that there was none and Americanisation thus never occurred. Such rhetorical constructions, as White warns us, can act as particularly effective political encodations serving the exercise of power – history as ideology. To this end, when written as history, Turner's frontier thesis is ultimately integrated into his definition of America by emphasising its essential nationalising characteristic, which he defines as 'the existence of an area of free land'.

These tropologically determined or prefigured strategies of explanation allow us as historians an inventory from which to choose in order to construct narrative explanations or interpretations of the past – even for those among us whose desire it is to know what actually happened, or who wish to confirm our own particular constructionist explanation. This logic is translated by White into his argument that the actual choice of emplotment is ultimately the product of the episteme in which it is written, because it draws upon contemporary cultural reference points, or as he calls them archetypal story forms, which themselves accord with the dominant (and/or subordinate) myths and needs of society as cast at the tropic or metahistorical level from which our written history emerges. The American frontier experience, as emplotted by Frederick Jackson Turner in the 1890s, chimed with the needs of the dominant entrepreneurial social formations at that time to create a useful heroic pioneer identity for themselves. Hence, in what to us in our episteme may appear to be a rather implausible notion, that the recession of the frontier provided the forces by which the composite nationality of the United States was created, his emplotment nevertheless served at the time important nationalistic ends in a period of cultural crisis. It did this by providing the story of the pioneer-hero – the archetypal individualistic American transmuted into the entrepreneur – whose frontier-inspired powers would eventually resolve the many problems that beset America in the turbulent 1890s. For Turner, history itself became the ultimate metaphor.

The context of Turner's history supports White's contention that the most convincing stories told by historians will be those that echo contemporary cultural myths and beliefs, as they conform to the recognisable and dominant Western story-types of romance, tragedy, comedy and satire. Hence, the story fashioned by the historian tropically prefigures the way in which the traces of the past are connected together through the kinds of figurative reductions or integrations I noted above. The emplotment, for example, is selected as a result of the historian's conception of the power of action of the hero or protagonist over his or its environment. Because, in White's view, no set of historical circumstances is inherently tragic or comic, the emplotment is written by the impositionalist historian as a consequence of imposing a judgement on the nature of the sequence of events encountered by the designated hero or protagonist. The emplotment becomes the vehicle of his/her historical explanation.

In describing events as a romance, the historical emplotment is identified by the historian imagining the power of the historical agent/hero or protagonist as ultimately superior to his or its environment. History emplotted as a romance unfolds as a quest with final success, redemption or transcendence assured. In Western culture this history is usually described as a journey, a struggle, with eventual victory over adversity for the hero or protagonist, whether nation, state, individual, class, or whatever. Emplotment as a satire is the polar opposite to romance in that the agent/hero or protagonist is imagined by the historian as being inferior, a captive of their world, and destined to a life of obstacles and negation. Tragic emplotments are similar to romance in as much as they identify the hero or protagonist as eventually thwarted by fate or their tragic personality flaw. The end result is failure, defeat or death. The fate of the bourgeoisie in Marxian history, for example, is usually cast as a tragic emplotment. In a comic emplotment, movement is imagined from obstruction to reconstruction, and the historian always hopes for at least a temporary victory over circumstance for the hero or protagonist through the process of reconciliation. Festivities at the closure of such historical narratives usually celebrate the coherence and consensus achieved with other men, women, races, nations or classes by the heroic figure.[37]

In addition to the narrative level of emplotment of events, there is another level on which the historian tries to explain 'the point of it all' or 'what it all adds up to', which is explanation by formal argument (formist, mechanistic, organicist and contextualist arguments).[38] Explanation by argument means that as historians we offer to our readers more or less convincing but always commonly accepted laws of historical change or human behaviour upon which we all draw to explain events. The arguments we use relate events, people and actions by the appeal we make to our own thinking processes of dispersion or integration. A formist argument, for example, identifies the unique, atomistic or dispersive character of events, people and actions in the past. Such an argument permits us graphically to represent vivid individual events from which it is possible to make significant generalisations. Thus the winning or losing of great battles or civil wars constitutes the origins of great historical change, or the special lives of great men and women are taken to signify the nature of historical change; a classic form of the latter is the genre of born in poverty to become president, or overcome social disadvantage to rise to statesman, or conquer prejudice to emerge as a race leader. Organicist arguments, which are integrative, allow us to identify past events, people and actions as components of a synthetic process in a microcosmic–macrocosmic relationship whereby a single event or an individual is just one element among many – a factor that goes into making for complex historical change. Mechanistic arguments tend to be reductive rather than synthetic, usually cast in the form of an equivalent part–part relationship, and with which we identify events, people and actions as subject to deterministic extra-historical laws. As the term suggests, contextualist arguments are moderately integrative and are employed by those historians wishing to identify events, people and actions in the past by their presumed connections to others in webs of colligatory relationships within an era, or within a complex process of interconnected change.

A little thought produces many examples of rhetorical constructionism operating as explanatory argument. White himself offers the example of the relationship between Marx's base and superstructure as a classic mechanistic 'law'. According to this 'law', transformations in the economic base ultimately determine changes in the social/ideological superstructure, but the reverse does not occur (part to part). Thus, the tragedy of Marx's mechanistic explanation of historical change lies in the failure of the heroic proletariat to successfully overthrow their bourgeois oppressors in Europe and America in the late nineteenth century. Another rhetorical construction could have it differently, as in the case of the Russian Revolution which might be imagined as a successful romance of proletarian victory. So, historical disputes are less about what did or did not actually happen, and more about how we emplot or invoke 'laws'/social theories to explain the past.

There is, however, the third level in White's formal model of historical explanation, and this final strategy of explanation is the ideological. As White's description suggests, the ideological is the moral implication of our choice of emplotment and argument. Accordingly, in the historical narrative the ideological level projects 'the ethical element in the historian's assumption of a particular position on the question of the nature of historical knowledge and the implications that can be drawn from the study of past events for the understanding of present ones'.[39] In this way White acknowledges the presentism of history and its construction as a contemporary cultural discourse. He acknowledges that no historian can stand aside from history and suspend his/her capacity for or exercise of moral judgement. The nature of our impositionalism means that there are no disinterested historians. White makes this very clear when he defines ideology as a set of 'prescriptions for taking a position in the present world of social praxis and acting upon it (either to change the world or to maintain it in its current state)'. He postulates four basic ideological positions (borrowing from the German philosopher Karl Mannheim) – anarchism, radicalism, conservatism and liberalism. These four basic positions all claim to be rational or scientific in the modernist sense of having to make such claims to the master narrative of science in order to be heard.[40] The ultimately ideological nature of empiricist history lies in the way in which it attempts to make us all read its works as if they were realistic – this is the truth of the matter, or we really must face the facts – and thus we can respond only in certain ways.

In spite of the seemingly pre-eminent or determining power of the troping process, White is unsure that ideology is absolutely the result of form, that is, that the trope ultimately determines ideological positions.[41] At one point he says that the four primary ideological positions are less influenced by troping (between reduction, dispersion and integration) than by the historian's attitude towards what is desirable in the nature and pace of social change, that is, that the historian has a free moral choice unencumbered by the power of figuration, and that, therefore, all four ideological positions in their differences as to the desirability of its direction and pace may be autonomous. Briefly, conservatives are most suspicious of change, the others less so. Conservatives oppose rapid change by supporting the evolutionary elaboration of existing social institutions. Anarchists demand rapid, perhaps even cataclysmic, social change in order to establish a new society. Liberals prefer the fine tuning of society to secure moderately paced social change, while radicals welcome imminent social change, but unlike anarchists are more aware of what White calls the 'inertial pull of inherited institutions' and are, therefore, much more exercised by the means to effect change than are anarchists. All four positions thus carry preferences for the distribution of power and the criteria by which power is exercised. What this means is that the ideology of the historian is refracted through the history he/she writes, and as to the question of ultimate determination – trope or ideology – the answer is always likely to remain disputed.

Nevertheless, White's model is clear that the explanatory historical narrative depends not on the facticity of events for its functioning, but rather upon creating a story, deploying arguments, and taking up moral positions that the reader can follow and understand in shared contemporary cultural terms. Precision in the generation of facts is literally meaningless unless and until those facts (as propositions or events under a description) are turned into stories, explained further with arguments, and offered as sustained and coherent ideological positions. Louis Mink, quoting the literary critic Barbara Hardy, makes an important point in this respect:

Narrative, like lyric or dance, is not to be regarded as an aesthetic invention used by artists to control, manipulate and order experience, but as a primary act of mind transferred to art from life. . . . More important than the artifices of fiction are the qualities which narrative shares with the story-telling of lived experience: 'for we dream in narrative, daydream in narrative, remember, anticipate, hope, despair, believe, doubt, plan, revise, criticise, construct, gossip, learn, hate, and love by narrative'.[42]

Now, although the level of understanding to which narratives aim is for Mink a primary act of mind, he draws back from the final logic of Hardy's position, and here White agrees with his conclusion that

Stories are not lived but told. Life has no beginnings, middles or ends: there are meetings, but the start of an affair belongs to the story we tell ourselves later, and there are partings, but final partings only in the story. There are hopes, plans, battles, and ideas, but only in retrospective stories are hopes unfulfilled, plans miscarried, battles decisive, and ideas seminal. Only in the story is it America which Columbus discovers, and only in the story is the kingdom lost for want of a nail. . . . So it seems truer to say that narrative qualities are transferred from art to life. We could learn to tell stories of our lives from nursery rhymes, or from culture-myths if we had any, but it is from history and fiction that we learn how to tell and to understand *complex* stories, and how it is stories answer questions.[43]

In spite of this anti-narrativist assertion by White, we must at least be permitted to ask once more, is history really only the fiction that historians tell as they order the evidence, or is there not a cultural resonance between history as it is lived and as it is told?

CONCLUSION

According to the formalism of White's tropic model, history is a process of continuous intertextual reinscription composed and conducted by the historian – it is primarily an act of literary creation. Because the character of historical interpretation resides in its narrative structure, historical knowledge is generated by the constant debates between narratives (interpretations) rather than the primeval, uninscripted and uncontextualised traces of the past. F.R. Ankersmit makes the point well with his claim that all we historians have is the 'intertextual' interplay between our historical narratives.[44] All debates in history – who started the Cold War, how successful were the Chartists in achieving their aims, to what extent was the recession of the American frontier culturally significant in American history? – are debates between competing narrative interpretations. Moreover, because the historical imagination itself exists intertextually within our own social and political environment, the past is never discovered in a world set aside from everyday life. History is designed and composed in the here and now.

Whether the impositionalism of the historian is ultimately structured by ideology or trope is impossible to determine by either the evidence or criticism. The historian's position may be morally and/or rhetorically inflected. What is important, however, is that the historical imagination is both a lightning rod and a conductor of culture, past and present. Alongside the tropically prefigured epistemic model of cultural formation provided by Michel Foucault, White's formalist theory of historical narrative offers a morphology for the study of the past. Agreeing with White that historical understanding as derived from evidence lies not at the level of individual referential statement but in its emplotted arrangement, leaves open the question that in the past there may have been dominant and tropically constituted epistemic narrative structures that mediated the nature of historical change. This leads me to the conclusion that the real poverty of empiricism resides in its strenuous refusal to acknowledge the power of figuration in the narrativisation of the past as exercised then as well as later by the historian. The implications of this contention for the deconstructive consciousness forms the basis of my summary in the concluding chapter.

9 Conclusion

INTRODUCTION

In this book I have asked how can what the content of the past means be influenced by the form of its presentation? I pursued this by asking four key questions about epistemology, evidence, social theory and narrative. My thoughts on these questions were facilitated by describing the three dominant current approaches towards the historical enterprise, the twin tendencies of empiricist reconstructionism and social theory constructionism, and what I have characterised as deconstructionism. Each offers a distinctive methodological orientation towards the four questions. As we have seen, the three methodological orientations not only signpost the complexities and varieties of historical method available today, but they also reveal the fundamental differences among historians over the nature and roles of objectivity, explanation, truth, description and meaning in historical understanding.

The deconstructive historical consciousness does not suggest that, because we cannot have a direct and unalloyed access to the actuality of the past, history must be characterised as either a purely mental or purely linguistic entity. We can still talk about the past and what we think happened in it. But what I have proposed is that, despite the closest scrutiny of the evidence, and in the absence of a direct correspondence to the reality of the past, the way in which history is interpreted and reported as a narrative is of primary importance to the acquisition and character of our historical knowledge. While it is unproblematic to accept that the reality of the past once existed, it is also reasonable to argue that we cannot gain access to it solely or even primarily through the empirical method. Deconstructionist historians doubt whether we can *really* know the past *as it actually happened* by following the six points of the mainstream charter. This is not anti-history, but is a conception of history as what it palpably is: a self-conscious narrative composition written in the here and now that recognises its literary form as its essential cognitive medium, and not merely its mode of report. Following on from this I have asked if the past itself was constituted as a narrative by people in the course of their lived experience, a process that may be imprinted in the evidence. I have, therefore, questioned the degree to which historians discover the past, or can choose to write either *the* past, or *a* past, in the shape of *the* story, or *a* story. This led to my contention that we must always distinguish the past from history. My understanding of the importance of the form of history to the nature of historical change, as well as the historian's account of it, I examined by reference to the strategic combination of Michel Foucault's conception of the epistemic/tropic social infrastructure, and Hayden White's formalistic model of the historical imagination.[1] I will now move to the implications for the discipline of history of this rethinking of its nature.

EPISTEMOLOGY

In our postmodern millennial climate of doubt and dispute many things once held to be certain are questioned, and, among many other things, the empirical grand narrative is not exempt from this interrogation. Specifically, deconstructionist history focuses the growing objection of many historians and critical thinkers on Western thought's modernist belief in the representational or correspondence theory linking the word and the world.[2] Although the philosopher of history Louis Mink has argued that to explain historical events does not now depend on any supreme model of explanation, whether empiricist, covering law or, for that matter, deconstructionist, the main development in the philosophy of history in the past generation has surely been the proposal that history's primary cognitive device may reside in its power of narration.[3] Until relatively recently few history texts were so epistemologically self-referential as to draw deliberate attention to their rhetorical form, preferring instead to foreground the presumed reality behind it. Consequently, texts like Emmanuel Le Roy Ladurie's *Montaillou*, Carlo Ginzburg's *The Cheese and Worms*, Natalie Zemon Davis's *The Return of Martin Guerre*, Simon Schama's *Dead Çertainties* and his recent *Landscape and Memory* are regarded as exemplars of a new historical genre because they draw attention to themselves either through their content as studies of the trivial, the anecdotal, the apparently historically marginal, or in respect of their form, as illustrations of where history transgresses the border into fiction through the particular ways in which they organise the content of the past.[4]

Books like these do not purport to refer to the truth of the past which we can know objectively through the forensic study of the evidence. As Natalie Zemon Davis said, her book was intended to question the point at which history ceases to be reconstruction and becomes invention, concluding that she chose to advance her arguments 'as much by the ordering of narrative, choice of detail, literary voice, and metaphor as by topical analysis'.[5] It is at this point that the historian disobeys the traditional rules by replacing the authority of the source with the form of its organisation. Through this the past is liberated because it is no longer the captive of the reconstructionist–constructionist intellectual establishment. Postmodern or deconstructionist history converges no longer on the past as such, but on the disjuncture between pastness and presentness. The historian from the conservative reconstructionist mainstream is an empiricist who believes in a knowable historical reality independent of the mind of the historian – subject and object are separated just as mind and knowledge are presumed to be. The text is there merely to convey, as explicitly as possible, the meaning of the past. However, all texts conceal the past through the ideologically inflected intentionality of the author-historian. Instead of being there but not examined, the text is now the focus for our study of the past. This does not mean, as Derrida would have us believe, that there is nothing beyond the text, for the text is not the end of history, it is the beginning.

The deconstructionist historian is always uncertain about history. Although it may be difficult to overcome old historians' habits, it is not essential to establish either teleological or total explanations. In objection to the certaintist and naturalistic myths of reconstructionist-contextualist empiricism, or the empirically founded social theorising of constructionists, the deconstructive awareness of history's invented nature does not allow that *the past* and *history* are the same. That there are no natural links, only assumed epistemological ones, between real events in the past and the way in which we describe them is the force of F.R. Ankersmit's contention that history is best viewed through the perspective of a narrativist rather than an epistemological philosophy of history.[6]

The past does not dwell 'out there', with an existence independent of the historian and his/her use of language. If this is so, say reconstructionists, how can we tell good from bad history and without the transcendent benchmark of empiricism, the anchors of factualism and the forensic study of the evidence, are we not adrift in a sea of relativism? How can we trust the history we read? Posing such questions reveals much about the methodological limits to empiricism. Such worries announce the reconstructionist's uncited investment in the trope of the real. Many, hopefully most, historians today would not accept Gertrude Himmelfarb's argument, derived from philosophical realism, that our impositionalism must mean that we construct the past without any sense of what is morally right just because we do not know what is true. This is a bleak argument that does not do justice to the dissenting and questioning nature of much historiography.

The challenge mounted by Barthes and Derrida to the referential relationship of the word and the world has formed a part of the broader objections of the likes of White, Megill, LaCapra, Jenkins, Ankersmit, Kellner, Rüsen and Foucault to the traditional paradigms. Unlike Himmelfarb, these critics refuse the Baconian belief that we can gain entrance to the Real World of the Past through the bits of reality scattered through the archives. Instead of the presumption of getting closer to the evidence, and hence through it to the truth of what actually happened, an alternative historical understanding is offered. This deconstructive epistemology recognises the existence of the reality-effect rather than the fantasy notion of historical truth, denies that we can discover the intentionality of the author, accepts chains of interpretative signification rather than recoverable original meaning, refuses the seductions of the easy referent, disputes the objectivity of the historian as he/she works within the figurative structure of narrative, accepts the sublime nature of the past imagined as a sense of 'the other', and admits that the form and content relationship is more complex than many in the twin main tendencies often allow.

In 1990 the Africanist historian Elizabeth Tonkin, in pursuit of the multiple voices of the past, claimed no longer to use the word 'history', preferring the term 'representations of pastness' because, as she understands the nature of historical knowledge, histories are simply chains of words 'either spoken or written, ordered in patterns of discourse that represent events'. She continued: 'Arguments and opinions too are forms of words. When we grasp a historical fact or interpretation, we have ourselves made an extremely complex set of interpretations to do so.'[7] The deconstructive consciousness makes us epistemologically aware that the way in which we metaphorically prefigure, organise, emplot, explain and make moral judgements about the past is our only access to it. If the reader is persuaded by the general approach of the historian, accepts his/her practices and his/her methodological orientation, then no detectable gap exists between reader, text and understanding. If the linguistic customs and conventions employed by the historian, and shared with the reader, are those of reconstructionism, then again there is no detectable fissure between the historical account and what is *believed* to have actually happened. Either way, the historian has to tap into the epistemological assumptions of his/her readership. If historical explanation does not work within one or more of the common intellectual currencies of the present in which it is written, it can never explain anything to anyone.

White's primary contention that history is a rhetorical construction of the historian, as much invented as found, means the past as it actually happened must ultimately be unknowable. Rather than being able to grasp the past's real meaning as it is objectively filtered through the mesh of the evidence by the historian, and which is then absorbed by the reader, deconstructionist history stresses the interactive and impositionalist role of the historian, so that whatever knowledge we have of the past is provided not only by the past itself, but by the tropically prefigured, emplotted, argued and ideologically positioned narrative of the historian. The question remains, however, in spite of White's insistence that the past is not inherently emplotted, that if Foucault's trope–episteme link does exist, then is there an ultimate determination in history to be located as historians tell stories about the past? The universe of contemporary cultural and linguistic experience shared by historians is the ultimate epistemological constraint on not only what can be written as history, but how it is written.

EVIDENCE

I do not doubt that the past once existed, and that evidence of it remains in our present. However, the intractable epistemological problem of never knowing the past as it actually was, because all we can do is infer meaning through its traces, emphasises the need to readdress the mainstream working assumption of an adequate correspondence between evidence and the truthful knowledge of the past. This doubt informs my answer to the question: what is the character of historical evidence and what function does it perform? The naïve empiricist position, which necessarily assumes the existence of objective and judicial historians separated from the evidence, who keep their minds free from *a priori* assumptions, who avoid questions that beg answers, and who apply to the evidence forensic procedures for the critical evaluation of the evidence, is now more widely disputed than ever before.

I have tried to show how it is the reconstructionist belief that 'truth' corresponds to past reality via the mechanisms of referentiality and inductive inference (which I summarised as the six points or principles of the empiricist charter), which prompts historians like McCullagh, Elton, Stanford and Marwick to argue that historical truth can be discovered

by recovering the intentionality of the author of the evidence. This position, as developed but not rejected by reconstructionist moderates like
Kloppenberg, Appleby, Hunt, Jacob and Gordon, means that they seek
out *the* story that most faithfully represents *the* truth which can and
must eventually be found in *the* past through the undisputed factual
detail of past events. While they acknowledge narrative as the medium
for this empiricist reconstruction of the past, its power to invent is stren-
uously denied. Historians serve the evidence under all circumstances.
The same thinking applies to deductive social science theorising, so
much so that both deconstructionism and constructionism are viewed as
unnatural acts going against the grain of evidence-based historical
methodology.

We should by now be familiar with the Elton argument that history
is what results from the evidence as interrogated by the disinterested and
independent historian who, in asking appropriately framed questions,
remains particularly sceptical about paradigms of explanation proposed by both social theorists as well as deconstructionists. Among the
consequences assumed to flow from this method is not only the generation of incontestable facts derived from the discovery of the
intentionality of the author of the evidence, but also the emergence of
clear distinctions between history and value, fact and fiction.
Constructionist theories of history are thus rejected by hard-core reconstructionists because of the injuries they do to the relics of the past as
they are forced into strange shapes dictated by the needs of the hypotheses to be tested, and, as Elton has it, invariably confirmed. For both
conservative and mainstream historians the ultimate defence against
what is proclaimed as the relativism of deconstructionism resides in
the practice of *Quellenkritik* – the technical and detailed study of the
sources through the process of verification, comparison and colligation.

In the past half century, however, under E.H. Carr's influential vision
of history that the past is always imperfectly encountered, most practical realist or moderate mainstream historians have had little difficulty in
accepting what they call the provisional nature of their interpretations
and that proof and truth do not exist in history. This translates readily
into historical revisionism. The provisional nature of all historical interpretation rests on the continuous process of discovering new evidence,
treating it with increasingly sophisticated mechanisms of analysis and
conceptualisation, and constantly recontextualising it so that, for example, the evidence of Empire becomes, for the next generation of
historians, the evidence for a new post-colonial interpretation. Although
this happens, the available evidence is, of course, still believed to provide
a window on past reality. While new evidence always offers new win-

dows, revisionist views will still correspond to the reality found beyond the new windows. Revisionist constructions placed on the historical facts do not, therefore, destroy the knowability of past reality. Even given Collingwood–Carr relativism, the ultimate claim of reconstructionism remains intact, that *the* past is knowable through the evidence, and remains knowable even as it is constituted into *the* narrative, for it is then that we get to *the* story or true description of the past. For mainstreamers the aim remains to get ever closer to the *truest* possible description.

My response to this vision of the existence of a knowable historical reality has been to question the empiricist belief that the explanatory value of the evidence increases the more we turn up the magnification on the *Quellenkritik* microscope. I have submitted that it does not follow that the closer to the evidence we get, the more we see of the truth. I have not disputed that the correspondence of evidence with reality works reasonably satisfactorily at the basic level of the single sentence supported by the evidence (US President Abraham Lincoln was shot on 14 April and died in the early morning of 15 April 1865). But, such correspondence does not exist when we shift a gear to the level of interpretation through the imposition of an emplotment or argument (Abraham Lincoln was assassinated before he could put his reconstruction plans into effect). It bears repetition. the historical narrative is not *the* past, it is *a* history. While it may be possible to demonstrate a strong, even a probable correspondence between a single statement about the past and a single piece of evidence, sufficient to generate a factual statement, to then translate this inductive 'truth' to a whole historical interpretative narrative, so as to recover the past as it actually was, is a flawed practice.

That evidence does not correspond with past reality at the interpretative level makes discovering authorial intentionality particularly problematic. To argue, like Elton, that the detached historian can understand the intentions of people in the past by asking why did the evidence come into existence, displays an extraordinary level of artlessness. The innate imprecision of inductive inference ought to warn off all historians from such a belief, but clearly does not. Claiming to seek *the* truth inferentially may be psychologically and professionally satisfying, but it is always intellectually dangerous, and no more so than when someone believes they are getting ever closer to it, or have found it. The steel trap of certainty then closes over the inquiring mind. Always to doubt and to question is to welcome the inherently discontinuous nature of the writing of the past – a position that may lead to a more encompassing form of historical analysis that is less likely to close off the marginalised and the 'other'.

The most thoughtful and mature appreciation of what constitutes mainstream history today is to be found in the work of the historians like Appleby, Hunt and Jacob who argue that their commitment to the study of the evidence is to discover the truth of (in their case) a pluralistic and multicultural American history that will necessarily reinforce (what they choose to believe is) America's essential democratic heritage. That is their view of real American history, and so be it. But to cast it as part of the search for *the* ultimate truth of *the* American historical experience, especially when such a search is undertaken and described as part of a self-styled practical realist perspective, is clearly an ideologically freighted conception produced by their social, political, and intellectual agenda. This is not, of course, problematic if practical realism with, in this case, its multicultural objective is acknowledged to be just another set of ideological positions as represented in their narrative. Their book title, *Telling the Truth About History*, suggests that they are mustering an arbitrarily contextualised, constructed and historicised narrative which imposes a particular set of signifying relationships on the past. Appleby, Hunt and Jacob do in fact recognise their presentist agenda in their attack on deconstructionist history with their claim that it is 'The legacy of Cold War science . . . [that] helps explain the cynicism, even nihilism, and certainly the intellectual relativism, that greet even the mention of truth and objectivity.'[8] So for them it seems that empirically derived truth remains transcendental, while the deconstructionist questioning of its truth-value and reality-effect is epistemic and presumably transient, a product in this case of the psychologically destabilising effects of the Cold War. That this may or may not be unfair is one thing, but what is important is that we always bear in mind that they are telling us their version of the truth about history.

The historicisation of *Telling the Truth About History* is a clear example of Foucault's argument that the past imagined as history exists only in the contemporary discourses of historians. History remains a construction, whether it is viewed as a rhetorical representation or as empirically tested social theorising. Books with a claim to historical truth, like *Telling the Truth About History*, confirm my doubts about anyone's ability to interpret and contextualise evidence as if in an ideology-free 'clean room'. As I have attempted to demonstrate in this book, the historian's dialogue with his/her evidence cannot be undertaken through an objective, non-intertextual, non-figurative and value-free medium. As David Harlan has suggested, this leaves us with as many different kinds of histories and methods as there are kinds of historical writing. And, as Foucault and White have suggested, the reasons for

constructing the form of history in a particular way are usually ideologically inspired.

As Foucault argued in his genealogical analysis of the treatment of
the insane and the exercise of power over the human body, history is a
central discourse instancing and ratifying the exercise of power.
History's authority is at its most potent when, in the hands of disinterested historians, it professes to reveal the objective truth of the past as
it actually was. What such history does in pursuit of this assertion is
represent a version of the past through what White called the shaping of
language *and* cultural self-interest. How the evidence is translated or
narrated into the historian's facts is basic to the exercise of power –
what White has designated the 'terminological determinism' of the figures of speech.[9] This fundamental inability of historians to get to *the*
truth of the evidence is not, indeed, a debilitating experience, instead it
permits a space to open up that cannot be so easily colonised for ideological purposes. Uncertainty in history is a form of protection against
what is politically right, wrong, correct or incorrect. Political certainty
is, I would suggest, always suspect. The deconstructionive consciousness
position that history is not a summary of the truth that emerges from
the evidence will upset only a few particularly naïve historians. But few
in the mainstream would accept that when we write history we are creating a verbal/textual fictive artifact generating what I have called a
historical truth – the reality or truth-effect. They would not accept that
the reality of the past resides in the truth-effect or plausibility of the
stories they tell as history, but would insist that the evidence must
remain the ultimate and absolute measure of the facts.

THEORIES OF HISTORY: CONSTRUCTING THE PAST

On the question of the construction of social (or rhetorical) frameworks with which to interrogate the evidence, the deconstructive
consciousness recognises this as the impositionalism of the historian.
The suspicions of naïve empiricists about critical approaches to historical understanding are amply demonstrated in their antipathy towards
idealist and relativist philosophers of history like Collingwood, Croce,
Beard, Becker and E.H. Carr, as well as innumerable deterministic
social, cultural and Marxist-inspired constructionist historians, but
most recently to narrativists ranging from Michel Foucault, Hayden
White and Dominick LaCapra to Louis Mink and Frank Ankersmit.
The common link between these relativist historians is their assumption
not only that they are in an interrogative dialogue with evidence but that
they are directly interventionist. In their different ways, all recognise

that the past *becomes* history *only* when it is construed through the filter of the historian's strategies of explanation. As a general position, mainstream historians accept the relativism inherent in constructionism, short of taking it to its deconstructionist conclusion that effectively abandons the foundation of empiricism.

Constructionists understand past events through a variety of methods, econometric and statistical, employing anthropological and sociological deductive–inductive generalisations as covering laws, even Collingwood's empathic rethinking of the past. While for reconstructionists the evidence offers up the truth through the examination of its fine detail, for positivists it is prised out through the leverage of appropriate theory. For the mainstream, these two extremes have been compromised by E.H. Carr's popular but, from the deconstructive perspective, unconvincing view that while it is historians who write history and create models of explanation, they do so according to the dictates of the evidence. Carr's method means that the continuous process of rapid shifting between text and context is always informed by the structures and patterns, offered up as the theories/models/concepts of class, race, gender, and so forth, that are to be found/discovered in the evidence. For E.H. Carr the evidence suggests certain appropriate explanatory models of human behaviour which will then allow for ever more truthful historical explanation. Most historians in the mainstream would likely accept this description of what they do.

Because, however, the demarcation between where empiricism ends and hypothesis testing begins is usually too hard to calculate, and increasingly we accept as reasonable that historians are always active in the creation of the past through model-building, then why is it unreasonable to take into account our prefigured narrative emplotments, arguments and their ideological implications? Although hard-core reconstructionists in particular always maintain that moral decisions have no place in the objective reconstruction of the past, I would contend that because no history is written that is free from prefigured emplotment and argument, or moral and ethical positioning, a fuller understanding of the past can emerge only when the impositionalist role of the historian is *fully* appreciated as being that of an author rather than that of a reporter.

Empirically founded constructionism today encompasses many new modes of analysis and conceptualisations acquired from cognate disciplines like sociology and anthropology. John Tosh's description of history as the product of hypotheses to be 'tested against the evidence' attests to the complexities of mainstream history today. But history has burst the banks of the mainstream as many practitioners try to bridge fact and fiction by borrowing analytical techniques from literary critical theory and by viewing history as a literary genre. Although cast as worries, the comments of Lawrence Stone are more than adequate evidence for this development. Rather than a cause for concern, it seems to me that historians should move in this direction, especially given Philippe Carrard's recognition that not even the most positivist-inspired constructionist historians can escape the power of narrative and emplotment – writing without tropes is hard to do.[10]

As I have tried to explain, the emphasis on the constitutive role of the historian's narrative derives from our insights into the nature of language and the arbitrary nature of the sign. Historical narrative depends more on rhetorical rather than logical argument, working as it does by collapsing the link between signifier and referent to produce the illusion of language transparently representing or corresponding with the events of the past, and thus showing them in their 'true light'. The models that we construct are similarly produced. It is at this point that Hayden White's tropically prefigured model of historical narrative assumes its significance. Once we do away with the notion of the unclouded connection of the word and the world, and view it as the trope of realism, we can start to appreciate the importance of the narrative strategies that White suggests enable historical interpretation.

Where deconstructionism parts company with constructionism is in the latter's positivist insistence that it is possible to relate and understand discrete events only by reference to a grand narrative of explanation like a covering law, or generalisations about human behaviour that generally hold in given material situations or contexts. In this sense, constructionist *a priorism* elicits as little conviction in the deconstructionist mind as it does in that of the reconstructionist. Constructionists are effectively claiming that truth emerges *more realistically* through their particular empirically derived social theory than it does through the reconstructionist recovery of fine detail, or, for that matter, through the deconstructionist preoccupation with the truth- or reality-effects of narratives. In spite of his early flirtation with the *Annales* school, Foucault's intention to undermine logocentrism was, I have argued, eventually exemplified in his model of the rhetorically and socially constructed episteme. It was his aim to locate the means by which knowledge is produced linguistically within society. His search turned him towards the historical rules of social change. In doing this, unlike most historians who view change over time as the discovery of the linear or diachronic unfolding of a coherent narrative or interconnected process, Foucault views it as a network or synchronic structure of power relationships, the aim of which is to create knowledge, and in particular historical knowledge. As he insists, history is not about factual discovery but about the literary and textual creation of knowledge for the purpose of the exercise of power, or to counter such exercise as a form of literary dissent. In this sense we historians, like the literary critic, or any overtly committed intellectual, are entangled in the webs of signification that we and society have created – historical knowledge is always implicated in discourse and culture.

Foucault, like White, draws on the tradition of Vico and assumes that historical change results from the interaction of human consciousness with its social and natural context, and this makes literary and cultural artifacts, such as our written history, little more than the hindsight rationalisations of human beings interacting in social situations. This original insight of Vico, built on the incapacity of humanity ever to understand fully the natural world as well as we can know our own social creations, has inspired much social science theorising. But the positivism of the majority of constructionist historians, particularly stage theorists like Marxists, effectively ignores Vico's insight that history, as a literary art, necessitates a distinctive conceptual approach to the analysis of past social and human phenomena, quite different to the deductivism that characterises the study of their natural or social worlds.

Like Vico, White and Foucault both accept the creative power of language. The complex manner in which we use language and language uses us to mediate past reality suggests that no amount of sophisticated social science hypothesis-testing can avoid the interactive relationship between the historian, the word and the world. Narrative is not simply the representation of the world of past reality, a reproduction of things and the relations subsisting between them. While language is used by mainstream historians as if it were capable of reproduction, it is primarily an innovative medium that has the power to invent and create our knowledge of the past. Both White and Foucault, like Vico before them, have found this explanatory power of narrative in its metaphoric or troping nature.

NARRATIVE

I have argued in favour of narrative as history's primary cognitive device working in the mind of the historian as he/she imagines, shapes and represents the past. The emplotment of history as a story, with its supporting arguments and ethical strategies of explanation, is a highly complex form of explanation of historical change, but it is not history as it actually happened. How the past is configured hangs on the historian's capacity to match a type of emplotment with the historical events that he/she wishes to furnish with a meaning of a particular kind. Narrative explanation is more than recording a flow of events in their order of occurrence. Lemon's definition, 'this happened, and *then* that', signals the sophisticated level of interpretation that is rapidly entailed beyond mere sequencing. The historian's function, noted by Gallie as the essence of historical understanding, is to offer a story that is followable. Such followability emerges when the stories that historians tell are coherent and appear plausible in the light of the available evidence. The reality of the past does not already exist in the unhewn marble, requiring only the historian's skill to chip away to reveal the object existing within. This is certainly White's position, but we can again pose the question: is there a narrative in the past to be retold?

Even though Collingwood and E.H. Carr admitted the existence of a constant interplay between the historian and the events described, they were still ultimately unwilling to accept that the resulting history was primarily a fictive enterprise. For them and others, more recently Richard T. Vann, White's argument that history is a tropically prefigured literary artifact, a story as much invented as found, remains unacceptable because without the anchor of a determining meaning to be discovered in the evidence, facts cannot emerge and there is no standard against which the truth of those facts can be measured. They take to heart Louis Mink's comment 'if alternative emplotments are based only on preference for one poetic trope rather than another, then no way remains for comparing one narrative structure with another in respect of their truth claims as narratives'.[11] But accepting Mink's argument must not blind us to the problematic nature of our enterprise. The fundamental empiricist tenet that the truth is 'out there' remains the basic flaw in our understanding of what it is we do, and how we do it. History as a written discourse is not indifferent to the forces that create the past. Because the past is irrecoverable, its secondary written record is at least as important to our historical understanding as the evidence of the past itself. Our only access to the past is through the imaginative narrative and the intellectual operations registered in the tropes, the theory of which provides us with a radical and promising basis for categorising the historical imagination in any given episteme.[12]

The human troping capacity is complex. I have indicated how tropes operate in the imaginations of historians by reductions and integrations to represent the nature of change in the past. The important point of Foucault's historical method is the way in which he takes the tropological foundation to human consciousness as a model through which to evaluate how history emerges from the exchange between reality and language, or, as White describes the relationship, between 'transitions in societies and the tropological transformations of speech'.[13] In this fashion it seems reasonable to me to argue that narrative, as the linguistic medium of human consciousness, may facilitate historical change over time, not merely our description of it. Taken together, Foucault and White offer the figurative process as a model through which historical change is lived *and* can be explained.

I have argued that because it is the tropological model of narrative that frames the interpretation of the evidence, rather than the other way round, historical understanding is as much the product of literary artifice as it is a knowable historical reality. The rejection of the correspondence theory does not mean that we are completely free to select any tropic–emplotment–argument–ideological configuration for the evidence, and then proceed to some ultimate historical version of literary deconstruction that allows any meaning to be imposed on the past while declaiming any responsibility for it. What we have instead is a recognition that there is a substantial degree of reciprocity between the mental prefigurative process and the evidence, in as much as each narrativised piece of evidence is already an intertext that has previously been interpreted and textualised by other historians working within the archive and their episteme. No historian can work in ignorance of previous interpretations or emplotments of the archive.

Naïve realism does not take sufficient notice of the great power of language to describe and invent. Empiricism necessarily sells history short. As White says, language 'used to describe a field of historical occurrences in effect constitutes the field itself' and, therefore, limits the kind of methods that can be used 'to analyse the events occurring within the field'.[14] That this great power of language resides in its metaphoric and figurative (tropological) structure can be understood through an illustration. Comparing Theodore Roosevelt, upon his return from big game hunting in Africa in 1910, with Halley's Comet is a legitimate historical interpretation, from which we infer that Roosevelt was akin to a spectacular force of nature (technically this is a synecdoche used to signify Roosevelt's quality of character). But, while this description explains and interprets Roosevelt, it in no way ties the language that the historian uses to the events discussed.[15] There is no natural correspondence between Theodore Roosevelt and a comet. In the course of employing this image, the historian vividly paints a picture of Roosevelt that brings him to life and places him within his context (Halley's Comet appeared in 1910). It also evidences White's view that the historical narrative 'does not *image* the thing it indicates; it *calls to mind* images of the things it indicates'.[16] In other words, the metaphor cannot constitute a genuine image of the object it aspires to describe, and offers instead a cognitive map for the reader to find the appropriate (and explanatory) associative images. Comparing Teddy Roosevelt to Halley's Comet is not referential nor less mimetic, but it remains meaningful *because* of its poetic character. The reality-effect takes over – not to subvert reality but to create meaning.

The influence of deconstructionist history is seen today in the wide acceptance that the past, as written history, is a textual product of its age, and, given the central organising role of the historian, is inevitably inflected by presentist ideological demands and the current dispensations of power. It is increasingly accepted that the historian, through his/her narrative description, is fully implicated in any written representation of pastness. Few see history as a matter of following the evidence like footprints in the sands of time towards truth. More and more historians today feel much happier asking not just how did historical actors understand their own lives and events which shaped them, but how can those observer-historians build again their subjective world-views and explain their actions? Where the mainstream diverges from deconstructionism is not over the fact that history is concerned primarily with debates between narrative interpretations, but over the deconstructionist insistence that objectivity is impossible to achieve. The mainstream will not take that deconstructionist step that offers 'Man' (his actions, thoughts, behaviour, decisions) as being what history is about; the historian inevitably and unavoidably must give it a form or shape by inventing, for example, the proletarian, the 'de-natured woman', 'the origins of American Revivalism', 'a century of war', '1921: the end of Soviet idealism', the post-colonial 'other', the first industrial nation, the Third American Revolution, the Age of Equipoise, the Uncle Tom race leader, or the father of the nation. All these are objects created by the historical imagination because it seemingly cannot capture and reproduce past realities. As Megill points out, no amount of empiricist flag-waving can deny that written history requires a discursive form of interpretation, what Ankersmit calls the constitution of a linguistic object, and White the 'poetical understructure' of written history.

CONCLUSION

So, to return to the question I posed at the outset: to what extent is history, as a discipline, the accurate recovery and representation of the content of the past, through its popular form of the narrative? My answer has been that as a vehicle for historical explanation the adequacy of its narrative structure must be judged within the wider postmodern critique of the nature of meaning and language. The overarching implication is that history can be no more, nor less, than a representation of pastness. Such a conception explicitly rejects written history primarily as an empirical discipline that purports objectively to represent a presumed past historical reality. The issue is the nature of representation, not the empirical research process as such. The problem is to warn against the belief that we can truly know the reality of the past through its textual representation. There is still a strong tendency for history in its narrative form to become more real than the reality, like America's frontier experience represented through the frontier thesis of Frederick Jackson Turner. To Americans this history became so important as a metaphor for American individualism and democracy that it took on an essential but wholly mythic dimension. As the history text becomes more real than the past itself, all the traditional notions of truth, referentiality and objectivity, which, paradoxically, gave rise to its status as historical truth, fade.

The past is not discovered or found. It is created and represented by the historian as a text, which in turn is consumed by the reader. Traditional history is dependent for its power to explain like the statue pre-existing in the marble, or the *trompe l'œil* principle. But this is not the only history we can have. By exploring how we represent the relationship between ourselves and the past we may see ourselves not as detached observers of the past but, like Turner, participants in its creation. The past is complicated and difficult enough without the self-deception that the more we struggle with the evidence the closer we get to the past. The idea of the truth being rediscovered in the evidence is a nineteenth-century modernist conception and it has no place in contemporary writing about the past.

Glossary

A priori **knowledge**   A term popular in philosophy that assumes knowledge to be independent of experience.

Argument   A set of premises and the conclusion drawn or inferred from them. An argument is said to be valid (not the same as true) if the conclusion follows either **inductively** or deductively from the premise(s).

Cliometrics   The application of mathematics and statistics to the data of the past in order to facilitate interpretation. Popular in the 1960s, especially in economic history, but somewhat in decline in the 1990s.

Colligation   In history, the process of explaining an event by bringing together a set of otherwise apparently separate events under a general description or principle, e.g. the inventions of the eighteenth and nineteenth centuries under the description of the revolution in scientific thought. The process is similar, but not identical, to **emplotment** which identifies a pattern in the sequence of events. For historians who reject the notion of emplotment in favour of colligation, its outcome is usually assumed to be the more or less accurate **reconstruction** of the past as history, because of the identification of causes. The danger is that historians may be tempted to be too tidy in relating events, although reconstructionist historians would argue that creating meaning through the **context** avoids such difficulties.

Constructionism   The requirement of historians to propose rather than discover relationships between events in the past. In the twentieth century constructionism is most clearly found in the Marxist school which offers the construct of class exploitation as *the* model for historical understanding. The *Annales* school also produced a constructionist history that suggested alternative demographic and behavioural theories. Constructionist historians are to be clearly distinguished from the other two major categories of **reconstructionists** and **deconstructionists**.

Context   In history, the background to the events described, knowledge of which assists in the creation of meaning. In practice the context is the framework of other **facts**, events and preceding circumstances.

Correspondence theory of truth   The **argument** that propositions are true when they correspond with the facts. Although it is often difficult to establish what is factual, the commonsense idea of a correspondence (or reflection) between the word and world remains for many historians in the **reconstructionist** mainstream an attractive, if increasingly disputed, notion.

Covering laws   A model for historical explanation (directly related to establishing causes) developed by the American philosopher of history Carl Hempel (1905–), and founded on the insistence that an event may be explained when it is capable of being deduced from a law of nature or human behaviour. Very often its form is that of statistical probability.

Death of the author   Derived from the deconstructive study of literature originating with Roland Barthes (1915–1980) and employed extensively by Michel Foucault (1926–1984) that suggests that all texts precede their authors who are simply constructs who cannot privilege meaning. For the deconstructionist historian **evidence** does not denote a discoverable past reality as found in author intentionality, but offers instead only chains of significations and interpretations.

Deconstructionism   A term originating with Jacques Derrida (1930–) that suggests that understanding texts is not solely or exclusively dependent upon reference to the external reality of **empiricism**, God, reason, morality, objectivity or author intentionality (see **Death of the author**). This **logocentric** notion of an originating source of absolute meaning is disputed in favour of the assumption that meaning is arbitrary and figuratively produced.

Deconstructionist history   In history, a model of study that questions the traditional assumptions of **empiricism** couched as factualism, disinterested analysis, objectivity, truth, and the continuing division between history, **ideology**, fiction and perspective. Instead, deconstructionist history accepts that language constitutes history's content as well as the concepts and categories deployed to order and explain historical **evidence** through our linguistic power of figuration.

Determinism The notion that historical processes are structured according to forces beyond individual or group choice or influence, so that in effect all events are unexceptionably effects determined by prior events. The most famous example is the Marxian model which insists that history is the result of the class struggle.

Difference/*différance* Term coined by deconstructionist philosopher Jacques Derrida (1930–) as a play on the French verb 'différer' which means to differ and defer. The consequent slide of meaning as between signs means that we cannot distinguish a true or original point of meaning – there is no original site of meaning. A central **argument** in **post-structuralism**.

Discourse The result of the placement or insertion of a text (usually longer than a simple sentence) into its **context** so that it derives a coherent meaning shared by both author(s) and reader(s). As a shared language terrain, a discourse has reference to extra-linguistic dimensions as found in the material and ideological worlds of institutional and economic power.

Empathy Usually associated with the historical method espoused by the British historian R.G. Collingwood (1889–1943) in *The Idea of History* (1936), it means the state of being 'in touch with' the thoughts and situation of the historical agent. The route to this emotional and intellectual state is to interpret the historical **evidence** by literally rethinking the thoughts of people in the past within their known **context**. For many **reconstructionist** historians it is the empathic linkage of evidence and context that constitutes history. See also **hermeneutics**.

Empiricism The method whereby knowledge is gained through the use of the senses as we observe and experience life, or through statements or **arguments** demonstrated to be true. In the Anglo-American tradition of writing **reconstructionist** history, empiricism has been the central methodology with a particular insistence on the corollary of the objective observation of the reality to be discovered 'out there'. The problem usually encountered by empiricism is that thought does not simply emerge from experience, but actually provides us with concepts or mental categories that we utilise to organise and make sense of our experience. This inevitably leads to the question: how can we truly know the reality 'out there', given that our observations may well be only constructions of our mind or intuition? Most empiricists and moderate or practical realist **reconstructionists** today accept a middle position, that we observe but we also mentally process information, deploying *a priori* **knowledge** as appropriate and helpful. Empiricism can, of course, take the form of a denial of *a priori* **knowledge**.

Emplotment   The meaning of any historical or more overtly fictional **narrative** is provided by the emplotment (story line or plot structure), i.e. a narrative of events and their causal, **contextual** or **colligatory** connections. It is the role of the historian to turn a sequence of events (this happened, then that) into a story of a particular kind – romantic, comic, tragic or satiric, or some combination. Dependent upon the methodological inclination of the historian, the emplotment is produced with the intention of discovering *the* meaning or imposing *a* meaning on the events. All histories have emplotments.

Enlightenment (the)   A widespread intellectual, cultural and technological/scientific movement, being the seedplot of the Modern Era. It began in the early seventeenth century in England (with Francis Bacon, John Locke and Thomas Hobbes) and ended at the close of the eighteenth in France and Germany (with Descartes, Voltaire, Diderot and Lessing), but was found throughout Europe. European thought was characterised in what was a time of great technological and scientific change by an acceptance of new concepts like **positivism** and experimentation in science, by the close observation of natural phenomena, reason and rationality promoting explanation, by new ideas concerning government through contract rather than force (based on the emerging doctrine of Liberalism with its central tenets of popular sovereignty and equality of opportunity), and by a new conception of the marketplace as a rational economic mechanism. Its impact on history is seen in its very creation as a discipline founded on the belief that it was the record of progress and human perfectibility. Perhaps inevitably the thought it generated eventually turned in on itself, promoting a questioning of its own central tenets in succeeding centuries, notably in the present (or **postmodern** age).

Episteme   Michel Foucault (1926–1984) in *The Order of Things* (1966) uses the term to designate how a culture acquires and organises knowledge in a given historical period. The episteme connects all the separate **discourses** (religious, scientific, historical, medical, etc.) into a more or less coherent structure of thought founded on a set of shared assumptions about how such knowledge is obtained and deployed. The shared assumptions are fixed through the troping process (**trope/figuration**) which takes place at the deep level of the human consciousness, and which is basic to the **emplotments** that historians generate. Knowledge is thus organised within each of the four distinctive historical epistemes, which Foucault maintains existed from the sixteenth to the twentieth centuries. For the historian these assumptions or attitudes, as they characterise each age's dominant form of **narrative representation**, are displayed in our narratives and directly influence our access to the 'reality' in the **evidence** through our metaphoric encodation of similarity or dissimilarity.

Epistemology   The theory of knowledge. Among its concerns are how it is discovered/constructed through various mechanisms/methods like **empiricism** or *a priori* **knowledge**, how we can justify what we believe (as opposed to what we know), and scepticism in knowledge acquisition. It remains one of the central concerns of philosophers, and is increasingly a growing interest among historians because of the disputed role of empiricism as the historical method.

Evidence   Traditionally, the sources, both documentary (primary) or written by historians (secondary), upon which authoritative historical explanations are founded. Evidence cannot be considered as separate from the process of its interpretation through **inference**, its constitution as **fact**(s) by an initial verification and comparison attesting to its authenticity, and by being set within its **context**.

Fact   The concept of the fact is a complex and contentious one among historians. Traditionally, a fact is the actual and undisputed event, process or piece of social action upon which historians agree – the Battle of Waterloo occurred in 1815 – the **correspondence** of reality and description. Beyond this simple level of factual statement historians immediately enter the realm of interpretation. What do we do with the fact(s)? How do we **colligate** them? How do we **emplot**/narrate them? How do we sequence and explain them? Beyond the usual problems with the **evidence** – that it may be of doubtful authenticity, or unreliable (their authors lied (!)), or simply absent – historians have many difficulties in constituting facts. What criteria should be used by the **impositionalist** historian to winnow out that **evidence** judged to be irrelevant to the constitution of a fact? How reliable is **inference** as a method for establishing facts? Should historians all become **constructionists**

'testing' **evidence** against a hypothesis to establish a fact? What of the unreliable nature of the **signifier–signified–sign** equation?

Hermeneutics   Literally the art of interpretation of texts (**evidence**). A technical skill used by post-Reformation Protestants to interpret the Bible, modern hermeneutics began with the efforts of Friedrich Schleirmacher (1768–1834) to understand texts grammatically and what the authors are likely to have intended when writing them (grammatical and psychological elements). The hermeneutic circle is the loop between the text and the author. As a process of interpretation it was extended by Wilhelm Dilthey (1833–1911) to include drawing analogies between the likely intentions of the author of the evidence and our own experiences. This formed the basis of R.G. Collingwood's (1889–1943) notion of **empathy**. In the twentieth century Martin Heidegger (1889–1976) further extended hermeneutics to include the interpretation of our own being and existence as interpreters.

Historical interpretation   A **narrative** account of the events, occurrences, texts and people in the past that makes the content understandable and/or plausible. The process at some point involves all aspects of scrutiny of the **evidence** and historical method, how so ever it is defined by the historian – **inference, colligation, contextualisation, emplotment, argument, impositionalism, empathy,** etc.

Ideology   A coherent set of socially produced ideas that lend or create a group consciousness. Ideology is time and place specific. Constituted as a dominant mode of explanation and rationalisation, ideology must saturate society and be transmitted by various social and institutional mechanisms like the media, Church, education and the law. In the view of some commentators, ideology is to be found in all social artifacts like narrative structures (including written history), codes of behaviour and patterns of belief. Ideology, according to Marxian theory, reflects and maintains the authority of the dominant social class by deliberately obscuring the reality of economic exploitation, thus ensuring that the economic relations of capitalist society appear natural and legitimate.

Impositionalism   The process whereby historians are implicated in the constitution of the past as history. Although rejected by naïve realists as a corruption of the historical enterprise, practical realists and **deconstructionist** historians recognise the unavoidable nature of the dialogue between the historian and his/her sources. The latter group, in particular, accept that historical interpretation means arranging ideas, sorting **evidence**, and imposing an explanatory **emplotment** or **argument** on the past. It follows that historical knowledge is produced as a linguistic text that has no direct access to past reality.

Induction/deduction   Induction is a form of explanation based upon **inference** from the particular to the general, or it may be described alternatively as generalising from observed instances. It is the traditional or common form of historical explanation. Deduction is explanation where a conclusion must follow logically from a set of premises. In practice, most historians employ both methods in explanation.

Inference   The thought process of moving from one set of beliefs to another based upon fresh information. Its two primary forms are **induction** and **deduction**.

Linguistic turn   An umbrella term describing a number of strands in Western thought in the twentieth century, but especially found in **poststructuralist** thought, stressing that the route to knowledge invariably centres upon the role of **discourse** and forms of **representation** in and through language. The linguistic turn centres on the opacity and figurative character of language, the manner in which subject positions as well as **reality-effects** are created within language.

Logocentrism   Term used frequently by Jacques Derrida (1930–) and advocates of **deconstructionism** in history, literature and philosophy to criticise the idea that there can be any fixed or centre to meaning established independently of language, and/or that language (especially the spoken word) can authentically represent reality.

Meta-narrative   Literally a **narrative** about narratives, the term was used by Jean-François Lyotard (1924–) in his book *The Postmodern Condition: A Report on Knowledge* (1984) in which he argued that meta-narratives or master-narratives, the stories told about how we gained knowledge and thus understood human progress and history (Hegelianism, Marxism, Liberalism, the **Enlightenment**), have reached the end of their useful life in what is now the **postmodern** era. The fact that we can no longer depend on such grand stories as universal benchmarks against which to measure or ensure truth characterises our postmodern condition. What we are left with are numerous 'little narratives' that effectively become self-legitimating.

Modernism/modernist   Historically, modernism describes the nineteenth-

and twentieth-century movement in the arts, culture and literature which in general terms criticised the **positivist**, objectivist, rationalist, **empiricist** and **referentialist** certainties of the **Enlightenment**. Confusingly, from the perspective of philosophy, modernism begins with René Descartes' (1596–1650) search for rationality in understanding, and is thus regarded as being co-terminous with the seventeenth- and eighteenth-century **Enlightenment**. Michel Foucault (1926–1984) conceives the Modern **episteme** as constituting an epistemological incongruity for humanity, with Man as both the product of his social experience while also being the constitutor of knowledge through deduction.

Narrative   A structure of explanation used to account for the occurrence of events and human actions. At its most basic the historical narrative is the vehicle for **colligation** because it explains how things happen, and in what order, according to the cause and effect of 'this happened, then that'. When the historical narrative is constructed around a selected **emplotment** it becomes the primary vehicle for the transmission, and arguably the constitution, of historical understanding. What is often disputed is the extent to which the historical narrative can **correspond** to the past as it actually was – that is, be able to recount *the* story.

New Historicism   The revival of interest since the early 1980s in the study of literary texts within their historical **contexts**. New Historicism is important to the writing of history because it draws upon that body of **post-structuralist** literary criticism that doubts the solidity of language as a clear medium capable of adequately representing the past material world. It also acknowledges that the historical text is generated intertextually within the wider social and institutional **context**, and that, as a consequence, there are no absolute or transcendent truths to be discovered, neither are there theories of explanation to be verified through empirical testing. The practical distinctions between factual and fictional texts are thus placed under doubt.

Positivism   A theory of knowledge developed by the French sociologist Auguste Comte (1798–1857) as part of his grand theory of progressive historical evolution over three stages, beginning with the theological, then the metaphysical, and ending with the scientific or positive stage. The final stage (which Comte saw himself as ushering in) is characterised by the verifiable or empirical measurement and predictability of the relationship between discrete phenomena. As an extension of established notions of **empiricism**, positivism insists on no speculation about natural phenomena. Because positivism assumes a uniformity in scientific method, it allows for the analytical study of human behaviour – scientific sociology. Positivism's legacy for the historian is plainly seen in crude forms of **constructionism** whereby historians must aggregate **evidence** from which our forensic skills will generate incontrovertible **facts** that operate according to laws of human behaviour (cf. **covering laws**). The historian is presumed to do this objectively without any **impositionalism** on his/her part.

Postmodernism   A term used in many different contexts (history, painting, literature, architecture, fashion, music) as a description of the various critiques of, and reactions against, the **Enlightenment** and its cultural product **modernism**. According to Jean-François Lyotard (1924–) in *The Postmodern Condition: A Report on Knowledge* (1984), postmodernism is characterised specifically by its rejection of overarching grand or **meta-narratives** deployed in the modern historical era to explain and justify human history and progress. The result is that the postmodern age is distinguished by its **post-structuralist**-inspired denial of transcendental realities, fixed meanings, **facts** and the **correspondence theory of truth**. Postmodernism as an approach to understanding thus produces, among other things, tentative beliefs, playfulness, style and vogue, neo-pragmatism in philosophy, the **linguistic turn**, presentism, **relativism**, the **reality-effect**, **deconstructionism** and self-reflexivity in history and literature, doubts about **referentiality**, and the ultimate failure of **narrative** as an adequate mode of **representation**. Postmodernism encourages doubt and uncertainty, challenges hierarchy and authority, and promotes the acceptance of 'the other' as legitimate.

Post-structuralism   Claimed, as a part of the **postmodernist** movement, to be the successor to (and reactive against) **structuralism**. The inspiration for the so-called **linguistic turn** in historical writing and understanding, post-structuralism insists that language, as *the* cultural and intellectual form, is the medium of exchange for power relationships (e.g. Michel Foucault [1926–1984] and power/knowledge) and the ultimate constitutor of 'truth'. Post-structuralism can trace its lineage through the work of various philosophers, historians and thinkers such as Friedrich Nietzsche (1844–1900), Benedetto Croce (1866–1953), Martin Heidegger (1889–1976), Hans-Georg Gadamer (1900–), Jacques Derrida (1934–), Michel Foucault (1926–1984) and Julia Kristeva (1941–).

Reality-effect   A concept explored at some length by Roland Barthes

(1915–1980) in his essay 'The Discourse of History' (1967). Barthes' **argument** that the connection between language and history does not rely on any genuine conformity between **evidence** and its constitution as historical **fact**, means that what historians take for the past as it actually was, is only a reality-effect generated by our assumption that the **correspondence theory of truth** allows us to adequately **reconstruct** the past. As a result, the idea of historical truth becomes ever more problematic for **deconstructionist** historians.

Reconstructionism   One of the three major strands in historical inquiry (cf. **constructionist** and **deconstructionist** history). Reconstructionist historians range from conservative empiricists to practical realists dependent primarily upon their attitude towards the validity and practice of commonsense **empiricism** as the fundamental historical method. More precise characterisation is complex, given its dependence upon the historians' attitudes towards the uses of **evidence**, **referentiality**, etc., but particularly upon how they envisage the role of language and **narrative** as cognitive elements in the reconstruction of the past.

Referentiality   A term used to designate a general belief in the largely unproblematic or adequate match between reality (event, person, thing, process) and its description (linguistic expression). **Structuralism** teaches that words are not **signifiers** that relate in any natural fashion to their referents – the things to which they refer in that the relationship between the word and the world is arbitrary (socially provided) – and so it follows that any referentiality assumed in language is the result of it being fixed in language by conventional usage. This situation complicates the translation of **facts** into interpretation in as much as referentiality cannot be assumed to extend beyond the most basic level.

Relativism   The idea that a precise measurement against a fixed benchmark is impossible in practice leads to the notion of uncertainty. In history, the relativist debate has been enjoined over many years between conservative **empiricist-** and/or **positivist-** inspired **reconstructionists** and their ideal of a stable and objective history of the past, and those who believe that the history they write is as much the product of their **narrative** and their present, as it is of past reality.

Representation   Any sign, word, sentence, **discourse**, picture, sound or action intended to depict or characterise another is an act of representation. The **correspondence theory of truth** takes representation to be closer to reflectionism rather than, say, resemblance. For historians, representation is an important concept in that it forms the mechanism that allows **empiricism** to work. There is a working assumption that language is, by and large, an adequate medium of representation for the **reconstruction** of the past. The empiricist foundation of history thus repudiates the **deconstructionist** assumption that **facts** are literary arti-facts and, therefore, open like all texts to the **post-structuralist** criticisms levelled at the taken-for-granted link between reality and its represen-tation in language.

Signifier–signified–sign   According to the **structuralist** model of lan-guage proposed by Ferdinand de Saussure (1857–1913), words are 'signs' defined in their differentiation from other words, and not because of any natural link with the real world of objects/things. Signs are built of the signifier and the signified, with the word or concept as the signi-fier and the thing represented as the signified = signifier–signified–sign. The arbitrary nature of the signifier–signified–sign relationship flows from its social or cultural constitution. Although historians constantly use words as if they were strictly **referential**, they are based on invented meanings often derived from widely accepted cultural values, and as Michel Foucault (1926–1984) argues, related to institutionalised power relationships within social structures. This inherent uncertainty in meaning prompted Jacques Derrida (1930–) to argue that it is impos-sible to write truthful **narratives** as historical explanations because there is no certain origin in linguistic meaning.

Structuralism   A broad intellectual movement the high point of which was reached in France in the 1960s. Basic is the idea, derived from the work of Ferdinand de Saussure (1857–1913) in linguistics, that the rela-tionship between all **discourses**, cultural forms, belief and behaviour systems can be understood employing the structure of language as the model. In practice, this means social meaning is generated according to the contrast between inherent binary opposites operationalised at the deep level of human consciousness and revealed in the real world in the structure of grammar, myths, sexual relationships, etc. For history this means its data is primarily understood through our linguistic mental structures rather than found in the external **empirical** data. Inevitably this casts doubt on notion of evolutionary change, scientific objectivity, the disinterested search for truth, and **referentiality**. Structuralism's descent into **post-structuralism** has probably had a greater impact on the writing of **deconstructionist** history.

Trope/figuration   Taken as figures of speech (primarily metaphor, metonymy, synecdoche and irony, but we could also include the variants simile, litotes, periphrasis and hyperbole) that deploy words in such a way as to turn or translate meaning. Troping operates at the deep level of human thought in Saussure's sense of creating meaning through binary opposition, and as employed by Michel Foucault (1926–1984) in the sense of otherness, or **difference** in any historical period. In his book *Metahistory* (1973), Hayden White (1928–) examined the theory of tropes and troping as a means to distinguish the dominant modes of historical imagination in nineteenth-century Europe. By extrapolation to the cultural level we may identify the deep and surface structures of the historical imagination. The troping process may be extended to include the creation of large-scale metaphors, like the base-superstruc-ture metaphor of Marx as the basis of a total explanation of historical change, or to create other models of historical change that rely upon the basic relationships of part–whole/whole–part. The tropes may thus be regarded as being at the heart of every historical period *and* in its description.

Guide to further reading

The notes and references indicate the sources and thinking behind my arguments and conclusions. This short guide is intended to signpost where you can turn for a more detailed study of the book's key issues, about the character of history, the two methodological historical mainstreams and their deconstructive challenge. We began with history's traditional empirical or reconstructionist method. The basic principles of this school are nowhere better expounded than by G.R. Elton in *The Practice of History* (London, Fontana, 1967) and in his statement of the faith of the conservative empiricist in *Return to Essentials* (Cambridge, Cambridge University Press, 1991). A firm grounding in the classic approach to reconstructing the past is offered by Arthur Marwick in his *The Nature of History* (London, Macmillan, 1970, third edition, 1989) which remains one of the most popular introductions to history imagined as a craft. Moving more towards the empiricist centre are John Tosh, *The Pursuit of History* (London, Longman, second edition, 1991) and Peter Charles Hoffer and William W. Stueck, *Reading and Writing American History: An Introduction to the Historian's Craft* (2 vols, Lexington, D.C. Heath, 1994). Defending the philosophical foundation of the reconstructionist approach is C. Behan McCullagh, *Justifying Historical Descriptions* (Cambridge, Cambridge University Press, 1984) and Chris Lorenz, 'Historical Knowledge and Historical Reality: A Plea for "Historical Realism"', *History and Theory*, Vol. 33, No. 3, 1994, pp. 297–327. Taken to be somewhat more relativist in his approach to the creation of the past is E.H. Carr, *What is History?* (London, Penguin, second edition, 1987). Confronting the postmodern or deconstructive challenge to the classic paradigm is Gertrude Himmelfarb, 'Some Reflections on the New History', *American Historical Review*, Vol. 94, No. 3, June 1989, pp. 661–670.
  Possibly the best current introduction to the methodologies available in history today is Michael Stanford, *A Companion to the Study of*

History (Oxford, Basil Blackwell, 1994). The most comprehensive exploration of the modern development of the American history profession and its methodological concerns is Peter Novick, *That Noble Dream: The 'Objectivity Question' and the American Historical Profession* (Cambridge, Cambridge University Press, 1988). The debate on historical objectivity is to be found in the *AHR* Forum, 'The Objectivity Question and the Future of the Historical Profession', *American Historical Review*, Vol. 96, No. 3, June 1991, pp. 675–708. More general philosophy of history texts include William H. Walsh, *An Introduction to Philosophy of History* (London, Hutchinson, third edition, 1967), William Dray (ed.), *Philosophical Analysis and History* (New York, Harper & Row, 1966) and Leon Goldstein, *Historical Knowing* (Austin, University of Texas Press, 1976). A basic survey of the varieties of history is to be found in J. Gardiner (ed.), *What is History Today?* (London, Humanities Press International, 1988). The practical realist element of the reconstructionist mainstream is ably represented by Jerzy Topolski, 'Towards an Integrated Model of Historical Explanation', *History and Theory*, Vol. 30, No. 3, 1991, pp. 324–338 and Joyce Appleby, Lynn Hunt and Margaret Jacob, *Telling the Truth About History* (New York, Norton, 1994). Although an increasing number of texts published in the mid-1990s have taken the linguistic turn into account in their exploration of historical method, early notable examples are Dominick LaCapra and Steven L. Kaplan, *Modern European Intellectual History: Reappraisals and New Perspectives* (Ithaca, Cornell University Press, 1982), Lynn Hunt, *The New Cultural History* (Berkeley, University of California Press, 1989) and Keith Jenkins, *Re-Thinking History* (London, Routledge, 1991). Also useful, and critical of White, is Saul Friedlander (ed.), *Probing the Limits of Representation: Nazism and the 'Final Solution'* (Cambridge, Massachusetts, Harvard University Press, 1992). The most recent texts include Michael S. Roth, *The Ironist's Cage: Memory, Trauma, and the Construction of History* (New York, Columbia University Press, 1995), David D. Roberts, *Nothing But History: Reconstruction and Extremity after Metaphysics* (Berkeley, University of California Press, 1995), Robert Berkhofer, *Beyond the Great Story: History as Text and Discourse* (Cambridge, Massachusetts, Harvard University Press, 1995), Clayton Roberts, *The Logic of Historical Explanation* (University Park, Pennsylvania University Press, 1996), Beverley Southgate, *History: What and Why* (London, Routledge, 1996) and Roger Chartier, *On the Edge of the Cliff: History, Language and Practice* (Baltimore and London, Johns Hopkins University Press, 1997).

On the general relationship between postmodernism as an intellectual movement and the writing of history see Stephen Bann, *The Clothing of Clio: A Study of the Representation of History in Nineteenth Century Britain and France* (Cambridge, Cambridge University Press, 1984), Derek Attridge, Geoff Bennington and Robert Young (eds), *Post-Structuralism and the Question of History* (Cambridge, Cambridge University Press, 1987), David Harvey, *The Condition of Postmodernity: An Enquiry into the Origins of Cultural Change* (Oxford, Basil Blackwell, 1989), Steven Connor, *Postmodernist Culture: An Introduction to Theories of the Postmodern* (Oxford, Basil Blackwell, 1989), F.R. Ankersmit, 'Historiography and Postmodernism', *History and Theory*, Vol. 28, No. 2, 1989, pp. 137–153, Elizabeth Deeds Ermath, *Sequel to History: Postmodernism and the Crisis of Historical Time* (Princeton, Princeton University Press, 1992) and Hans Bertens, *The Idea of the Postmodern: A History* (London, Routledge, 1995). On the intellectual history of postmodernism see Joyce Appleby *et al.* (eds), *Knowledge and Postmodernism in Historical Perspective* (London, Routledge, 1996) which provides an excellent introduction to the key texts of, among others, Nietzsche, Ricoeur, White, Foucault, Derrida and Rorty.

The debate on social theory constructionism in history is well covered in Alex Callinicos, *Theories and Narratives: Reflections on the Philosophy of History* (Oxford, Oxford University Press, 1995), Christopher Lloyd, *The Structures of History* (Oxford, Basil Blackwell, 1993), Peter Burke (ed.), *New Perspectives on Historical Writing* (University Park, Pennsylvania University Press, 1992) and *History and Social Theory* (Ithaca, Cornell University Press, 1993). Among the classic expositors of social theory history is Clifford Geertz; see his 'Thick Description: Toward an Interpretive Theory of Culture', and 'Deep Play: Notes on the Balinese Cockfight', in *The Interpretation of Cultures* (New York, Basic Books, 1973), pp. 3–31, 412–454 and *Local Knowledge: Further Essays in Interpretative Anthropology* (New York, Basic Books, 1983). Another example of this mainstream approach is Fernand Braudel, *On History* (London, Weidenfeld & Nicolson, 1980).

On narrative and the character of writing history it is advisable to start with W.B. Gallie, *Philosophy and the Historical Understanding* (New York, Schocken Books, second edition, 1968) and Peter Gay, *Style in History: Gibbon, Ranke, Macaulay, Burckhardt* (New York, Basic Books, 1974). Informed by the most recent thinking are R. Canary and H. Kozicki (eds), *The Writing of History: Literary Form and Historical Understanding* (Madison, University of Wisconsin Press, 1978), Arthur Danto, *Narration and Knowledge* (New York, Columbia University Press, 1985), David Carr, *Time, Narrative and History*

194   *Guide to further reading*

(Bloomington, Indiana University Press, 1986), F.R. Ankersmit, *History and Tropology: The Rise and Fall of Metaphor* (Berkeley, University of California Press, 1994), M.C. Lemon, *The Discipline of History and the History of Thought* (London, Routledge, 1995) and F.R. Ankersmit and Hans Kellner (eds), *A New Philosophy of History* (Chicago, University of Chicago Press, 1995). There are several important articles in this area; see, for example, Lawrence Stone, 'The Revival of Narrative', *Past and Present*, No. 85, 1979, pp. 3–24. For a Marxist response see E. Hobsbawm, 'Some Comments', *Past and Present*, No. 86, 1980, pp. 3–8 and David Carr, 'Narrative and the Real World: An Argument for Continuity', *History and Theory*, Vol. 25, No. 2, 1986, pp. 117–131. One of the most influential pieces is John E. Toews, 'Intellectual History after the Linguistic Turn: The Autonomy of Meaning and the Irreducibility of Experience', *American Historical Review*, Vol. 92, No. 4, October 1987, pp. 879–907. Further important comments on history after the linguistic turn can be found in the *AHR* Forum, 'Intellectual History and the Return of Literature', *American Historical Review*, Vol. 94, No. 3, June 1989, pp. 581–621. To understand fully the contribution of Lawrence Stone to the issue of postmodernism and history see his 'History and Post-Modernism', *Past and Present*, No. 131, 1991, pp. 217–218 and 'History and Post-Modernism', *Past and Present*, No. 135, 1992, pp. 187–194. Also of value is Perez Zagorin, 'Historiography and Postmodernism: Reconsiderations', *History and Theory*, Vol. 29, No. 3, 1990, pp. 263–274, Andrew P. Norman, 'Telling It Like It Was: Historical Narratives on Their Own Terms', *History and Theory*, Vol. 30, No. 2, 1991, pp. 119–135 and Gabrielle M. Spiegel, 'History and Post-Modernism', *Past and Present*, No. 135, 1992, pp. 197–198. More recent is Dominick LaCapra, 'History, Language and Reading: Waiting for Crillon', *American Historical Review*, Vol. 100, No. 3, June 1995, pp. 799–828, and in the same issue Dorothy Ross's examination of the emplotting of American history, 'Grand Narrative in American Historical Writing: From Romance to Uncertainty', pp. 651–677.

   This book has argued that central to the relationship between postmodernist intellectual developments in representing the past and writing history is the work of Michel Foucault and Hayden White. Michel Foucault's key texts include 'The Order of Discourse', Inaugural Lecture at the Collège de France, 2 December 1970, *The Archaeology of Knowledge* (New York, Harper & Row, 1972), *The Order of Things: An Archaeology of the Human Sciences* (New York, Random House, 1973), *Madness and Civilization: A History of Insanity in the Age of Reason* (London, Tavistock, 1973), *The Birth of the Clinic* (New York, Vintage

Books, 1975), *Counter-Memory, Practice: Selected Essays and Interviews* (Ithaca, Cornell University Press, 1979), *Power/Knowledge: Selected Interviews and Other Writings* (Brighton, Harvester Press, 1980). The best commentaries on Foucault are J.G. Merquior, *Foucault* (London, Fontana, 1985), Jan Goldstein, *Foucault and the Writing of History* (Oxford, Basil Blackwell, 1994) and Mitchell Dean, *Critical and Effective Histories: Foucault's Methods and Historical Sociology* (London, Routledge, 1994). An excellent introduction to Foucault as a historian is provided by Hayden White, 'Structuralism and Popular Culture', *Journal of Popular Culture*, Vol. 7, 1974, pp. 759–775 and 'Foucault Decoded: Notes From Underground', *History and Theory*, Vol. 12, 1973, pp. 23–54. A very comprehensive list of Foucault's works is provided in James Bernauer and Thomas Keenan, 'The Works of Michel Foucault, 1954–1984', in James Bernauer and David Rasmussen (eds), *The Final Foucault* (Cambridge, Massachusetts, MIT Press, 1988). Also of value in exploring Foucault are Hubert L. Dreyfus and Paul Rabinow, *Michel Foucault: Beyond Structuralism and Hermeneutics* (Brighton, Harvester Press, second edition, 1983), Mark Poster, *Foucault, Marxism and History* (London, Polity Press, 1984) and his 'The Reception of Foucault by Historians', *Journal of the History of Ideas*, Vol. 48, 1987, pp. 117–141, Gary Gutting, *The Cambridge Companion to Foucault* (Cambridge, Cambridge University Press, 1994) and Alan Sheridan, *Michel Foucault, The Will to Truth* (London, Routledge, reprint, 1994). In another *AHR* Forum on Russian history, Foucault's historical method came under close scrutiny; see the articles by Laura Engelstein, Rudy Koshar and Jan Goldstein, *American Historical Review*, Vol. 98, No. 2, April 1993, pp. 338–381. More recently, Gerard Noiriel examined the contribution of Foucault to historical understanding in his 'Foucault and History: The Lessons of a Disillusion', *Journal of Modern History*, Vol. 66, September 1994, pp. 547–568.

Hayden White's contribution to the study of the past is to be found in his three key texts: *Metahistory: The Historical Imagination in Nineteenth Century Europe* (Baltimore, Johns Hopkins University Press, 1973), *Tropics of Discourse: Essays in Cultural Criticism* (Baltimore, Johns Hopkins University Press, 1978) and *The Content of the Form: Narrative Discourse and Historical Representation* (Baltimore, Johns Hopkins University Press, 1987). The latter two texts are collections that contain his major articles. For a recent debate on the Whitean approach to history as a way of knowing, see Arthur Marwick, 'Two Approaches to Historical Study: The Metaphysical (Including Postmodernism) and the Historical', *Journal of Contemporary History*,

Vol. 30, No. 1, January 1995, pp. 5–36 and White's riposte 'Response to Arthur Marwick', *Journal of Contemporary History*, Vol. 30, No. 2, April 1995, pp. 233–246. The engagement with White can also be seen in Hans Kellner, 'White's Linguistic Humanism', *History and Theory*, *Beiheft* 19, 1980, pp. 1–29, Gregor McLennan, 'History and Theory: Contemporary Debates and Directions', *Literature and History*, Vol. 10, No. 2, Autumn 1984, pp. 139–164, Paul A. Roth, 'Hayden White and the Aesthetics of Historiography', *History of the Human Sciences*, Vol. 5, 1992, pp. 17–35, Alun Munslow, *Discourse and Culture: The Creation of America, 1870–1920* (London, Routledge, 1992), Wulf Kansteiner, 'Hayden White's Critique of the Writing of History', *History and Theory*, Vol. 32, No. 3, 1993, pp. 273–295 and Keith Jenkins, *On 'What is History?'* (London, Routledge, 1995) and his *Postmodern History Reader* (London, Routledge, 1997).

Notes

1 INTRODUCTION

1 Quoted in Richard T. Vann, 'Louis Mink's Linguistic Turn', *History and Theory*, Vol. 26, No. 1, 1987, pp. 1–14. See also Louis Mink, 'History and Fiction as Modes of Comprehension', *New Literary History*, Vol. 1, 1970, pp. 541–558. While strongly objecting to Hayden White's placing of literary form before historical content as the central organisational feature of written history, a helpful introduction to the relationship of form and content in historical explanation is to be found in Saul Friedlander (ed.), *Probing the Limits of Representation: Nazism and the 'Final Solution'* (Cambridge, Massachusetts, Harvard University Press, 1992).

2 A lucid though unsympathetic introduction to this issue is to be found in Alex Callinicos, *Theories and Narratives: Reflections on the Philosophy of History* (Cambridge, Polity Press, 1995), Introduction, pp. 2–4. See also Keith Jenkins, *Re-Thinking History* (London, Routledge, 1991), pp. 10–13.

3 M.C. Lemon, *The Discipline of History and the History of Thought* (London, Routledge, 1995), p. 131.

4 Ibid., p. 144.

5 Ibid.

6 This is a well-established position. See Richard Rorty, *Philosophy and the Mirror of Nature* (Princeton, Princeton University Press, 1979), Peter Charles Hoffer and William W. Stueck, *Reading and Writing American History: An Introduction to the Historian's Craft* (Lexington, D.C. Heath, 1994) and Keith Jenkins, *On 'What is History?'* (London, Routledge, 1995).

7 Arthur Danto, *Narration and Knowledge* (New York, Columbia University Press, 1985), p. 202.

8 Lemon, op. cit., p. 133. See also Philip Stewart, 'This is Not a Book Review: On Historical Uses of Literature', *Journal of Modern History*, Vol. 66, No. 3, September 1994, pp. 521–538.

9 This description is to be found in Thomas A. Bailey and David M. Kennedy, *The American Pageant* (Lexington, D.C. Heath, tenth edition, 1994), p. 225.

10 William H. Walsh, 'Colligatory Concepts in History', in Patrick Gardiner (ed.), *The Philosophy of History* (New York, Oxford University Press, 1974), p. 136; William Dray, *Philosophy of History* (Englewood Cliffs, Prentice-

Hall, second edition, 1993), pp. 89–113; Hayden White, *Metahistory: The Historical Imagination in Nineteenth Century Europe* (Baltimore, Johns Hopkins University Press, 1973), pp. ix–x.

11 R.G. Collingwood, *The Idea of History* (originally published 1946, Oxford, Oxford University Press, revised edition 1994), pp. 302, 390–395.

12 Neville Kirk, 'The Continuing Relevance and Engagement of Class', *Labour History Review*, Vol. 60, No. 3, winter 1995, pp. 2–15.

13 The term used by the philosopher of history Michael E. Hobart to describe this attention to the role of narrative in writing history is rhetorical constructionism, while White describes it variously as the 'metahistorical' or an 'essentially poetic act' in which the historian 'prefigures the historical field'. See Hobart, 'The Paradox of Historical Constructionism', *History and Theory*, Vol. 8, No. 1, 1989, pp. 43–58. The only full application and critique of White's methodology of history is to be found in Alun Munslow, *Discourse and Culture: The Creation of America, 1870–1920* (London, Routledge, 1992). The most recent assessment of the role of narrative in writing the past and other issues concerning the postmodern condition of history is to be found in Robert F. Berkhofer, *Beyond the Great Story: History as Text and Discourse* (Cambridge, Massachusetts, Harvard University Press, 1995); David R. Roberts, *Nothing But History: Reconstruction and Extremity After Metaphysics* (Berkeley, University of California Press, 1995); Michael S. Roth, *The Ironist's Cage: Memory, Trauma, and the Construction of History* (New York, Columbia University Press, 1995); Joyce Appleby (ed.), *Knowledge and Postmodernism in Historical Perspective* (London, Routledge, 1996); Keith Jenkins, *The Postmodern History Reader* (London, Routledge, 1997) and Roger Chartier, *On the Edge of the Cliff: History, Language and Practice* (Baltimore and London, Johns Hopkins University Press, 1997).

14 W.B. Gallie, *Philosophy and the Historical Understanding* (New York, Schocken Books, second edition, 1968), p. 105. See also Louis Mink, 'Narrative Form as a Cognitive Instrument', in R. Canary and H. Kozicki (eds), *The Writing of History: Literary Form and Historical Understanding* (Madison, University of Wisconsin Press, 1978), pp. 129–149.

15 David Carr, 'Narrative and the Real World: An Argument for Continuity', *History and Theory*, Vol. 25, No. 2, 1986, pp. 117–131; Michel de Certeau, *The Writing of History* (trans. Tom Conley, New York, Columbia University Press, 1988); Paul Ricoeur, *Time and Narrative* (Chicago, University of Chicago Press, 3 vols, 1984, 1985).

16 Paul Veyne, *Writing History: Essays on Epistemology* (Middletown, Wesleyan University Press, 1984); Hayden White, 'The Historical Text as Literary Artifact', in *Tropics of Discourse: Essays in Cultural Criticism* (Baltimore, Johns Hopkins University Press, 1978), p. 82.

17 Hayden White, *The Content of the Form: Narrative Discourse and Historical Representation* (Baltimore, Johns Hopkins University Press, 1987), p. 81. See also the collection by F.R. Ankersmit, *History and Tropology: The Rise and Fall of Metaphor* (Berkeley, University of California Press, 1994), pp. 25–28, and his two articles 'The Dilemma of Contemporary Anglo-Saxon Philosophy of History', pp. 44–74, and 'Historical Representation', pp. 97–124, both of which originally appeared in the American philosophy of history journal *History and Theory.*

18 Michel Foucault, *Power/Knowledge* (Brighton, Harvester Press, 1981), pp. 131–132.
19 White, *Content of the Form*, op. cit., p. 87.
20 George A. Reisch, 'Chaos, History, and Narrative', *History and Theory*, Vol. 30, No. 1, 1991, pp. 1–20.
21 Peter Novick, *That Noble Dream: The 'Objectivity Question' and the American Historical Profession* (Cambridge, Cambridge University Press, 1988), p. 523.
22 Jean-François Lyotard, *The Postmodern Condition* (Manchester, Manchester University Press, 1984), p. 21.
23 This is a point made by the literary critic Robert Young in his study of the deconstruction of the concept of 'the West' in his book *White Mythologies: Writing History and the West* (London, Routledge, 1990), pp. 1–20.
24 Jenkins, *On 'What is History?'*, op. cit., p. 6.
25 F.R. Ankersmit, 'Historiography and Postmodernism', *History and Theory*, Vol. 28, No. 2, 1989, pp. 137–153.
26 Ignacio Olábarri, '"New" New History: A Langue Durée Structure', *History and Theory*, Vol. 34, No. 1, 1995, pp. 1–29.

2 THE PAST IN A CHANGING PRESENT

1 Philosopher of history Christopher Lloyd maintains that 'The writing of economic and social history is now a multifarious, voluminous, and cacophonous business'; see Christopher Lloyd, *The Structures of History* (Oxford, Basil Blackwell, 1993), p. 66. See also Lynn Hunt, *The New Cultural History* (Berkeley, University of California Press, 1989), Introduction, p. 1; Robert Darnton, 'Intellectual and Cultural History', in Michael Kammen (ed.), *The Past Before Us: Contemporary Historical Writing in the United States* (Ithaca, Cornell University Press, 1980), pp. 327–354. See also Peter Burke (ed.), *New Perspectives on Historical Writing* (University Park, Pennsylvania University Press, 1991), p. 1 and *History and Social Theory* (Ithaca, Cornell University Press, 1992). A basic survey of the varieties of history is to be found in J. Gardiner (ed.), *What is History Today?* (London, Humanities Press International, 1988).
2 This debate between postmodernity and history is now well established. See Frank R. Ankersmit, 'The Reality Effect in the Writing of History: The Dynamics of Historical Topology', in *History and Tropology: The Rise and Fall of Metaphor* (Berkeley, University of California Press, 1994), pp. 125–161; Gertrude Himmelfarb, 'Some Reflections on the New History', *American Historical Review*, Vol. 94, No. 3, June 1989, pp. 661–670; Lawrence Stone, 'History and Post-Modernism', *Past and Present*, No. 131, May 1991, pp. 217–218; C. Behan McCullagh, 'Metaphor and Truth in History', *Clio*, Vol. 23, No. 1, Fall 1993, pp. 23–49; Elizabeth Tonkin, 'History and the Myth of Realism', in Raphael Samuel and Paul Thompson (eds), *The Myths We Live By* (London, Routledge, 1990), pp. 25–35; Philippe Carrard, *Poetics of the New History: French Historical Discourse from Braudel to Chartier* (Baltimore, Johns Hopkins University Press, 1992); Alun Munslow, *Discourse and Culture: The Creation of America, 1870–1920* (London, Routledge, 1992); Barbara Melosh (ed.),

Gender and American History Since 1890 (London, Routledge, 1993); Alex Callinicos, *Theories and Narratives: Reflections on the Philosophy of History* (Oxford, Oxford University Press, 1995) and Keith Jenkins, *On 'What is History?'* (London, Routledge, 1995).

3 Peter Gay, *Style in History: Gibbon, Ranke, Macaulay, Burckhardt* (New York, Basic Books, 1974), p. 3.

4 G.R. Elton, *The Practice of History* (New York, Crowell, 1967); John Tosh, *The Pursuit of History* (London, Longman, second edition, 1991); J.H. Hexter, *Re-Appraisals in History* (Evanston, Northwestern University Press, 1961).

5 Marshal Sahlins, *Historical Metaphors and Mythical Realities* (Ann Arbor, University of Michigan Press, 1981), *Islands of History* (Chicago, University of Chicago Press, 1985), *Boundaries: The Making of France and Spain in the Pyranees* (Berkeley, University of California Press, 1989); Anthony Giddens, *New Rules of Sociological Method: A Positive Critique of Interpretative Sociologies* (New York, Basic Books, 1976); Clifford Geertz, 'Thick Description: Toward an Interpretive Theory of Culture' and 'Deep Play: Notes on the Balinese Cockfight', in *The Interpretation of Cultures* (New York, Basic Books, 1973), pp. 3–31, 412–454, and *Local Knowledge: Further Essays in Interpretative Anthropology* (New York, Basic Books, 1983).

6 Harvey Kaye, *The British Marxist Historians: An Introductory Analysis* (New York, Polity Press, 1984) and *The Education of Desire: Marxists and the Writing of History* (London, Routledge, 1992).

7 For a basic introduction see Dominick LaCapra and Steven Kaplan (eds) *Modern European Intellectual History: Reappraisals and New Perspectives* (Ithaca, Cornell University Press, 1982); Dominick LaCapra, *Rethinking Intellectual History: Texts, Contexts, Language* (Ithaca, Cornell University Press, 1983); David Harlan, 'Intellectual History and the Return of Literature', a contribution that lent its title to the AHR Forum, *American Historical Review*, Vol. 94, No. 3, June 1989, p. 585; Joan W. Scott, *Gender and the Politics of History* (New York, Columbia University Press, 1988) and 'History in Crisis? The Others' Side of the Story', AHR Forum, *American Historical Review*, Vol. 94, No. 3, June 1989, pp. 680–692; Stephen Bann, *The Clothing of Clio: A Study of the Representation of History in Nineteenth Century Britain and France* (Cambridge, Cambridge University Press, 1984) and Roger Chartier, *On the Edge of the Cliff: History, Language and Practice* (Baltimore and London, Johns Hopkins University Press, 1997).

8 Tosh, *The Pursuit of History*, op. cit., p. 48.

9 G.R. Elton, *Return to Essentials* (Cambridge, Cambridge University Press, 1991), pp. 6, 77–98.

10 Ibid., p. 12.

11 Chris Lorenz, 'Historical Knowledge and Historical Reality: A Plea for "Historical Realism"', *History and Theory*, Vol. 33, No. 3, 1994, pp. 297–327.

12 Elton, *Return to Essentials*, op. cit., p. 67.

13 Ibid., pp. 67–68.

14 Ibid., p. 10.

15 Arthur Marwick, *The Nature of History* (London, Macmillan, third edition, 1989), pp. 105–106.

16 Lawrence Stone, 'Dry Heat, Cool Reason: Historians Under Siege in England and France', *Times Literary Supplement*, 31 January 1992.
17 Burke (ed.), *New Perspectives*, op. cit., pp. 2, 9.
18 Mark Cousins, 'The Practice of Historical Investigation', in Derek Attridge, Geoff Bennington and Robert Young (eds), *Post-Structuralism and the Question of History* (Cambridge, Cambridge University Press, 1987), pp. 126–136.
19 Lawrence Stone, 'The Revival of Narrative', *Past and Present*, No. 85, 1979, pp. 3–24. For a Marxist constructionist response see E. Hobsbawm, 'Some Comments', *Past and Present*, No. 86, 1980, pp. 3–8.
20 Lawrence Stone, 'History and Post-Modernism', *Past and Present*, No. 131, 1991, pp. 217–8.
21 Lawrence Stone, 'History and Post-Modernism', *Past and Present*, No. 135, 1992, pp. 187–194.
22 Roger Chartier, *Cultural History: Between Practices and Representations* (Cambridge, Cambridge University Press, 1988), p. 42 and *On the Edge of the Cliff*, op. cit., pp. 28–38.
23 The best recent introduction to the history and impact of all major aspects of postmodernism is Hans Bertens, *The Idea of the Postmodern: A History* (London, Routledge, 1995), pp. 45, 67, 71–74.
24 Chartier, *Cutural History*, op. cit., p. 43.
25 Jacques Derrida, *Of Grammatology* (trans. G.C. Spivak, Baltimore, Johns Hopkins University Press, 1976), *Writing and Difference* (trans. A. Bass, Chicago, University of Chicago Press, 1978), 'Différance', *Speech and Phenomena: and Other Essays on Husserl's Theory of Signs* (trans. David B. Allison, Evanston, Northwestern University Press, 1973), pp. 129–160.
26 A useful summary of constructionism is provided by Michael Stanford in *A Companion to History* (Oxford, Basil Blackwell, 1994), pp. 128–129. Barbara Melosh is very much aware that in her book *Gender and American History Since 1890* she has edited a collection that is epistemologically self-conscious, as she says 'these essays demonstrate the influence of post-structuralist attention to language', Melosh, op. cit., p. 5.
27 Raymond Williams, *Keywords* (Oxford, Oxford University Press, 1983), pp. 304–306.
28 Ferdinand de Saussure, *Course de Linguistic Générale* (1916, trans. Wade Baskin, London, Fontana, 1959). See also Tim Dant, *Ideology and Discourse* (London, Routledge, 1991), p. 101.
29 On this important issue see Christopher Norris, *Deconstruction: Theory and Practice* (London, Methuen, 1982), pp. 1–55. A number of philosophers of history and practising historians have explored the nature of narrative as historical explanation; see, for example, William H. Walsh, *An Introduction to Philosophy of History* (London, Hutchinson, 1958) and Leon Goldstein, *Historical Knowing* (Austin, University of Texas, 1976).
30 Roland Barthes, *Mythologies* (London, Jonathan Cape, 1972), *Elements of Semiology* (New York, Hill & Wang, 1967), *S/Z* (New York, Hill & Wang, 1975) and *Image–Music–Text* (New York, Hill & Wang, 1977). This issue will be taken up further below.
31 The term new historicism emerged in Michael McCanles, 'The Authentic Discourse of the Renaissance', *Diacritics*, Vol. 10, No. 1, Spring 1980, pp. 77–87. The phrase was recoined by Stephen Greenblatt in his essay

'The Forms of Power and the Power of Forms in the Renaissance', *Genre*,
Vol. 15, Nos 1–2, 1982, pp. 1–4, and has been subsequently elaborated in
Greenblatt's *Shakespearean Negotiations: The Circulation of Social Energy
in Renaissance England* (Berkeley, University of California Press, 1988). In
1989 Greenblatt suggested that the movement could be defined as 'an openness to the theoretical ferment of the last few years' and that this openness
'is what distinguishes the new historicism from the positivist historical
scholarship of the early twentieth century', Stephen Greenblatt, 'Towards a
Poetics of Culture', in H. Aram Veeser (ed.), *The New Historicism* (London,
Routledge, 1989), pp. 1–14. For an alternative definition that stresses new
historicism as 'the next step past deconstructionism', see James A. Winn,
'An Old Historian Looks at the New Historicism', *Comparative Studies in
Society and History*, Vol. 35, No. 4, October 1993, pp. 859–870.
32 Veeser (ed.), *The New Historicism*, op. cit., Introduction, *passim*.
33 White, 'New Historicism: A Comment', in Veeser (ed.), *The New
Historicism*, op. cit., pp. 293–302.
34 Stone, 'History and Post-Modernism', *Past and Present*, No. 131, loc. cit.
35 Veeser (ed.), *The New Historicism*, op. cit., Introduction, p. xi.
36 Gay, *Style in History*, op. cit., p. 3.
37 Williams, *Keywords*, op. cit., p. 306.
38 Dant, *Ideology and Discourse*, op. cit., p. 7; Munslow, *Discourse and Culture*,
op. cit., pp. 1–3.
39 White, 'The Historical Text as Literary Artifact', in *Tropics of Discourse:
Essays in Cultural Criticism* (Baltimore, Johns Hopkins University Press,
1978), p. 82.
40 Carrard, *Poetics of the New History*, op. cit., pp. 18–19. The *dissertations
historiques* is the exacting French equivalent of Ph.D. level historical study.

3 HISTORY AS RECONSTRUCTION/CONSTRUCTION

1 Neville Kirk, 'The Continuing Relevance and Engagement of Class',
Labour History Review, Vol. 60, No. 3, Winter 1995, p. 4.
2 C. Behan McCullagh, *Justifying Historical Descriptions* (Cambridge,
Cambridge University Press, 1984), p. 2.
3 Ibid., p. 4.
4 C. Behan McCullagh, 'Can Our Understanding of Old Texts be Objective?',
History and Theory, Vol. 30, No. 3, 1991, pp. 302–323.
5 McCullagh, *Justifying Historical Descriptions*, op. cit., p. 6.
6 McCullagh, 'Can Our Understanding', op. cit., p. 302.
7 James T. Kloppenberg outlined a list similar to this in 'Objectivity and
Historicism: A Century of American Historical Writing', *American
Historical Review*, Vol. 94, No. 4, October 1989, pp. 1011–1030.
8 Joyce Appleby, Lynn Hunt and Margaret Jacob, *Telling the Truth About
History* (New York, Norton, 1994), p. 248 and Joyce Appleby (ed.),
Knowledge and Postmodernism in Historical Perspective (London,
Routledge, 1996), p. 14.
9 Appleby *et al., Telling the Truth*, op. cit., p. 249.
10 Arthur Marwick, *The Nature of History* (London, Macmillan, third
edition, 1989), p. 21.

11 Arthur Marwick, 'Two Approaches to Historical Study. The Metaphysical (Including Postmodernism) and the Historical', *Journal of Contemporary History*, Vol. 30, No. 1, January 1995, pp. 5–36.
12 G.R. Elton, *Return to Essentials* (Cambridge, Cambridge University Press, 1991), p. 51.
13 John Tosh, *The Pursuit of History* (London, Longman, second edition, 1991), p. 53.
14 Elton, *Return to Essentials*, op. cit., p. 52.
15 Ibid., p. 55.
16 Ibid., p. 62.
17 Ibid., p. 66.
18 Ibid., p. 70.
19 Michael A. Stanford, *A Companion to History* (Oxford, Basil Blackwell, 1994), p. 124.
20 David Hollinger, 'The Return of the Prodigal: The Persistence of Historical Knowing', *American Historical Review*, Vol. 94, No. 3, June 1989, p. 613.
21 Elton, *Return to Essentials*, op. cit., p. 11.
22 E.H. Carr, *What Is History?* (London, Penguin, second edition, 1987), p. 65.
23 Ibid., p. 22.
24 Peter Burke, *History and Social Theory* (Ithaca, Cornell University Press, 1993), p.1.
25 Ibid., p. 28.
26 Ibid., p. 29.
27 Appleby *et al.*, *Telling the Truth*, op. cit., p. 304.
28 Alex Callinicos, *Theories and Narratives: Reflections on the Philosophy of History* (Cambridge, Polity Press, 1995), p. 77.
29 Appleby *et al.*, *Telling the Truth*, op. cit., p. 304.
30 Callinicos, *Theories and Narratives*, op. cit., p. 82.
31 James Harvey Robinson, *The New History: Essays Illustrating the Modern Historical Outlook* (New York, Free Press, 1965).
32 Frederick Jackson Turner quoted in Peter Novick, *That Noble Dream: The Objectivity Question and the American Historical Profession* (Cambridge, Cambridge University Press, 1988), p. 92.
33 Philippe Carrard, *Poetics of the New History: French Historical Discourse from Braudel to Chartier* (Baltimore, Johns Hopkins University Press, 1992), pp. 1–28.
34 Christopher Lloyd, *The Structures of History* (Oxford, Basil Blackwell, 1993), p. 83.
35 Carrard, *Poetics of the New History*, op. cit., p. 31.
36 Carl Hempel, 'The Function of General Laws in History', *The Journal of Philosophy*, Vol. 34, 1942, reprinted in Patrick Gardiner (ed.), *Theories of History* (New York, Free Press, 1959).
37 Ibid., p. 351. See also Murray G. Murphey, 'Explanation, Causes, and Covering Laws', *History and Theory, Beiheft* 25, 1986, pp. 43–57.
38 Anthony Giddens, *Profiles and Critiques in Social Theory* (Berkeley, University of California Press, 1982) and *Social Theory and Modern Sociology* (Stanford, Stanford University Press, 1987); Ernest Gellner, *Culture, Identity and Politics* (Cambridge, Cambridge University Press, 1987); Charles Tilly, *From Mobilisation to Revolution* (Reading, Massachusetts, Addison-Wesley, 1978) and *Big Structures, Large Processes,*

Huge Comparisons (New York, Russell Sage Foundation, 1984); Clifford Geertz, *The Interpretation of Cultures* (New York, Basic Books, 1973) and *Local Knowledge* (New York, Basic Books, 1976); Fernand Braudel, *The Mediterranean and the Mediterranean World in the Age of Philip II* (New York, Harper & Row, 1972) and *The Identity of France* (New York, Harper & Row, 1988–90); Emmanuel Le Roy Ladurie, *The Peasants of Languedoc* (Paris, Flammarion, 1969) and *Montaillou* (New York, G. Braziller, 1978); Robert Darnton, *The Great Cat Massacre and Other Episodes in French Cultural History* (New York, Basic Books, 1985); Roger Chartier, *Cultural History: Between Practices and Representations* (Cambridge, Polity Press, 1988); W.G. Hoskins, *The Making of the English Landscape* (London, Penguin, 1955); Harry Braverman, *Labor and Monopoly Capitalism* (New York, Monthly Review Press, 1974); James Weinstein, *The Corporate Ideal in the Liberal State* (Boston, Beacon Press, 1968); Gabriel Kolko, *The Roots of American Foreign Policy* (Boston, Beacon Press, 1969); Herbert Gutman, 'Work, Culture and Society in Industrialising America, 1820–1920', *American Historical Review*, Vol. 78, No. 3, 1973, pp. 531–587; David Montgomery, *Workers' Control in America: Studies in the History of Work, Technology and Labor Struggles* (Cambridge, Cambridge University Press, 1980); Eric Hobsbawm, *The Age of Empire* (New York, Pantheon Books, 1987); Eugene Genovese, *In Red and Black: Marxian Explorations in Southern and Afro-American History* (New York, Vintage Books, 1971); Sheila Rowbotham, *Hidden From History* (London, Pluto Press, 1983) and Catherine Hall, *White, Male and Middle Class: Explorations in Feminism and History* (Cambridge, Polity Press, 1992).

39   J.H. Hexter, 'The Rhetoric of History', *International Encyclopaedia of the Social Sciences* (1968), first quotation in Novick, *That Noble Dream*, op. cit., p. 623, and Hexter, *The History Primer* (New York, Basic Books, 1971), pp. 108, 222.

40   Ibid., pp. 137–138.

41   M.C. Lemon, *The Discipline of History and the History of Thought* (London, Routledge, 1995), pp. 184–186.

42   Hayden White, 'The Question of Narrative in Contemporary Historical Theory', in *The Content of the Form: Narrative Discourse and Historical Representation* (Baltimore, Johns Hopkins University Press, 1987), pp. 26–57; Andrew Norman, 'Telling It Like It Was: Historical Narratives on Their Own Terms', *History and Theory*, Vol. 30, 1991, pp. 119–135 and William H. Dray, *Philosophy of History* (Englewood Cliffs, Prentice-Hall, second edition, 1993), pp. 91–95.

43   Lawrence Stone, 'Revival of Narrative', *Past and Present*, No. 85, 1979, pp. 3–4, 19.

44   Ibid., p. 19.

45   W.B. Gallie, *Philosophy and the Historical Understanding* (New York, Schocken Books, second edition, 1968), p. 105. See also Arthur Danto, *Narration and Knowledge* (New York, Columbia University Press, 1985).

46   Carrard, *Poetics of the New History*, op. cit., p. 75.

47   Appleby *et al.*, *Telling the Truth*, op. cit., p. 238.

48   Ibid., pp. 234–235.

49   Stanford, *A Companion to History*, op. cit., p. 95.

50   Ibid., p. 102.

51 Ibid., p. 104.
52 Phyllis Deane, *The First Industrial Revolution* (Cambridge, Cambridge University Press, 1965); Clive Trebilcock, *The Industrialisation of the Continental Powers 1780–1914* (London, Longman, 1981) and Vicki L. Ruiz and Ellen Carol DuBois (eds), *Unequal Sisters* (London, Routledge, 1994).
53 Elton, *Return to Essentials*, op. cit., p. 12.
54 McCullagh, *Justifying Historical Descriptions*, op. cit., pp. ix–x.

4 HISTORY AS DECONSTRUCTION

1 Mark Poster, 'Foucault and History', *Social Research*, Vol. 49, 1982, p. 120; Jan Goldstein, *Foucault and the Writing of History* (Oxford, Basil Blackwell, 1994) and Mitchell Dean, *Critical and Effective Histories: Foucault's Methods and Historical Sociology* (London, Routledge, 1994).
2 Allan Megill, 'Foucault, Structuralism, and the Ends of History', *Journal of Modern History*, Vol. 51, September 1979, p. 451.
3 Charles Beard, 'Written History as an Act of Faith', *American Historical Review*, Vol. 39, No. 2, 1934, pp. 219–231 and 'That Noble Dream', *American Historical Review*, Vol. 41, No. 1, 1935, pp. 74–87.
4 Rudy Koshar, 'Foucault and Social History: Comments on "Combined Underdevelopment"', *American Historical Review*, Vol. 98, No. 2, April 1993, pp. 354–363.
5 Roland Barthes, 'Le discours de l'histoire', *Information sur les sciences sociales*, Vol. 6, No. 4, 1967, pp. 65–75, translated as 'Discourse of History' with an introduction by Stephen Bann, *Comparative Criticism – A Yearbook*, Vol. 3 (University Park, Pennsylvania University Press, 1981), pp. 3–20.
6 Quoted by Bann in ibid., p. 3.
7 Ibid., p. 5.
8 Barthes, 'Discourse of History', op. cit., p. 7.
9 Ibid., p. 11.
10 Barthes, 'Discourse of History', op. cit., p. 16.
11 Ibid., p. 17. See also Stephen Bann, 'Analysing the Discourse of History', *Renaissance and Modern Studies*, Vol. 27, 1983, pp. 61–84.
12 Barthes, 'Discourse of History', op. cit., p. 18. See Richard J. Ellis and Alun Munslow, 'Narrative, Myth and the Turner Thesis', *Journal of American Culture*, Vol. 9, No. 2, 1987, pp. 9–17 and Alun Munslow, *Discourse and Culture: The Creation of America, 1870–1920* (London, Routledge, 1992), pp. 68–88.
13 See Hayden White, 'The Question of Narrative in Contemporary Historical Theory', *History and Theory*, Vol. 23, No. 1, 1984, pp. 1–33.
14 Andrew P. Norman, 'Telling It Like It Was: Historical Narratives on Their Own Terms', *History and Theory*, Vol. 30, No. 2, 1991, pp. 119–135.
15 Roland Barthes, 'The Death of the Author', quoted in David Harlan's 'Intellectual History and the Return of Literature', a contribution that lent its title to the AHR Forum, *American Historical Review*, June 1989, p. 585.
16 F.R. Ankersmit, 'Historiography and Postmodernism', *History and Theory*, Vol. 28, No. 2, 1989, p. 146.
17 Hayden White, 'The Context in the Text: Method and Ideology in

Intellectual History', in *The Content of the Form: Narrative Discourse and Historical Representation* (Baltimore, Johns Hopkins University Press, 1987), p. 192.

18 G.R. Elton, *Return to Essentials* (Cambridge, Cambridge University Press, 1991), p. 49.

19 Hayden White, 'The Burden of History', in *Tropics of Discourse: Essays in Cultural Criticism* (Baltimore, Johns Hopkins University Press, 1978), p. 47.

20 R.G. Collingwood, *The Idea of History* (Oxford, Oxford University Press, revised edition, 1994), pp. 282–302.

21 Ibid., p. 302.

22 Ibid.; see Elton's commentary, *Return to Essentials*, op. cit., p. 43.

23 The original examination of the character of general or covering laws in historical explanation is to be found in C.G. Hempel, 'The Function of General Laws in History', *Journal of Philosophy*, Vol. 39, 1942, reprinted in Patrick Gardiner, *Theories of History* (New York, Free Press, 1959), pp. 344–356.

24 Frederick Jackson Turner, *Rise of the New West, 1819–1829* (1906), a volume in the series *The American Nation; The United States, 1830–1850: The Nation and Its Sections* (New York, H. Holt & Co., 1935) with an introduction by Avery Craven; *The Frontier in American History* (1920, New York, reprinted by Holt, Rinehart & Winston, 1962); Martin Ridge, 'Frederick Jackson Turner, Ray Allen Billington, and Frontier History', *Western Historical Quarterly*, Vol. 19, January 1988, pp. 5–20; Munslow, *Discourse and Culture*, op. cit., pp. 68–88; John Mack Faragher, 'The Frontier Trail: Rethinking Turner and Reimagining the American West', *American Historical Review*, Vol. 98, No. 1, February 1993, pp. 106–117 and Peter Stoneley, 'Signifying Frontiers', *Borderlines*, Vol. 1, No. 3, March 1994, pp. 237–253.

25 Turner, 'The Significance of the Frontier in American History', in *The Frontier in American History*, op. cit., pp. 2–3.

26 Benedetto Croce, *Aesthetics as Science of Expression and General Linguistic*, translated by Douglas Ainslie with a new Introduction by John McCormick (New Brunswick, Transaction Publishers, 1995).

27 Carl Becker quoted in Peter Novick, *That Noble Dream: The Objectivity Question and the American Historical Profession* (Cambridge, Cambridge University Press, 1988), p. 98.

28 Karl Popper, *The Logic of Scientific Discovery* (London, Hutchinson, 1959). According to Allan Megill, 'Recounting the Past: "Description", Explanation, and Narrative in Historiography', *American Historical Review*, Vol. 94, No. 3, June 1989, pp. 627–653, 'the positivist programme still retains an aura of prestige' in historical explanation, p. 636. See also '"Grand Narrative" and the Discipline of History', in Frank Ankersmit and Hans Kellner (eds), *A New Philosophy of History* (Chicago, Chicago University Press, 1995).

29 Collingwood, *The Idea of History*, op. cit., p. 130.

30 Dorothy Ross, 'Grand Narratives in American Historical Writing: From Romance to Uncertainty', *American Historical Review*, Vol. 100, No. 3, June 1995, pp. 651–677.

31 Christopher Tilley (ed.), *Reading Material Culture* (Oxford, Basil Blackwell, 1990), pp. 281–347.

32 Quoted in Norman, 'Telling It Like It Was', op. cit., p. 130.
33 White, 'The Question of Narrative', op. cit., p. 19.
34 W.H. Dray, 'On the Nature and Role of Narrative in Historiography', *History and Theory*, Vol. 10, 1970, pp. 153–171.
35 Quoted in Norman, 'Telling It Like It Was', op. cit., p. 117.
36 Harlan, 'Intellectual History', op. cit., p. 600.
37 A.R. Louch, 'History as Narrative', *History and Theory*, Vol. 8, 1969, pp. 54–70.
38 William Dray, 'Mandelbaum on Historical Narrative', *History and Theory*, Vol. 8, 1969, p. 290, quoted in Leon Goldstein, *Historical Knowing* (Austin, Texas, 1976), p. 140.
39 Ibid., Introduction, p. xix. See also Goldstein, 'Impediments to Epistemology in the Philosophy of History', *History and Theory, Beiheft* 25, 1986, pp. 82–100.
40 Ibid., Introduction, pp. xx–xxiii.
41 William Gallie, *Philosophy and the Historical Understanding* (New York, Schocken Books, second edition, 1968), pp. 105–125 and M.C. Lemon, *The Discipline of History and the History of Thought* (London, Routledge, 1995), pp. 42–79.
42 Lemon, *The Discipline*, op. cit., p. 133.
43 Paul Ricoeur, *Hermeneutics and the Human Sciences*, ed. by J.B. Thompson (Cambridge, Cambridge University Press, 1981), p. 275.
44 Hayden White, 'Response to Arthur Marwick', *Journal of Contemporary History*, Vol. 30, No. 2, April 1995, pp. 233–246.
45 Roland Barthes, 'Introduction to the Structural Analysis of Narrative', quoted in White, 'The Question of Narrative', op. cit., p. 1. See also Paul Ricoeur, 'Explanation and Understanding: On Some Remarkable Connections Among the Theory of the Text, Theory of Action, and Theory of History', quoted in ibid., p. 26. See also Michel Foucault, 'The Order of Discourse', Inaugural Lecture at the Collège de France, 2 December 1970, *The Archaeology of Knowledge* (New York, Harper & Row, 1972), *The Order of Things: An Archaeology of the Human Sciences* (New York, Random House, 1973), *Madness and Civilisation: A History of Insanity in the Age of Reason* (London, Tavistock, 1973), *The Birth of the Clinic* (New York, Vintage Books, 1975), *Language, Counter-Memory, Practice: Selected Essays and Interviews* (Ithaca, Cornell University Press, 1979) and *Power/Knowledge: Selected Interviews and Other Writings* (Brighton, Harvester Press, 1980).
46 F.R. Ankersmit, *History and Tropology: The Rise and Fall of Metaphor* (Berkeley, University of California Press, 1994), p. 83.
47 Hayden White, 'Structuralism and Popular Culture', *Journal of Popular Culture*, Vol. 7, 1974, pp. 759–775, 'The Tropics of History: The Deep Structure of the *New Science*' and 'Foucault Decoded: Notes From Underground', in *Tropics of Discourse*, op. cit., pp. 197–217, 230–260; Munslow, *Discourse and Culture*, op. cit., pp. 1–4.
48 'Otherness' as a historical construct has been much explored by deconstructionist historians and critical theorists like Luce Irigaray, *This Sex which is not One* (Ithaca, Cornell University Press, 1979), and also see Hayden White, *Metahistory: The Historical Imagination in the Nineteenth Century* (Baltimore, Johns Hopkins University Press, 1973), pp. 133–425. A

culture results from the bargaining between dominant and subordinate groups and is represented through the metaphors, icons and images employed by such groups. On tropes and their cultural significance see Paul Ricoeur, *The Rule of Metaphor: Multi-Disciplinary Studies of the Creation of Meaning in Language* (Toronto, Toronto University Press, 1978), pp. 44–64 and Stephen Bann, *The Clothing of Clio: A Study of the Representation of History in Nineteenth Century Britain and France* (Cambridge, Cambridge University Press, 1984).

49 White, *The Content of the Form*, op. cit., Introduction, pp. 1–23.
50 White, *Tropics of Discourse*, op. cit., Introduction, p. 19.
51 Roland Barthes, *Mythologies* (London, Cape, 1972), p. 129.
51 The anthropologist Clifford Geertz has been one of the main advocates of the textual model for understanding culture. See his 'Thick Description: Toward an Interpretative Theory of Culture' and his 'Deep Play: Notes on the Balinese Cockfight' in his collection *The Interpretation of Cultures* (New York, Basic Books, 1973), pp. 3–30, 412–453.
53 White, 'The Context in the Text', in *The Content of the Form*, op. cit., p. 188.
54 White, 'The Absurdist Moment in Contemporary Literary Theory', in *Tropics of Discourse*, op. cit., pp. 261–282.
55 White, 'Historicism, History, and the Figurative Imagination', in ibid., p. 117.
56 Ibid.
57 Hayden White, 'The Metaphysics of Narrativity: Time and Symbol in Ricoeur's Philosophy of History', in *The Content of the Form*, op. cit., p.173.
58 Ricoeur, *Hermeneutics and the Human Sciences*, op. cit., p. 279. See also Robert Scholes and Robert Kellogg, *The Nature of Narrative* (New York, Oxford University Press, 1966) and Saul Friedlander (ed.), *Probing the Limits of Representation: Nazism and the 'Final Solution'* (Cambridge, Massachusetts, Harvard University Press, 1992).
59 Hayden White, 'The Metaphysics of Narrativity', op. cit., p.173.
60 Ibid., p. 181.
61 Ibid.

5 WHAT IS WRONG WITH DECONSTRUCTIONIST HISTORY?

1 Fred A. Olafson, 'Hermeneutics, "Analytical" and "Dialectical"', *History and Theory, Beiheft* 25, 1986, pp. 28–42.
2 John Tosh, *The Pursuit of History* (London, Longman, second edition, 1991), p. 108.
3 Joyce Appleby, Lynn Hunt and Margaret Jacob, *Telling the Truth About History* (New York, Norton, 1994), pp. 160–197.
4 T.S. Kuhn, *The Structure of Scientific Revolutions* (Chicago, University of Chicago Press, 1961).
5 Appleby *et al.*, *Telling the Truth*, op. cit., pp. 195–196.
6 Michel Foucault, 'What is Enlightenment?', in Paul Rabinow, *The Foucault Reader* (New York, Random House, 1984), pp. 32–50.
7 Appleby *et al.*, *Telling the Truth*, op. cit., p. 212.

8 Linda Gordon, 'Comments on That Noble Dream', *American Historical Review*, Vol. 96, No. 3, June 1991, pp. 683–687.
9 G.R. Elton, *Return to Essentials* (Cambridge, Cambridge University Press, 1991), p. 29.
10 Michael Stanford, *A Companion to the Study of History* (Oxford, Basil Blackwell, 1994), p. 91.
11 Arthur Marwick, 'Two Approaches to Historical Study: The Metaphysical (Including Postmodernism) and the Historical', *Journal of Contemporary History*, Vol. 30, No. 1, January 1995, pp. 18–20.
12 Appleby *et al.*, *Telling the Truth*, op. cit., p. 227.
13 James T. Kloppenberg, 'Objectivity and Historicism: A Century of American Historical Writing', *American Historical Review*, Vol. 94, No. 4, October 1989, p. 1017.
14 Richard Rorty, *Philosophy and the Mirror of Nature* (Princeton, Princeton University Press, 1980) and *Consequences of Pragmatism* (Minneapolis, University of Minnesota Press, 1982); Richard J. Bernstein, 'The Resurgence of Pragmatism', *Social Research*, Vol. 59, 1992, pp. 825–826.
15 Kloppenberg, 'Objectivity and Historicism', op. cit., p. 1018.
16 Quoted in ibid., p. 1020.
17 Ellen Nore, 'Charles A. Beard's Act of Faith: Context and Content', *The Journal of American History*, Vol. 66, No. 4, March 1980, pp. 850–866 and *Charles A. Beard: An Intellectual Biography* (Carbondale, Southern Illinois University Press, 1983).
18 Leon Goldstein, 'Impediments to Epistemology in the Philosophy of History', *History and Theory*, Beiheft 25, 1986, p. 96.
19 Marwick, 'Two Approaches', op. cit., pp. 20–23. See also John M. Ellis, *Against Deconstruction* (Princeton, Princeton University Press, 1989), p. 138.
20 Tosh, *The Pursuit of History*, op. cit., p.137.
21 Marwick, 'Two Approaches', op. cit., p. 21.
22 C. Behan McCullagh, 'Metaphor and Truth in History', *Clio*, Vol. 23, No. 1, Fall 1993, p. 36.
23 Ibid., p. 37.
24 Ibid.
25 E.H. Carr, *What Is History?* (London, Penguin, second edition, 1987), p. 11.
26 Ibid., p. 11.
27 R.G. Collingwood, *The Idea of History* (Oxford, Oxford University Press, revised edition, 1994), p. 244.
28 Carr, *What is History?*, op. cit., pp. 12–13.
29 See Keith Jenkins' treatment of the Carr–Elton debate in *On 'What is History?'*(London, Routledge, 1995), pp. 42–96, *passim*.
30 Peter Gay, *Style in History* (New York, Norton, 1974), p. 198.
31 Ibid., pp. 199, 217; Peter Novick, *That Noble Dream: The 'Objectivity Question' and the American Historical Profession* (Cambridge, Cambridge University Press, 1988), p. 611.
32 McCullagh, 'Metaphor and Truth', op. cit., p. 43.
33 Carr, *What is History?*, op. cit., p. 14.
34 Tosh, *The Pursuit of History*, op. cit., p. 139.
35 Elton, *Return to Essentials*, op. cit., p. 19.
36 F.J. Turner, 'Social Forces in American History', in *The Frontier in American*

History (New York, Holt, Rinehart & Winston, 1920, reprinted 1962), pp. 311–334. This was the speech he delivered to the American Historical Association after his election as President of the Association in 1910.

37 Elton, *Return to Essentials*, op. cit., p. 6.
38 Ibid., pp. 9–11.
39 Ibid., pp. 15, 19.
40 Gertrude Himmelfarb, 'Some Reflections on the New History', *American Historical Review*, Vol. 94, No. 3, June 1989, p. 665, *The New History and the Old* (Cambridge, Massachusetts, Harvard University Press, 1987).
41 Gertrude Himmelfarb, 'The New History', *New York Times Review of Books*, Vol. 17, August 1980, p. 3, quoted in Novick, *That Noble Dream*, op. cit., p. 610.
42 Ibid.
43 Lawrence Stone, letter to *Harper's Magazine*, Vol. 268, June 1984, pp. 4–5, quoted in ibid.
44 Lawrence Stone, 'The Revival of Narrative', *Past and Present*, No. 85, 1979, p. 4.
45 Ibid., pp. 4–8.
46 Ibid., p. 23.
47 Ibid., p. 19.
48 Lawrence Stone, 'History and Post-Modernism', *Past and Present*, No. 135, May 1992, p. 217.
49 Ibid.
50 Ibid., pp. 189–190.
51 Ibid., p. 192.
52 Ibid., pp. 193–194.
53 Gabrielle M. Spiegel, 'History and Post-Modernism', *Past and Present*, No. 135, May 1992, pp. 197–198.
54 Ibid., p. 203.
55 Tosh, *The Pursuit of History*, op. cit., p. 138.
56 Ibid., p. 139.
57 A.J.P. Taylor, 'Fiction in History', *Times Literary Supplement*, 23 March 1973, p. 327.
58 Ibid., p. 328.
59 Ibid.
60 Robert F. Berkhofer, *Beyond the Great Story: History as Text and Discourse* (Cambridge, Massachusetts, Harvard University Press, 1995), pp. 38–50.
61 Richard T. Vann, 'Theory and Practice in Historical Study', *Guide to Historical Literature*, Beth Norton and Pamela Gerardi (eds) (New York, American Historical Association, 1995), pp. 1–4.
62 Ibid., p. 4.
63 Collingwood, *The Idea of History*, op. cit., p. 391.
64 C. Behan McCullagh, *Justifying Historical Descriptions* (Cambridge, Cambridge University Press, 1984), pp. 8–10 and 'Metaphor and Truth', op. cit., pp. 43–44.
65 Olafson, 'Hermeneutics', op. cit., p. 40.
66 David Carroll, 'Poetics, Theory, and the Defence of History', *Clio*, Vol. 22, No. 3, 1993, pp. 273–289, a review of Philippe Carrard's *Poetics of the New History*, op. cit.
67 Ibid., p. 277.

68 Ibid., p. 289. See also William Cronon, 'A Place for Stories: Nature, History, and Narrative', *Journal of American History*, Vol. 78, March 1992, pp. 1347–1376, who very much doubts that radically different multiple interpretations using the same evidence are viable.

69 Appleby *et al.*, *Telling the Truth*, op. cit., pp. 254–257.

70 Arthur Danto, *Narration and Knowledge* (New York, Columbia University Press, 1985), p. 177.

71 Andrew P. Norman, 'Telling It Like It Was: Historical Narratives On Their Own Terms', *History and Theory*, Vol. 30, No. 2, 1991, pp. 133–134.

72 Appleby *et al.*, *Telling the Truth*, op. cit., p. 229.

73 Ibid.

74 Ibid., pp. 229–230.

75 Ibid., p. 230.

76 Eric Hobsbawm in Felix Gilbert and E.R. Graubard (eds), *Historical Studies To-Day* (New York, Norton, 1972), p. 9, quoted in Stanford, *A Companion*, op. cit., p. 106.

77 Alasdair MacIntyre, 'Epistemological Crisis, Dramatic Narrative, and the Philosophy of Science', *The Monist*, Vol. 60, 1978, p. 457, quoted in Norman, 'Telling It Like It Was', op. cit., p. 131.

78 Alex Callinicos, *Theories and Narratives: Reflections on the Philosophy of History* (Cambridge, Polity Press, 1995), p. 71. See also Hayden White, 'Historical Emplotment and the Problem of Truth', in Saul Friedlander (ed.), *Probing the Limits of Representation* (Cambridge, Massachusetts, Harvard University Press, 1992), pp. 37–53.

79 Collingwood, *The Idea of History*, op. cit., p. 32.

80 James A. Winn, 'An Old Historian Looks at the New Historicism', *Comparative Studies in Society and History*, Vol. 35, No. 4, October 1993, pp. 867–868.

81 Collingwood, *The Idea of History*, op. cit., p. 251.

6 WHAT IS WRONG WITH RECONSTRUCTIONIST/CONSTRUCTIONIST HISTORY?

1 Jerzy Topolski, 'Towards an Integrated Model of Historical Explanation', *History and Theory*, Vol. 30, No. 3, 1991, pp. 324–338.

2 Joan W. Scott, 'History in Crisis? The Others' Side of the Story', *American Historical Review*, Vol. 94, No. 3, June 1989, pp. 680–692.

3 Hans Kellner, *Language and Historical Representation: Getting the Story Crooked* (Madison, University of Wisconsin Press, 1989), p. vii.

4 Perez Zagorin, 'Historiography and Postmodernism: Reconsiderations', *History and Theory*, Vol. 29, No. 3, 1990, pp. 263–274.

5 Jörn Rüsen quoting Ranke in 'Rhetoric and Aesthetics of History: Leopold Von Ranke', *History and Theory*, Vol. 29, No. 2, 1990, pp. 190–204.

6 David A. Hollinger, 'Postmodernist Theory and *Wissenschaftliche* Practice', AHR Forum, *American Historical Review*, Vol. 96, No. 3, June 1991, pp. 688–692.

7 Mark Bevir, 'Objectivity in History', *History and Theory*, Vol. 33, No. 3, 1994, pp. 328–344.

8 Gabrielle M. Spiegel, *Romancing the Past: The Rise of Vernacular Prose Historiography in Thirteenth Century France* (Berkeley, University of California Press, 1992) and Carol Douglas Sparks, 'The Land Incarnate: Navajo Women and the Dialogue of Colonialism, 1821–1870', in Nancy Shoemaker (ed.), *Negotiators of Change: Historical Perspectives on Native American Women* (New York, Routledge, 1995), pp. 135 156.
9 James R. Kincaid, *Child Loving: The Erotic Child and Victorian Culture* (New York, Routledge, 1992), p. 5.
10 Sparks, 'The Land Incarnate', op. cit., pp. 136–137.
11 Roger Chartier, *Cultural History: Between Practices and Representations* (Cambridge, Polity Press, 1988), p. 42.
12 J.G.A. Pocock, *Virtue, Commerce and History: Essays on Political Thought and History Chiefly in the Eighteenth Century* (Cambridge, Cambridge University Press, 1985), pp. 8–15.
13 Mark Bevir, 'The Errors of Linguistic Contextualism', *History and Theory*, Vol. 31, No. 3, 1992, pp. 276–298.
14 Peter Burke (ed.), *New Perspectives on Historical Writing* (Cambridge, Cambridge University Press, 1991), p. 238.
15 Gabrielle M. Spiegel, 'History and Post-Modernism', *Past and Present*, No. 135, May 1992, p. 197.
16 David Harlan, 'Intellectual History and the Return of Literature', *American Historical Review*, Vol. 94, No. 3, June 1989, pp. 581–609.
17 Ibid., p. 609.
18 Ibid.
19 Alex Callinicos, *Theories and Narratives: Reflections on the Philosophy of History* (Cambridge, Polity Press, 1995), pp. 95–96.
20 Paul Ricoeur, *Time and Narrative* (trans. K. McLaughlin and D. Pellauer, 2 vols, Chicago, University of Chicago Press, 1983–84), p. 138.
21 Philippe Carrard, *Poetics of the New History: French Historical Discourse from Braudel to Chartier* (Baltimore, Johns Hopkins University Press, 1992), pp. 74–82, esp. p. 75.
22 Robert F. Berkhofer, *Beyond the Great Story: History as Text and Discourse* (Cambridge, Massachusetts, Harvard University Press, 1995), p. 58.
23 Callinicos, *Theories and Narratives*, op. cit., p. 76.
24 Lawrence Stone, 'History and Post-Modernism', *Past and Present*, No. 131, 1991, p. 191.
25 Ibid., p. 192.
26 Simon Schama, *Landscape and Memory* (London, HarperCollins, 1995), p. 624.
27 Marshal Sahlins, *Islands of History* (Chicago, University of Chicago Press, 1985).
28 Burke, *New Perspectives on Historical Writing*, op. cit., p. 240.
29 Ibid., pp. 240–241.
30 Ibid., p. 241.
31 Claire Sanders in interview with Natalie Zemon Davis, 'The Truth About Fiction', *Times Higher Education Supplement*, 10 November 1995, p. 21.
32 Schama, *Landscape and Memory*, op. cit., p. 7.
33 James A. Henretta, 'Social History as Lived and Written', *American Historical Review*, Vol. 84, No. 5, December 1979, pp. 1318–1319.
34 Ibid.

35 I explore the idea of history as representing cultural memory in Alun Munslow, 'Imagining the Nation: The Frontier Thesis and the Creating of America', in Philip John Davies (ed.), *Representing and Imagining America* (Keele, Keele University Press, 1996), pp. 15–23.
36 F.R. Ankersmit, 'Historiography and Postmodernism', *History and Theory*, Vol. 28, No. 2, 1989, p. 152.
37 R.G. Collingwood, *The Idea of History* (Oxford, Oxford University Press, revised edition, 1994), p. 434.
38 David Carroll, 'Poetics, Theory, and the Defence of History', *Clio*, Vol. 22, No. 3, 1993, pp. 273–289.

7 MICHEL FOUCAULT AND HISTORY

1 For a definitive listing of Foucault's work see James Bernauer and Thomas Keenan, 'The Works of Michel Foucault, 1954–1984', in James Bernauer and David Rasmussen (eds), *The Final Foucault* (Cambridge, Massachusetts, MIT Press, 1988). Among the most accessible commentaries on Foucault the historian are Hayden White, 'Structuralism and Popular Culture', *Journal of Popular Culture*, Vol. 7, 1974, pp. 759–775 and 'Foucault Decoded: Notes From Underground', *History and Theory*, Vol. 12, 1973, pp. 23–54, reprinted in *Tropics of Discourse: Essays in Cultural Criticism* (Baltimore, Johns Hopkins University Press, 1978). See also Hubert L. Dreyfus and Paul Rabinow, *Michel Foucault: Beyond Structuralism and Hermeneutics* (Brighton, Harvester Press, second edition, 1983); Mark Poster, *Foucault, Marxism and History* (London, Polity Press, 1984); J.G. Merquior, *Foucault* (London, Fontana, 1985); Allan Megill, *Prophets of Extremity: Nietzsche, Heidegger, Foucault, Derrida* (Berkeley, University of California Press, 1985) and 'The Reception of Foucault by Historians', *Journal of the History of Ideas*, Vol. 48, 1987, pp. 117–141; Gary Gutting, *The Cambridge Companion to Foucault* (Cambridge, Cambridge University Press, 1994); Lois McNay, *Foucault, A Critical Introduction* (New York, Continuum, 1994); Alan Sheridan, *Michel Foucault, The Will to Truth* (London, Routledge, reprinted 1994); Gerard Noiriel, 'Foucault and History: The Lessons of a Disillusion', *Journal of Modern History*, Vol. 66, September 1994, pp. 547–568 and Michael S. Roth, *The Ironist's Cage: Memory, Trauma and the Construction of History* (New York, Columbia University Press, 1995), pp. 71–136.
2 Rudy Koshar, 'Foucault and Social History: Comments on "Combined Underdevelopment"', *American Historical Review*, Vol. 98, No. 2, April 1993, p. 358.
3 Michel Foucault, *The Order of Things: An Archaeology of the Human Sciences* (New York, Random House, 1973).
4 White, 'Foucault Decoded', in *Tropics of Discourse*, op. cit.
5 Quoted in Noiriel, 'Foucault and History', op. cit., p. 551.
6 Roth, *The Ironist's Cage*, op. cit., pp. 72–78 and Clayton Roberts, *The Logic of Historical Explanation* (University Park, University of Pennsylvania Press, 1996), pp. 183–192.
7 Roth, *The Ironist's Cage*, op. cit., p. 76.
8 One of the best analyses of Foucault's epistemology is to be found in

Dreyfus and Rabinow, *Michel Foucault*, op. cit., pp. 124–125. Michel Foucault, 'Nietzsche, Genealogy, History', in *Language, Counter Memory, Practice: Selected Essays and Interviews*, ed. by Donald F. Bouchard, and trans. by Donald F. Bouchard and Sherry Simon (Ithaca, Cornell University Press, 1977), pp. 139–164.

9 Ibid., p. 157.

10 Ibid., p. 158.

11 Michel Foucault, *The Archaeology of Knowledge* (New York, Harper & Row, 1972).

12 Michel Foucault, *The Birth of the Clinic: An Archaeology of Medical Perception* (New York, Vintage Books, 1975) and *Madness and Civilization: A History of Insanity in the Age of Reason* (London, Tavistock, 1973).

13 Patrick Joyce, *Democratic Subjects: The Self and the Social in Nineteenth Century England* (Cambridge, Cambridge University Press, 1994), p. 9.

14 White, 'Structuralism and Popular Culture', op. cit., p. 771.

15 Quoted in Lynn Hunt (ed.), *The New Cultural History* (Berkeley, University of California Press, 1989), p. 7.

16 Foucault, *The Archaeology of Knowledge*, op. cit., p. 191.

17 Ibid.

18 Ibid.

19 White, 'The Tropics of History' and 'Foucault Decoded' in *Tropics of Discourse*, op. cit., pp. 254, 197.

20 Ibid.

21 Louis Althusser, *Lenin and Philosophy and Other Essays* (New York, Monthly Review Press, 1971), p. 162. For a lengthier introduction see Alun Munslow, *Discourse and Culture: The Creation of America, 1870–1920* (London, Routledge, 1992), pp. 177–178.

22 Poster, *Foucault, Marxism and History*, op. cit., p. 71.

8 HAYDEN WHITE AND DECONSTRUCTIONIST HISTORY

1 John Passmore, 'Explanation in Everyday Life, in Science, and in History', *History and Theory*, Vol. 2, No. 2, 1962, pp. 122, 123, quoted by G. Roberts, 'Narrative History as a Way of Life', *Journal of Contemporary History*, Vol. 31, 1996, pp. 221–228. This issue also contains responses and replies to the Marwick–White dialogue.

2 F.R. Ankersmit, *History and Tropology: The Rise and Fall of Metaphor* (Berkeley, University of California Press, 1994), p. 3.

3 Keith Jenkins, *On 'What is History?'* (London, Routledge, 1995), pp. 134–179 and Keith Green and Jill LeBihan, *Critical Theory and Practice: A Coursebook* (London, Routledge, 1996), pp. 92–93, 100–101, 136–137. See also Raphael Samuel's empiricist dismissal of White in *Theatres of Memory* (London, Verso, 1994), pp. 8, 41–42 and Roger Chartier, *On the Edge of the Cliff: History, Language and Practice* (Baltimore and London, Johns Hopkins University Press, 1997), pp. 28–38.

4 Frederick A. Olafson, 'Hermeneutics: "Analytical" and "Dialectical"', *History and Theory*, Beiheft 25, 1986, pp. 28–42.

5 Hayden White, 'The Historical Text as Literary Artifact', in *Tropics of Discourse: Essays in Cultural Criticism* (Baltimore, Johns Hopkins University Press, 1978), p. 85.

6   Hayden White, 'Historicism, History and the Figurative Imagination', in ibid., pp. 101–120.
7   Hayden White, *The Content of the Form: Narrative Discourse and Historical Representation* (Baltimore, Johns Hopkins University Press, 1987), p. 209.
8   Robert Berkhofer, *Beyond the Great Story: History as Text and Discourse* (Cambridge, Massachusetts, Harvard University Press, 1995), pp. 134–135.
9   Alun Munslow, *Discourse and Culture: The Creation of America, 1870–1920* (London, Routledge, 1992) and Dorothy Ross, 'Grand Narratives in American Historical Writing: From Romance to Uncertainty', *American Historical Review*, Vol. 100, No. 3, June 1995, pp. 651–677.
10 Hayden White, 'Interpretation in History', 'The Tropics of History: The Deep Structure of the New Science' and 'Foucault Decoded: Notes From Underground', in *Tropics of Discourse*, op. cit., pp. 51–80, 197–217, 230–260 and 'Structuralism and Popular Culture', *Journal of Popular Culture*, Vol. 7, 1974, pp. 759–775; Munslow, *Discourse and Culture*, op. cit., pp. 1–4.
11 Hayden White, 'The Fictions of Factual Representation', in *Tropics of Discourse*, op. cit., p. 134.
12 White, 'The Historical Text as Literary Artifact', op. cit., pp. 84–85.
13 S. Monk, *The Sublime* (Ann Arbor, University of Michigan Press, 1960).
14 White, 'Interpretation in History', op. cit., p. 60.
15 Ankersmit, *History and Tropology*, op. cit., p. 41.
16 Ibid., pp. 34–36.
17 White, 'Interpretation in History', op. cit., pp. 55–56.
18 Jenkins, *On 'What is History?'*, op. cit., p. 85, quoting from White, *The Content of the Form*, op. cit., p. 1.
19 White, 'Interpretation in History', op. cit., p. 73.
20 Clayton Roberts, *The Logic of Historical Explanation* (University Park, University of Pennsylvania Press, 1996) is only the most recent attempt to reinstate positivism and covering laws in historical explanation.
21 Philippe Carrard, *Poetics of the New History: French Historical Discourse From Braudel to Chartier* (Baltimore, Johns Hopkins University Press, 1992), p. 75.
22 Alun Munslow, 'Imagining the Nation: The Frontier Thesis and the Creating of America', in Philip J. Davies (ed.), *Representing and Imagining America* (Keele, Keele University Press, 1996), pp. 15–23.
23 Hayden White, 'Response to Arthur Marwick', *Journal of Contemporary History*, Vol. 30, No. 2, April 1995, p. 240.
24 Ibid., p. 244.
25 Hayden White, *Metahistory: The Historical Imagination in the Nineteenth Century* (Baltimore, Johns Hopkins University Press, 1973), p. 30.
26 White, 'Historicism, History and the Figurative Imagination', op. cit., pp. 101–120.
27 The best introduction to the White model is found in Jenkins, *On 'What is History?'*, op. cit., pp. 146–173.
28 White, *Metahistory*, op. cit., p. 29.
29 Ibid., pp. 29–30.
30 White, 'Interpretation in History', op. cit., p. 71.
31 Ibid., p. 72.
32 White, *Metahistory*, op. cit., p. 34.

216   *Notes*

33 Ibid.
34 Ibid., p. 30.
35 Michael S. Roth, *The Ironist's Cage: Memory, Trauma and the Construction of History* (New York, Columbia University Press, 1995), p. 144.
36 White, 'Interpretation in History', op. cit., p. 73.
37 White, *Metahistory*, op. cit., pp. 7–11.
38 Ibid., p. 11.
39 Ibid., p. 22.
40 Ibid., p. 24.
41 Ibid.
42 Louis Mink, 'History and Fiction as Modes of Comprehension', *New Literary History*, Vol. 1, 1970, pp. 541–558.
43 Ibid., pp. 557–558.
44 Ankersmit, *History and Tropology*, op. cit., p. 72.

9 CONCLUSION

1 Peter De Bolla, 'Disfiguring History', in Suzanne Gearhart (ed.), *The Open Boundary of History and Fiction: A Critical Approach to the French Enlightenment* (Princeton, Princeton University Press, 1984), pp. 57–64 and Alun Munslow, *Discourse and Culture: The Creation of America, 1870–1920* (London, Routledge, 1992).
2 This is a view explicitly argued by Elizabeth Deeds Ermath in *Sequel to History: Postmodernism and the Crisis of Historical Time* (Princeton, Princeton University Press, 1992).
3 George A. Reisch, 'Chaos Theory and Narrative', *History and Theory*, Vol. 30, No. 1, 1991, pp. 1–20, esp. p. 1.
4 Cushing Strout, 'Border Crossings: History, Fiction, and Dead Certainties', *History and Theory*, Vol. 31, No. 2, 1992, pp. 153–162.
5 Natalie Zemon Davis, 'On the Lame', *American Historical Review*, Vol. 93, No. 3, 1988, pp. 572–575. See also the attack on Davis's *The Return of Martin Guerre* in the same issue, Robert Finlay, 'The Refashioning of Martin Guerre', pp. 553–571, in which Finlay describes the book as failing to reach the acceptable standards of reconstructionist historical scholarship.
6 F.R. Ankersmit, *History and Tropology: The Rise and Fall of Metaphor* (Berkeley, University of California Press, 1994), p. 44.
7 Elizabeth Tonkin, 'History and the Myth of Realism', in Raphael Samuel and Paul Thompson (eds), *The Myths We Live By* (London, Routledge, 1990), p. 27.
8 Joyce Appleby, Lynn Hunt and Margaret Jacob, *Telling the Truth About History* (New York, Norton, 1994), p. 279.
9 Hayden White, 'The Fictions of Factual Representation', in *Tropics of Discourse: Essays in Cultural Criticism* (Baltimore, Johns Hopkins University Press, 1978), p. 134.
10 Philippe Carrard, *Poetics of the New History: French Historical Discourse from Braudel to Chartier* (Baltimore, Johns Hopkins University Press, 1992), p. 18.
11 Quoted in Richard T. Vann, 'Louis Mink's Linguistic Turn', *History and Theory*, Vol. 26, No. 1, 1987, p. 12.

12 Hayden White, *Metahistory: The Historical Imagination in the Nineteenth Century* (Baltimore, Johns Hopkins University Press, 1973), p. 31.

13 Hayden White, 'The Tropics of History: The Deep Structure of the "New Science"', in *Tropics of Discourse*, op. cit., p. 208.

14 Hayden White, 'Response to Arthur Marwick', *Journal of Contemporary History*, Vol. 30, No. 2, April 1995, p. 239.

15 John Milton Cooper, Jnr, *Pivotal Decades: The United States, 1900–1920* (New York, Norton, 1990), p. 158.

16 White, *Tropics of Discourse*, op. cit., p. 90.

Index

a priori 27, 40, 48, 59–60, 74, 83, 84, 86, 109, 136, 167, 173, 179
Althusser, Louis 137
America 161–2, 170
American Civil War 6
American Historical Association 86, 92
Americanisation 156
analogy 132
anarchist 34, 154, 159–60; *see also* conservative; ideology; liberal; radical
Anderson, Perry 19
Ankersmit, F.R. 15, 19, 58, 62, 68, 71, 74, 100, 102, 113, 114, 140, 141, 145, 148, 161, 165, 166, 171, 177
Annales 8, 19, 23, 24, 48–9, 88–9, 109, 130, 173, 179
Anthropological (Modern) 132–3; *see also* episteme; Modern
anthropology 22, 24, 27, 47, 50, 88, 89, 110, 111, 151, 172
Appleby, Joyce 18, 38–9, 41, 46–7, 53–4, 76, 77, 78, 79, 80, 83, 90, 94, 95, 98, 168, 170; *see also* Hunt, Lynn; Jacob, Margaret; *Telling the Truth About History*
archaeology 124
Archaeology of Knowledge, The 124, 131; *see also* Foucault, Michel
argument 34–5, 67, 71, 95, 113, 136, 144, 148, 153, 154, 155, 158–60, 166, 167, 172–4, 176, 179; *see also* contextualist; formist; mechanist; organicist

Bacon, Francis 40, 58, 166
Bann, Stephen 60
Barthes, Roland 30, 58–63, 71, 72, 77, 111, 145, 166, 187–8
Beard, Charles 22, 65, 80, 102, 171
Becker, Carl 65, 80, 102, 171
Berkhofer, Robert F. 92, 109, 144
Bernstein, Richard J. 80
Bevir, Mark 103, 105
Birth of the Clinic, The 125; *see also* Foucault, Michel
Bloch, Marc 23
Braudel, Fernand 23, 49–50
Braverman, Harry 50
Burckhardt, Jacob 154
Burke, Peter 45, 105–6, 112

Callinicos, Alex 19, 40, 45–7, 55, 64, 96–7, 108–9
Carr, David 11, 68, 100, 116
Carr, E.H. 21, 44–6, 52, 64, 78, 81, 83, 84, 89–91, 97–8, 137, 168–9, 171, 172, 175
Carrard, Philippe 19, 34, 49, 53, 94, 109, 113, 151, 173
Carroll, David 93–4
causality 31, 33, 45, 53–4, 58, 64, 70, 92, 109, 111, 116, 118, 120, 132, 138, 140; *see also* covering law
Chaos Theory 13
Chartier, Roger 19, 25, 49–50, 105, 130
Chartists 161–2
Cheese and Worms, The 164; *see also* Ginsburg, Carlo
Child Loving: The Erotic Child and

Victorian Culture 104; *see also*
Kincaid, James R.
class 43, 45–8, 50, 53, 104, 111, 132,
134, 140, 152, 158, 172
Classical 132; *see also* episteme
cliometrics 88, 146, 179
Cold War 13, 69, 77, 116, 170
collection (of evidence) 153
colligation 56, 153, 159, 168, 179
Collingwood, R.G. 7, 20, 21, 44, 52,
63–5, 83, 85, 91, 93, 97, 98, 102,
103, 115, 137, 169, 171, 172,
175; *see also Idea of History,
The*
Columbus 161
comedy 34, 95, 143, 149, 154, 157–8;
see also emplotment; romance;
satire; tragedy
comparison 153, 168
Comte, Auguste 22, 186
conservative 34, 154, 159–60; *see also*
anarchist; ideology; liberal; radical
cal
constructionism 7–9, 16, 18, 19,
22–6, 31, 36–56 *passim*, 64–6,
74, 76, 78, 85, 86, 87, 89, 90–1,
96, 97–100, 108–12, 114, 117,
118, 129, 130, 131, 134, 137,
140, 141, 142, 148, 150–3, 157,
163, 165, 168–74, 179–80; *see
also* social theory
content 19, 30, 32, 57, 66–7, 74, 92,
99, 117, 123, 124, 129, 133, 138,
142–5, 149, 153, 163–4, 166,
177–8; *see also* form
context 180
contextualisation 7, 8, 24, 26, 29–34,
41–2, 49, 53, 58–9, 62, 64, 70–1,
73, 74, 81, 83, 85, 90, 94, 95, 97,
100, 105, 118, 126, 136, 137,
141, 146, 147, 152, 155, 156,
158–9, 161, 170, 172, 179; *see
also* reconstructionism
contextualist 34, 154, 158–9; *see also*
argument; formist; mechanist;
organicist
contiguity 128, 132
continuity 128, 132
correspondence 2, 5, 9, 11, 12, 16, 20,
25–8, 30, 32–3, 35–56 *passim*,

58–62 *passim*, 65, 68–70, 77, 78,
85, 91, 93, 99, 109–10, 117, 118,
122, 124, 126, 127, 130, 133–5,
139–41, 143, 144, 148, 149, 163,
164, 167–71 *passim*, 173, 176,
180
covering law 45, 49, 56, 63, 64–6, 77,
86, 109, 141, 151, 153, 164, 172,
173, 180; *see also* causality;
Hempel, Carl
Croce, Benedetto 20, 21, 65, 171, 187
cultural signature 136; *see also* tropic
signature

Danto, Arthur 5, 10, 53, 68, 69, 94
Darnton, Robert 19, 23, 50, 110
Davis, Mike 24
Davis, Natalie Zemon 23, 110, 112,
164–5; *see also Return of Martin
Guerre, The*
de Certeau, Michel 11
Dead Certainties 110, 164; *see also
Landscape and Memory*;
Schama, Simon
Deane, Phyllis 54
death of the author 62, 81, 116–17,
127, 180
deconstructionism 2, 22, 25, 34, 77,
79, 81, 86, 87–9, 93, 96–8, 102,
105, 109, 118, 130, 137, 138,
163, 168, 172, 173, 177, 180;
see also deconstructionist history
tory
deconstructionist history 9, 14, 16,
18, 19, 24–7, 31–6, 39–40, 53,
57–98 *passim*, 102, 104–5, 107,
110, 123, 130, 149, 164, 165,
168, 170, 177, 180–1; *see also*
deconstructionism
deconstructive consciousness 2, 16,
19, 29, 35, 56–8, 63, 66–7, 75,
76, 81, 87, 91, 94, 102–4, 107,
110, 112, 117–18, 143, 146, 162,
163, 165, 166, 171
deconstructive turn 68, 74, 78, 84,
99, 109–10, 115, 135
deduction 4, 36, 38–40, 43–5, 48–9,
80, 81, 85, 86, 114, 120, 133,
137, 168, 172, 174, 185
Deleuze, Gilles 122

Derrida, Jacques 2, 21–2, 25, 29–30,
    58, 73, 77, 80, 89, 103, 105, 111,
    143, 165, 166, 187, 189
Descartes, René 48, 130, 137, 186
determinism 181; see also linguistic
    determinism
diachronic 28, 132, 173
différance (différence) 29, 143, 181
difference 125, 128, 130, 133, 135,
    136, 181
Dilthey, Wilhelm 184
Discipline and Punish 129; see also
    Foucault, Michel
discourse 10, 24, 31–3, 54, 59–60, 66,
    68, 74, 79, 91, 94, 110, 121–3,
    125, 126, 127, 130, 132, 134,
    138, 146, 166, 170, 174, 175,
    181; see also historical discourse
Dray, W.H. 67
Dubois, Ellen Carol 54

Easthope, Antony 127–8
Elias, Norbert 19, 89
Elton, Geoffrey 18, 20–4, 39–42,
    44–5, 50–1, 55, 61, 63, 64, 76,
    78–80, 83–4, 98. 110. 139, 167,
    168, 169
empathy 92, 101, 172, 181
empiricism 1–3, 5, 7–12, 14, 17–20,
    22–3, 26–7, 31–3, 35–8, 40, 45,
    47, 50, 52, 57, 59, 63, 65–6,
    69–70, 74, 75, 77, 80–2, 85–8
    passim, 93, 94, 96–101, 103, 111,
    112, 114–17, 120–4, 126, 127,
    130, 133, 140, 141, 145, 146,
    148, 150, 151, 153, 156, 160,
    162–72, 175–8, 181–2
emplotment 5, 7, 9, 11, 32–5, 41, 50,
    52–3, 58–9, 71, 73–4, 79, 92, 93,
    95, 96, 97, 101, 106, 109–11,
    116, 117, 135, 136, 141, 143–9,
    151, 153, 154, 155, 157–9, 166,
    167, 169, 172–6 *passim*, 182; *see
    also* comedy; romance; satire;
    tragedy
Enlightenment, the 14, 137, 147, 182
episteme 71, 120–39 *passim*, 142,
    144, 145, 150, 153, 157, 164,
    167, 173, 175, 176, 182–3; *see
    also* Anthropological; Classical;

Foucault, Michel; postmodern;
    Renaissance
epistemic rules 135; *see also* trope
epistemology 3–6, 14, 16, 18, 20, 33,
    35–41, 43, 54–5, 58–63, 66, 68,
    70, 75, 76–81, 95, 99–104, 113,
    115, 121–6, 129, 133–5, 141–5,
    163–7, 183
Evans-Pritchard, E.E. 89
evidence 2, 3, 6–7, 9–10. 15–16. 18,
    20–21, 23, 25–6, 31–2, 34, 36–9,
    41–7 *passim*, 50–2, 57–60, 62–7,
    69–71, 74, 76, 81–6, 89–93, 95,
    97–8, 99, 100, 101, 104–8, 113,
    117, 118, 120, 122, 126–30, 131,
    138, 142, 145–50, 156, 161–3,
    165, 166, 167–72, 175–6, 183

fact(s) 1, 6, 7, 16, 25, 33, 35, 38, 41,
    43–6, 60–1, 63, 65, 69–71, 74,
    78–85 *passim*, 87, 90–2, 96–8,
    104, 109, 111, 117, 124, 126,
    127, 134, 145–6, 149, 160, 165,
    166, 168, 171, 173–5, 183–4; *see
    also* fiction
farce 93, 117
fascist history 12; *see also* fascism
fascism 15; *see also* fascist history
Febvre, Georges 48
feminist history 147
fiction 25, 29, 31–2, 38, 43, 55, 60–1,
    65, 70, 74, 78, 90, 92, 96, 97–8,
    112, 117, 124, 143, 161, 164,
    168, 173; *see also* facts
fiction of factual representation
    149–50; *see also* White, Hayden
fictive origins 105
Foner, Philip 23
form 19, 24, 30, 32, 51–8 *passim*, 60,
    62, 66–7, 70, 74, 95, 99, 122,
    127, 129, 130, 133, 135–6, 138,
    140, 153, 160, 164, 166, 171,
    177 8; *see also* content
formist 34, 154, 158–9; *see also* argu-
    ment; contextualist; mechanist;
    organicist
Foucault, Michel 9, 12–14, 27–9,
    32–4, 39, 59, 66, 71–3 *passim*,
    75, 77, 78, 96, 99–100, 111, 115,
    118, 120–39 *passim*, 141, 142,

144, 150, 151, 153, 155, 156,
162, 164, 166, 167, 170–1,
173–6, 186–7, 189, 190; *see also*
Archaeology of Knowledge, The;
Discipline and Punish; episteme;
History of Sexuality; *Order of*
Things, The
free land 64, 156–7
French Revolution 14
Friedlander, Saul 73
functionalism 88

Gadamer, Hans-Georg 107, 187
Gallie, W.B. 10, 53–4, 68, 113, 134–5,
175
Gay, Peter 17, 83–4
Geertz, Clifford 50, 72, 89, 110, 112
Gellner, Ernest 50
gender 45–7, 50, 55, 100, 104–5, 111,
172
genealogy 124, 125, 129, 171
Genovese, Eugene 19
Giddens, Anthony 19, 50
Ginsburg, Carlo 110, 164; *see also*
Cheese and Worms, The
Goldstein, Leon 68, 81, 100
Gordon, Linda 78, 80, 168
Great Chain of Being 132
Guide to Historical Literature 92
Gutman, Herbert 24, 50

Hall, Catherine 50
Halley's Comet 176–7
Handlin, Oscar 18, 40
Hardy, Barbara 160–1
Harlan, David 19, 68, 107–8, 170
Hegel, Friedrich 14, 154
Heidegger, Martin 184, 187
Hempel, Carl 49, 64; *see also* cover-
ing law
Henretta, James A. 113–14
hermeneutics 78, 80, 99, 127, 142,
145, 184
heteroglossia 106
Hexter, J.H. 18, 21, 40, 51–3, 68
Hill, Christopher 23
Himmelfarb, Gertrude 18, 40, 80,
87–8, 166
historian, the 5, 7–8, 12, 16, 19–24,
26–7, 33, 35, 37–9, 41, 43, 45–6,

50, 59–63, 67–8, 70, 73, 75, 76,
81–6 *passim*, 89, 90, 94–6
passim, 99–101, 103–5, 108,
113–15, 118, 121–4, 126, 130,
142–3, 145–9, 161, 165–8, 171,
172, 174–8
historical discourse 32–3, 126, 153,
170, 175; *see also* discourse
historical explanation 3–5, 8–9, 12,
36, 40, 47, 51–7 *passim*, 64–5,
67–8, 71, 99, 110, 141, 142, 153,
157–8, 163, 167, 172, 177–8
historical interpretation 6–8, 10–11,
26, 29, 31, 35, 38, 40, 42, 44,
51–6, 60, 61, 67, 70, 80, 85, 87,
104, 118, 123, 128, 150, 161,
173, 184
historical knowledge 3, 7, 14, 17–27,
32–3, 36, 40, 51–5 *passim*, 57,
66, 69, 85, 100, 101, 103, 104,
114, 137, 159–61, 163, 174
historical truth 1, 3, 5, 10, 12–13, 16,
25, 31, 33, 38, 51, 55, 59–61, 68,
74, 77–80 *passim*, 89, 93, 95, 98,
101, 118, 123, 126, 129, 136,
146, 163, 166, 170, 171; *see also*
truth
historical understanding 3, 6, 24,
51–6 *passim*, 109, 110, 142, 143,
163, 175
historicism 8, 27, 90, 130, 152,
170
historiography 16, 101, 166
History of Sexuality 129; *see also*
Foucault, Michel
Hobsbawm, Eric 50, 96
Hollinger, David 44, 102–3
Holocaust 97, 149
Hoskins, W.G. 50
Hunt, Lynn 18, 38–9, 41, 46–7, 53–4,
76, 77, 78, 79, 80, 83, 94, 95, 98,
168, 170; *see also Telling the*
Truth About History; Appleby,
Joyce; Jacob, Margaret
hypothesis testing 86, 91, 109, 153,
172, 174,

Idea of History, The 97; *see also*
Collingwood R.G.
idealism 87

ideology 5, 9, 12, 13, 18–21, 23, 28,
34–5, 39, 44–7, 57, 59, 61, 62,
63, 70–5 *passim*, 77, 82, 84,
93–6, 100, 110, 111, 116, 117,
122–5, 128, 130, 136–8, 140–1,
144, 146–8, 154–5, 159–60, 165,
167, 170, 171, 172, 176, 177,
184; *see also* anarchist; conservative; liberal; radical
imperialism 26
impositionalism (of the historian)
7–8, 21, 26, 39–40, 44, 47, 53,
59, 63, 81, 86, 90, 92, 96, 103,
111, 114, 118, 124, 137, 142,
145, 149, 157, 159, 162, 166,
167, 171, 172, 184–5
induction 36–56 *passim*, 59, 65, 80,
82, 85, 97, 120, 121, 127, 130,
134, 137, 167, 169, 172, 185; *see
also* inference
Industrial Revolution 69
inference 7, 20, 36–56 *passim*, 64–5,
82, 84–5, 100, 121, 127, 138,
145, 151, 167, 169, 176, 185; *see
also* induction
intentionality 3, 4, 6, 8, 10, 12, 23,
32, 37, 45, 49–50, 53, 62, 66, 67,
81, 87, 90, 102, 105, 108, 116,
118, 127, 140, 141, 145, 147,
165, 166, 168, 169, 170
intertextuality 90, 106, 118, 143,
161–2, 170, 176
irony 11, 12, 34, 77, 95, 136, 137,
143, 144, 145, 152, 154, 155,
156; *see also* metaphor;
metonymy; synecdoche; trope;
troping
Islands of History 111; *see also*
Sahlins, Marshal

Jacob, Margaret 18, 38–9, 41, 46–7,
53–4, 76, 77, 78, 79, 80, 83, 94,
95, 168, 170; *see also* Appleby,
Joyce; Hunt, Lynn; *Telling the
Truth About History*
Jenkins, Keith 11, 14, 19, 58, 166
Joyce, Patrick 19, 24, 127–8

Kellner, Hans 58, 68, 100, 101, 166
Kennedy, John F. 116

Kiernan, Victor 24
Kincaid, James R. 104–5; *see also
Child Loving: The Erotic Child
and Victorian Culture*
Kloppenberg, James 21, 76, 80, 168
knower and known 38, 63, 64–6, 79,
82, 126, 151
knowledge 33
Kolko, Gabriel 50
Kristeva, Julia 187
Kuhn, Thomas 77, 85

labour (socio-economic discourse)
131; *see also* wealth creation
LaCapra, Dominick 19, 68, 69, 84,
166, 171
Ladurie, Emmanuel Le Roy 23,
49–50, 110, 164; *see also
Montaillou*
Landscape and Memory 111, 164; *see
also Dead Certainties*; Schama,
Simon
language 6, 13, 17–20, 22, 24–30, 32,
47, 50–6 *passim*, 58–60, 66, 69,
71, 72–4, 77, 78, 79, 82, 86, 91,
92, 94–8 *passim*, 101, 103, 106,
111, 120, 121, 123, 125, 127,
130, 132–7, 140, 142, 146, 149,
152, 155, 156, 165, 171, 173,
174, 176, 178
language (cultural discourse) 125,
131
langue 28
Lemon, M.C. 4–5, 10, 52–3, 62,
68–9, 113, 115, 117, 175
Lévi-Strauss, Claude 153
liberal 34, 154, 159–60; *see also* anarchist; conservative; ideology;
radical
life (biological discourse) 125, 131
linguistic determinism 96, 121–3,
129, 134, 150–2, 173, 176; *see
also* determinism; linguistic turn
linguistic turn 16, 25, 86, 91, 100,
110, 111, 127, 135, 176, 177,
185; *see also* linguistic determinism; linguistics
linguistics 27, 88–9, 129, 132, 134,
145, 166
literature 4–5, 15, 18–19, 22, 25, 29,

31, 33–5, 37, 42, 51–5 *passim*, 58, 61, 69, 71, 74, 86, 95, 97, 104, 109, 112, 115, 118, 141, 142, 144, 150, 151, 155, 161, 171, 173–4, 176
Lloyd, Christopher 49
logical positivism 78
logocentrism 61, 87, 111, 120, 130, 173, 185
Lorenz, Chris 21
Louch, A.R. 68
Lyotard, Jean-François 14–15, 59, 77, 187; *see also Postmodern Condition, The: A Report on Knowledge*

McCullagh, C. Behan 21, 37–8, 49, 55, 82, 84, 93, 94, 100, 105, 167
MacIntyre, Alasdair 96
McMillan, James F. 76
Madison, James 6
madness 122, 128–9, 171
Madness and Civilization 125; *see also* Foucault, Michel
Mandelbaum, Maurice 68
Mannheim, Karl 160
Marwick, Arthur 18, 21, 22, 23, 39, 68, 79–83 *passim*, 98, 167
Marx, Karl 22, 92, 149, 159
Marxist history 8, 19, 87, 110, 146, 147, 151, 152, 158, 171, 179; *see also* Marxism
Marxism 15, 18, 21, 23, 45, 57, 88, 96, 109, 174
master narratives 14–15, 160; *see also* meta-narratives
mechanist 34, 53, 154, 158–9; *see also* argument; contextualist; formist; organicist
medicine 121–2, 125
Megill, Allan 19, 113, 166, 177
memory 103, 114, 121
Metahistory: The Historical Imagination in Nineteenth Century Europe 93, 142, 144–5, 152, 154, 190; *see also* White, Hayden
meta-narratives 8, 14, 15, 77, 185; *see also* master narratives
metaphor 9, 11, 12, 32, 34, 63, 68, 71,

72, 90, 106, 111, 113–15, 122, 127, 136, 138, 143–4, 146, 149, 152, 154, 155, 156, 165–6, 174, 176, 178; *see also* irony; metonymy; synecdoche; trope; troping
metonymy 11, 12, 34, 136, 138, 143, 144, 154–6; *see also* irony; metaphor; synecdoche; trope; troping
Michelet, Jules 154
microhistory 112
micronarrative 112
Mink, Louis 2, 10, 11, 67, 113, 140, 160–1, 164, 171, 175
Modern 133, 136; *see also* Anthropological; episteme
modernisation 8
Modernisation School 19, 23
modernism 1, 5, 9, 185; *see also* modernist
modernist 9, 10, 15–18, 20, 35, 100, 120, 123, 133, 135, 136, 137, 160, 164, 178, 185; *see also* modernism; modernist history
modernist history 133, 136; *see also* modernist
Montaillou 164; *see also* Ladurie, Emmanuel Le Roy
Montgomery, David 50
multiculturalism 170
myth 80, 121, 123, 124, 135, 136, 147–8, 157, 161, 178

narrative 1–6, 8, 9–18, 20, 23–4, 26, 32–5, 38, 40–1, 51–5, 59–66, 67–75, 76, 78, 81, 88, 89, 91–8, 99–104 *passim*, 106, 109–27 *passim*, 134–9, 140–64 *passim*, 166, 168, 171, 173–8, 186
narrative correspondence 141, 144; *see also* textual model of history
New Cultural History 9, 86, 111
New Economic History 8, 109
new historicism 24, 27, 30–2, 89, 98, 186
New History 22, 48, 53, 88, 109, 124, 151
New Science, The 136; *see also* Vico, Giambattista

Nietzsche, Friedrich 59, 65, 78, 120,
123, 124, 130, 187
Norman, Andrew P. 95
Novick, Peter 18, 80, 84, 102

object 94, 133, 153, 155, 156, 165
objectivity 1–2, 4–5, 7, 9–10, 14, 16,
18, 20–1, 25–7, 36–7, 43, 55,
59–61, 63, 65–8, 71, 73, 76–80
passim, 82–5 passim, 93, 94, 95,
98, 100, 102, 103, 104, 115–16,
119, 120, 123, 124, 126, 129,
130, 137, 146, 153, 156, 163,
166, 167, 170, 171, 172, 177, 178
objectivity effect 115–16; *see also*
objectivity
Olafson, Frederick A. 68, 76, 82, 142
Order of Things, The 121, 131; *see
also* Foucault, Michel
organicist 34, 154, 158–9; *see also*
argument; contextualist;
formist; mechanist
other, the 102, 105, 122, 166, 169

paradigm 1, 14, 16, 22, 42, 77, 78, 83,
99, 100, 101, 115, 123, 125, 166,
168
parole 28
Parrington, Vernon L. 22
part–part relationships 159
part–whole relationships 136, 155, 156
Past and Present 89
philosophy 27, 31, 37, 41, 45, 70, 88,
103, 113, 117, 121, 127, 130,
139, 141, 156, 164–6
Pocock, J.G.A 89
Popper, Karl 77, 78, 85
positivism 1, 37 24, 36, 45, 48–9, 58,
64–6, 74, 77, 89–91 passim, 94,
99, 113, 120, 130, 146, 147, 172,
173, 174, 186–7
Poster, Mark 138
postmodern 133, 136, 138, 164, 178;
see also episteme
*Postmodern Condition, The: A Report
on Knowledge* 185, 187; *see also*
Lyotard, Jean-François
postmodernism 1–2, 5, 14–17, 19–20,
24–6, 30, 34, 38, 53, 59, 62, 76,
77, 78, 86, 89, 96, 102, 103, 1 16,
121, 124, 129, 132, 135, 187
post-structuralism 8, 17, 22, 27,
29–30, 33, 58–9, 68, 86, 90, 94,
111, 120, 123, 138, 187
power 12–13, 25, 28–9, 33, 66, 72, 78,
104, 106–7, 120, 121, 122, 123,
128, 129, 130, 133, 134, 136,
151, 160, 171, 173–4, 177; *see
also* power–knowledge
power–knowledge 122, 151, 173–4;
see also power
problematization 124
psychohistory 52, 88

Quellenkritik 44, 81, 82, 109, 111,
148, 168, 169

race 45–7, 50, 104, 111, 172
radical 34, 154, 159–60; *see also*
anarchist; conservative; ideology; liberal
Ranke, Leopold von 20, 87, 101–2
realism 7, 14, 16, 60–1, 71, 78, 81, 85,
90, 96, 109, 148, 166, 173, 176
realistic (reality) effect 61, 82, 115,
138, 145, 160, 166, 170, 171,
173, 177, 187–8
reality 2–3, 5, 9, 12, 17, 23, 26, 31–3,
35–6, 38–9, 45, 52, 54, 59–61,
66–7, 69, 74, 77, 78, 79, 81, 84,
90, 95–8, 100, 103, 105, 106,
108, 111, 118, 120, 123, 124,
126, 127, 128, 132, 133, 135,
137, 142, 143, 147, 148, 149,
153, 156, 163, 165, 166, 167,
168, 169, 174–8
reconstructionism 1, 7, 10, 18, 20–3,
25–6, 30–3, 35–58 passim, 62–3,
65–6, 69–70, 73–4, 76, 79–87
passim, 90–1, 94, 96, 97–8, 99,
104, 107–8, 114, 116–18, 123,
124, 127, 129, 132, 140–3,
147–51, 163, 164–8, 172, 173,
188; *see also* contextualisation
referentiality 4, 11, 28, 30, 36, 38,
40, 58, 60–1, 65–6, 69–70, 82,
91, 100, 101, 110, 114, 117, 118,
121–3, 130, 140, 143, 148, 149,
152, 156, 166, 173, 177, 178,
188

relativism 19, 26, 39, 65–6, 72–3, 77–80 *passim*, 82–3, 88, 92, 93, 97, 98, 111, 123, 151, 152, 165, 168–72, 188
Renaissance 132, 136, 144; *see also* episteme
representation 2, 9, 16–17, 19, 24–6, 30–2, 34–5, 47, 57, 63, 65–6, 70, 72, 75, 78, 99, 101, 109, 111, 112, 114, 116, 118, 122, 123, 125, 126, 128, 129, 135–6, 139, 141–3, 148, 149, 152, 153, 156, 164, 166, 173, 174, 175, 178, 188–9
resemblance 125, 128, 132
rethinking history 137
Return of Martin Guerre, The 112, 164; *see also* Davis, Natalie Zemon
rhetoric 9, 31, 58, 60, 61, 70–2 *passim*, 84, 94, 115, 118, 128, 131, 136, 144, 147, 152–3, 155, 162, 164, 170, 171, 173
rhetorical constructionism 144, 146, 148, 150–2, 156, 159, 167; *see also* White, Hayden
Ricoeur, Paul 11, 69, 71, 73, 109, 116, 140
Roberts, David M. 18
Robinson, James, Harvey 22, 48
Roediger, David 24
romance 34, 93, 95, 117, 143, 149, 154, 157–8; *see also* comedy; emplotment; satire; tragedy
Roosevelt, Theodore 176–7
Rorty, Richard 47, 80
Roth, Michael 123
Rowbotham, Sheila 50
Rudé, George 19, 24
Ruiz, Vicki L. 54
Rüsen, Jörn 58, 100, 166

Sahlins, Marshal 19, 111; *see also* *Islands of History*
Samuel, Raphael 24
satire 34, 149, 154, 157–8; *see also* comedy; emplotment; romance; tragedy
Saussure, Ferdinand de 27–8, 71–2, 78, 89, 189

Saville, John 24
Schama, Simon 110, 113, 164; *see also Dead Certainties*; *Landscape and Memory*
Schleirmacher, Friedrich 184
scissors and paste 97
Scott, Joan W. 19, 99–100,
Second World War 77
semiotics 88
sign 61, 111, 121–2, 173; *see also* signified; signifier
signified 28, 33, 61, 78, 121, 128–30, 141; *see also* sign; signifier; transcendental signified
signifier(-signified–sign) 28–9, 33 61, 69–70, 78, 110, 121, 128–9, 141, 152, 173, 189; *see also* sign; signified
similarity 128, 130, 132, 156
Skinner, Quentin 40, 89
social construction of reality 106, 122
social theory 3, 7, 8, 9, 18, 22, 24, 45, 48, 50–2, 54, 63–4, 76, 81, 85, 88, 93, 96, 97, 111, 131, 141, 151, 152–3, 159, 163, 165, 168, 170, 173; *see also* constructionism
socialism 15
sociology 27, 47, 172
Sparks, Carol Douglas 104–5
Spencer, Herbert 22
Spiegel, Gabrielle M. 90, 106–7
Stanford, Michael 21, 43, 54, 79, 80, 167
Stone, Lawrence 18, 21, 24, 31, 52–3, 68, 88–90, 110, 173
structuralism 22, 27–9, 31, 52, 58, 68, 88, 111, 121, 132, 189
style 10, 11, 17, 30, 32, 52, 58, 68, 95, 115, 121, 136, 142
subject 9, 12, 25, 94, 133, 165; *see also* subjectivity
subjectivism 88, 90, 113
subjectivity 13, 63, 78, 88, 98
sublime 5, 12, 13, 146–7, 151, 166
synchronic 28, 132, 173
synecdoche 11, 12, 34, 136, 138, 143, 144, 154, 155, 156, 176; *see also* irony; metaphor; metonymy; trope; troping

Taylor, A.J.P. 91–2
teleology 51, 96, 120, 165
Telling the Truth About History 95,
    170; *see also* Appleby, Joyce;
    Hunt, Lynn; Jacob, Margaret
terminological determinism 171; *see
    also* White, Hayden
textual model of history 2, 24–5, 68,
    106–7, 111, 115–19, 134–9,
    140–5, 150, 161–2, 164, 167,
    175–6, 190; *see also* narrative
    correspondence; rhetorical con-
    structionism
theories of history 7
Third World 78
Thompson, E.P. 19, 23, 72
Tilly, Charles 50
Tolstoy, Leo 112
Tonkin, Elizabeth 166
Tosh, John 18, 41, 76, 82, 84, 91, 172
Toson, Shimizaki 112
tragedy 34, 93, 117, 143, 149, 154,
    157–8; *see also* comedy;
    romance; satire
transcendental signified 130
Trebilcock, Clive 54
Trevor-Roper, Hugh 18, 40
trompe l'œil 60, 79, 178
trope /figuration 11, 12, 34–5, 61,
    71–2, 79, 109–10, 114, 115, 121,
    125–7, 133–8 *passim*, 141, 144,
    148–51, 153–62 *passim*, 166, 167,
    173, 175, 176, 189–90; *see also*
    epistemic rules; irony; metaphor;
    metonymy; synecdoche; tropic
    signature; troping; White,
    Hayden
tropic signature 126; *see also* cultural
    signature
troping 11, 18, 33, 136, 144, 150, 155,
    156, 160, 174, 175; *see also* trope
truth 38, 40, 43, 59–60, 69–70, 77–80
    passim, 82, 84, 90, 93, 94, 97,

100–2, 104, 110, 113, 117, 121,
    124, 125, 128, 129, 136, 137,
    138, 140, 142, 146, 147, 148,
    153, 163, 167, 168, 169, 170,
    171, 177, 178; *see also* historical
    truth
truth-effect 40, 61, 70, 79, 94, 115,
    169, 171
Turner, Frederick Jackson 22, 49–50,
    64, 86, 152, 156–7, 178

Vann, Richard T. 92–3, 175
verification 56, 153, 168
Veyne, Paul 11
Vico, Giambattista 131, 136, 137,
    138, 155, 174; *see also New
    Science, The*

Warsaw Uprising 93
wealth creation (socio-economic dis-
    course) 125, 131; *see also* labour
    (socio-economic discourse)
Weinstein, James 50
White, Hayden 9–13, 19, 21, 27,
    31–4, 39, 58, 62–3, 66, 68–75
    passim, 79, 84, 93–7, 100, 110,
    113, 115, 116, 117, 118, 121,
    123, 128, 129, 134, 135, 136,
    137, 138, 139–62 *passim*, 164,
    166, 167, 170, 171, 173–6, 190;
    *see also Metahistory: The
    Historical Imagination in
    Nineteenth Century Europe;*
    rhetorical constructionism; ter-
    minological determinism; trope
whole–part relationships 136, 155,
    156
Williams, Raymond 27, 32
Winn, James A. 76, 79, 98
Wood, Gordon S. 18

Zagorin, Perez 101
Zeldin, Theodore 76–7